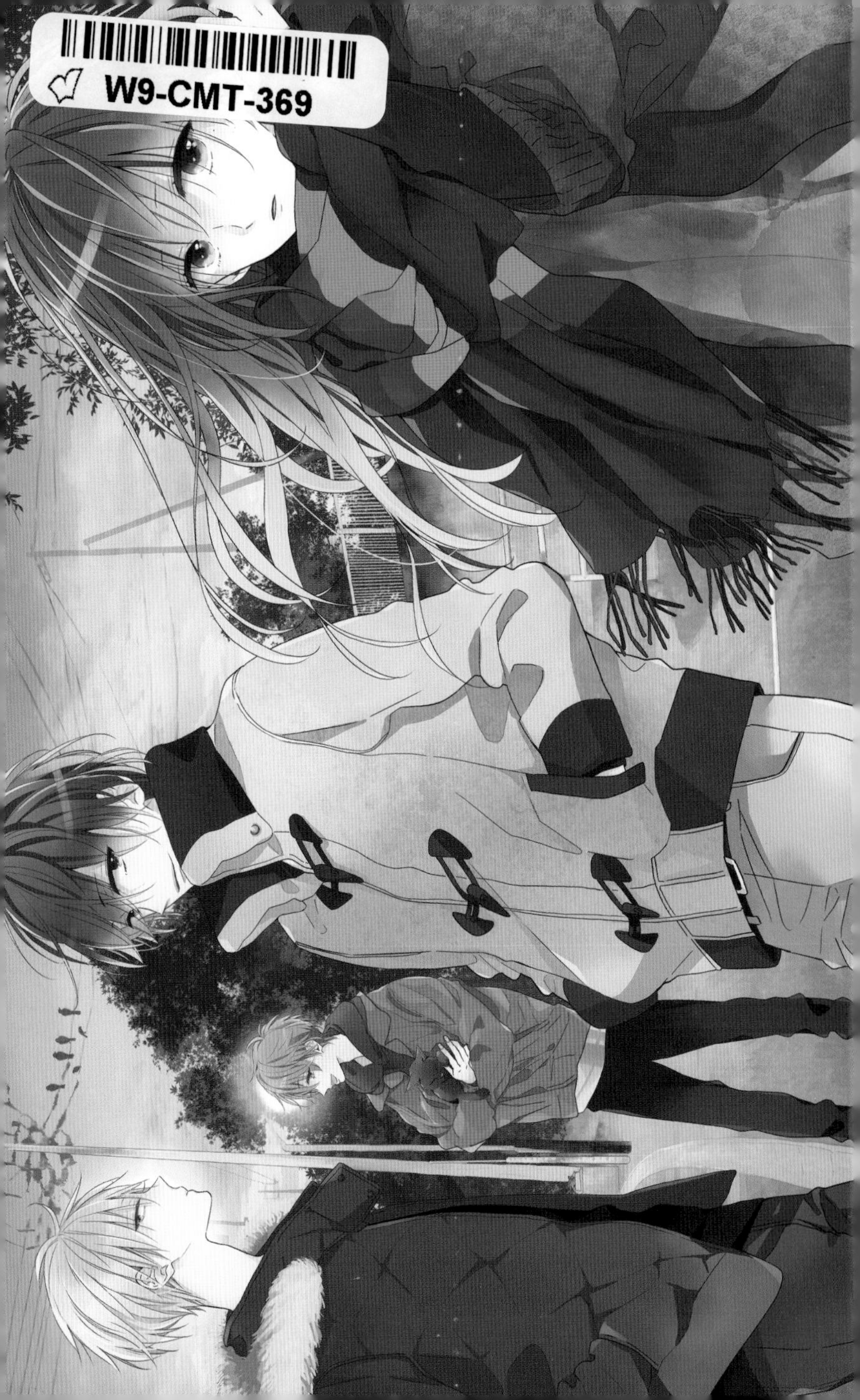

2

That Wolf-Boy is Mine!

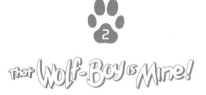

Contents

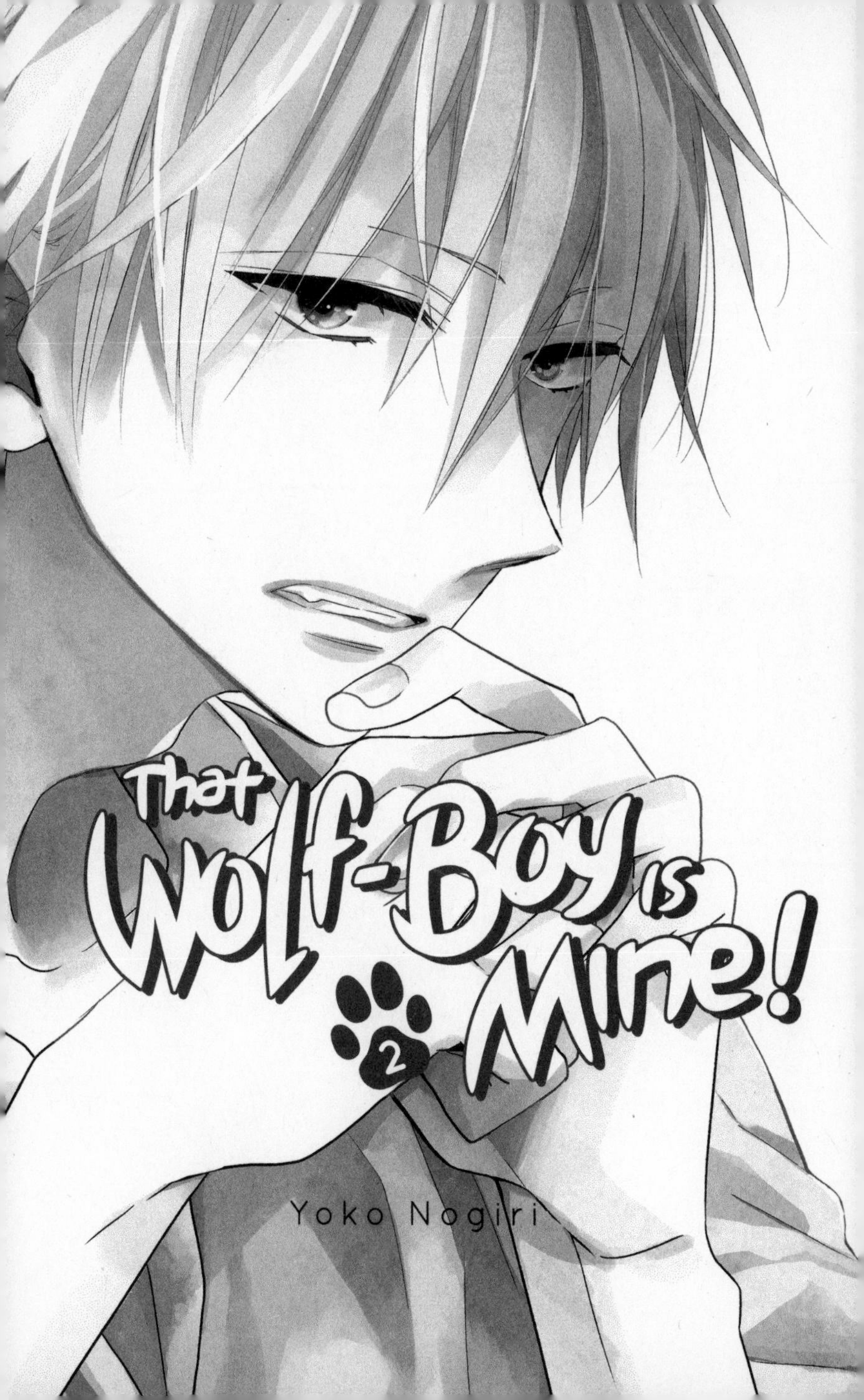
That Wolf-Boy is Mine!
2
Yoko Nogiri

CHARACTER & STORY

Sharing a secret with extraordinary boys?!

If you say no, I'll eat you up.

Komugi Kusunoki

A first-year high school student who transferred from Tokyo to Maruyama High School in Hokkaido. The one and only person who knows Ōgami's secret. She told him that she loves him, but he decided to pretend he didn't hear it...

Maruyama High School Idol No.1

Yū Ōgami

Very happy that Komugi decided to be his friend even after she learned his secret. Behind his kind smile hides a tragic past involving his mother. His true identity is a wolf.

Maruyama High School Idol No.2

Rin Fushimi

Noticed Komugi's interest in Ōgami and warned her not to fall in love with him. He's always tough on Komugi for some reason. His true identity is a fox.

Maruyama High School Idol No.3

Aoshi Awaji

A boy with down-turned eyes who likes to mess with people. He brings life to social gatherings and is amused at Komugi's appearance in their world. His true identity is a tanuki.

Maruyama High School Idol No.4

Senri Miyama

Cool and often lazy. He keeps his distance from humans and is indifferent to the fact that Komugi knows his secret. His true identity is a cat.

After having some social trouble at her high school in Tokyo, Komugi Kusunoki has moved to her father's home in Hokkaido.

On her first day of school, Yū Ōgami addresses her with the odd statement, "You smell good!" And it turns out he's not just an average guy—he's a wolf who can transform into a human!

Komugi learns that Ōgami's friends Rin, Aoshi, and Senri are all animals, too. However, their hypnotic powers fail to work on her, and their true identities become Komugi's own little secret.

As she interacts with the group and becomes closer, Komugi gradually finds herself thinking more and more about Ōgami...

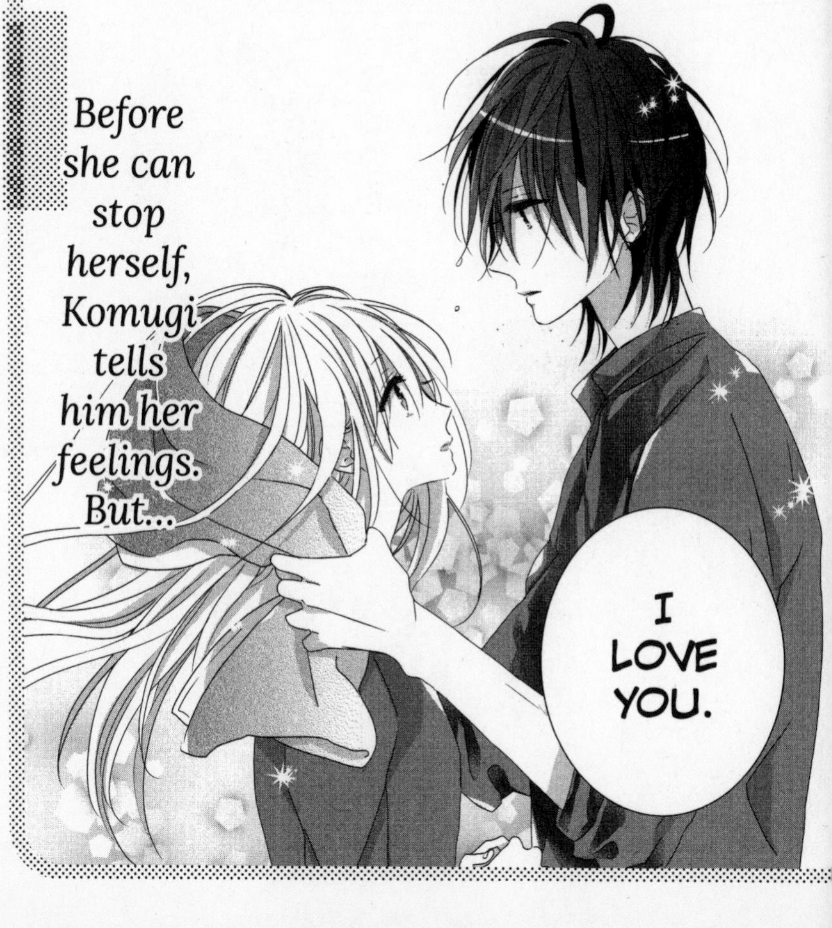
Before she can stop herself, Komugi tells him her feelings. But...
I LOVE YOU.

That Wolf-Boy is Mine!

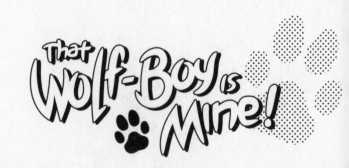

Chapter 5

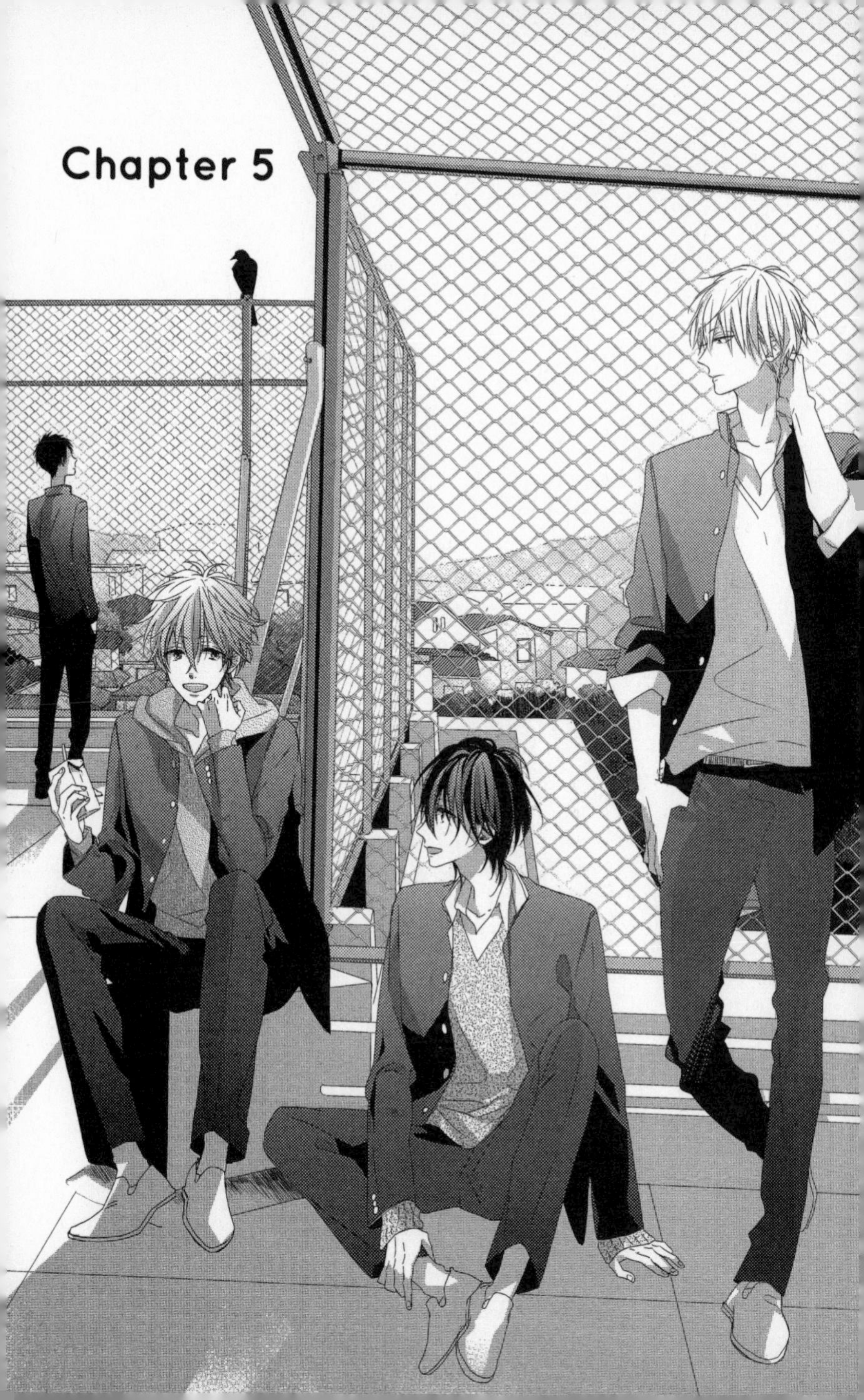

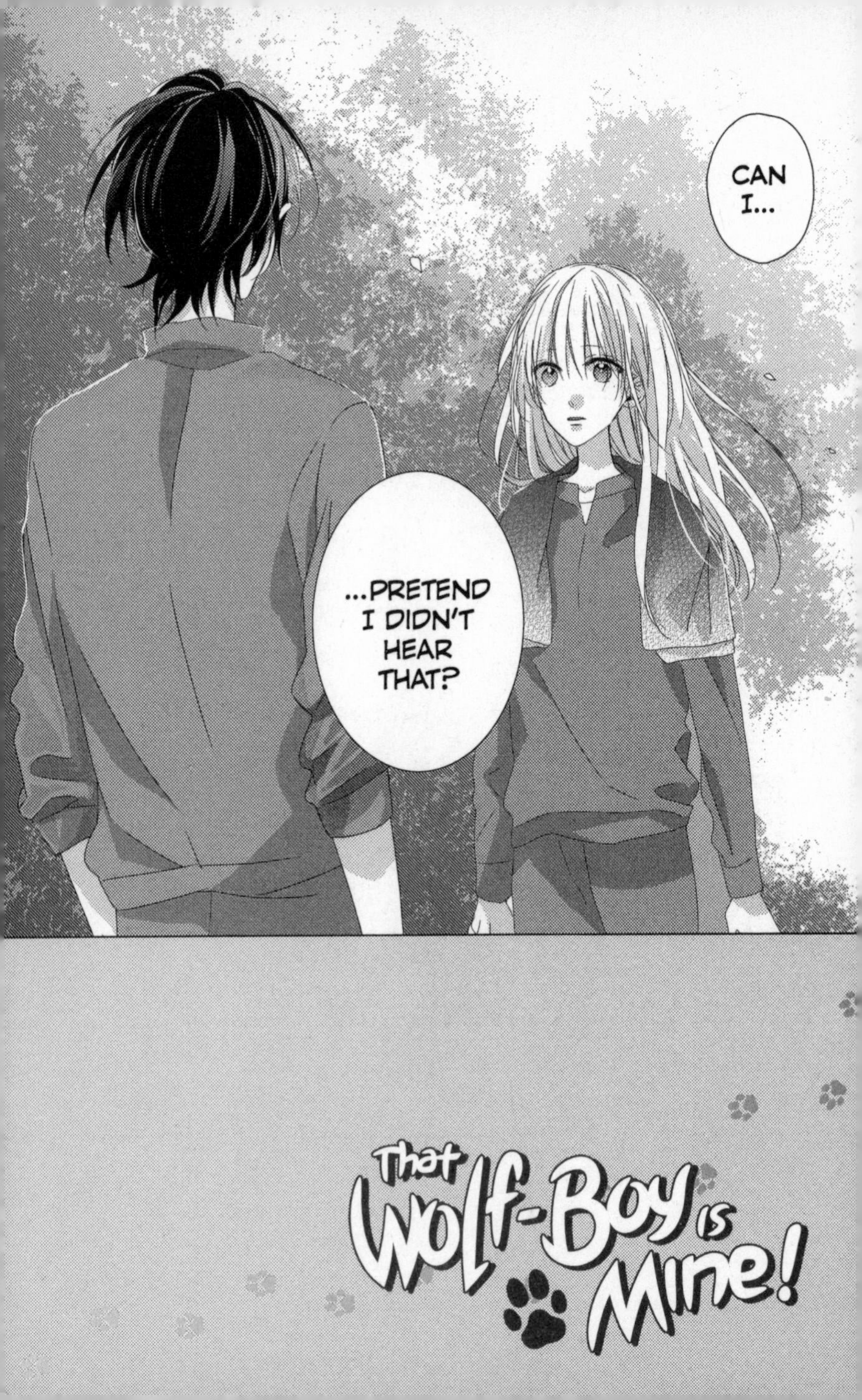
CAN I...
...PRETEND I DIDN'T HEAR THAT?

That Wolf-Boy is Mine!

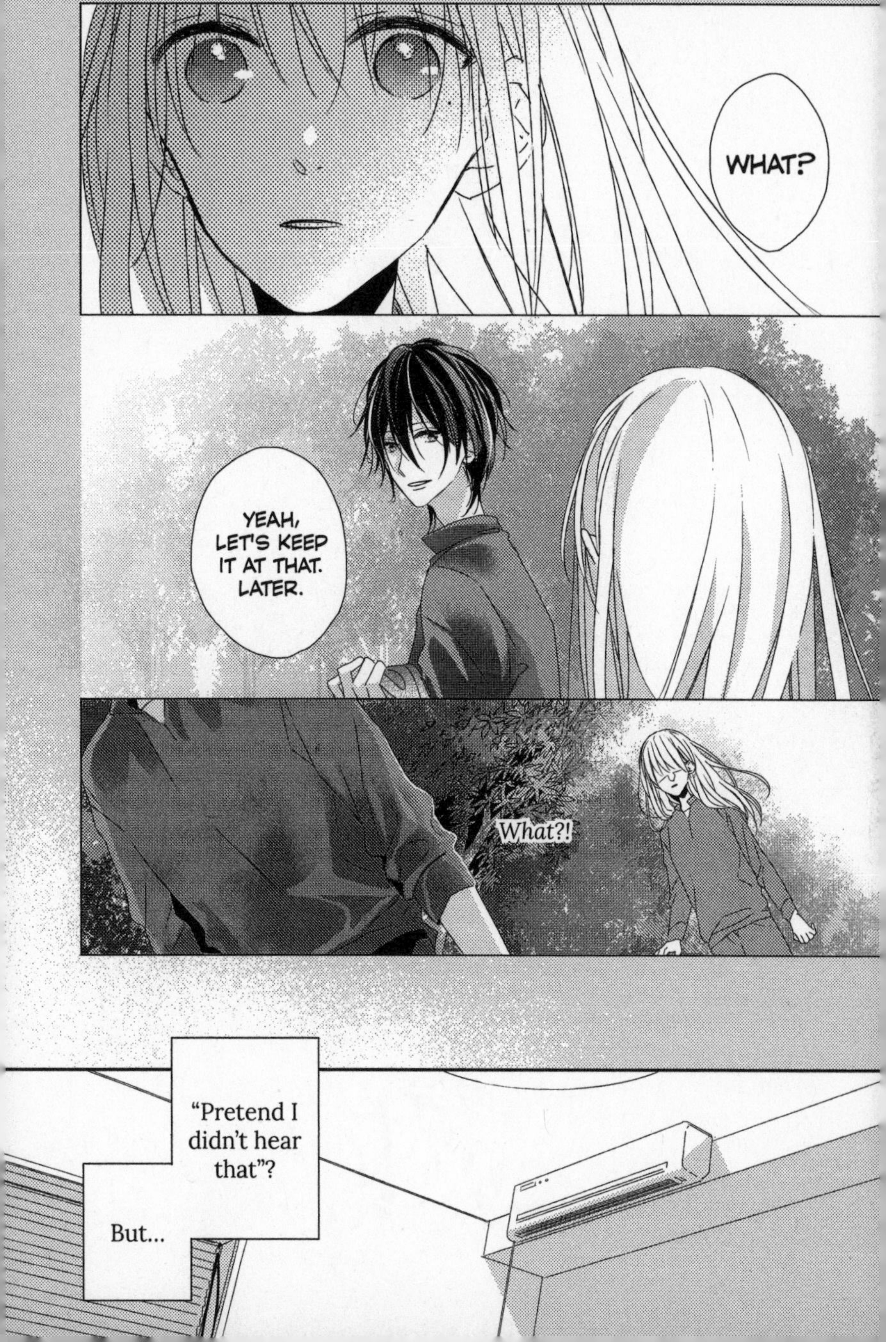
WHAT?
YEAH, LET'S KEEP IT AT THAT. LATER.
What?!
"Pretend I didn't hear that"?
But...

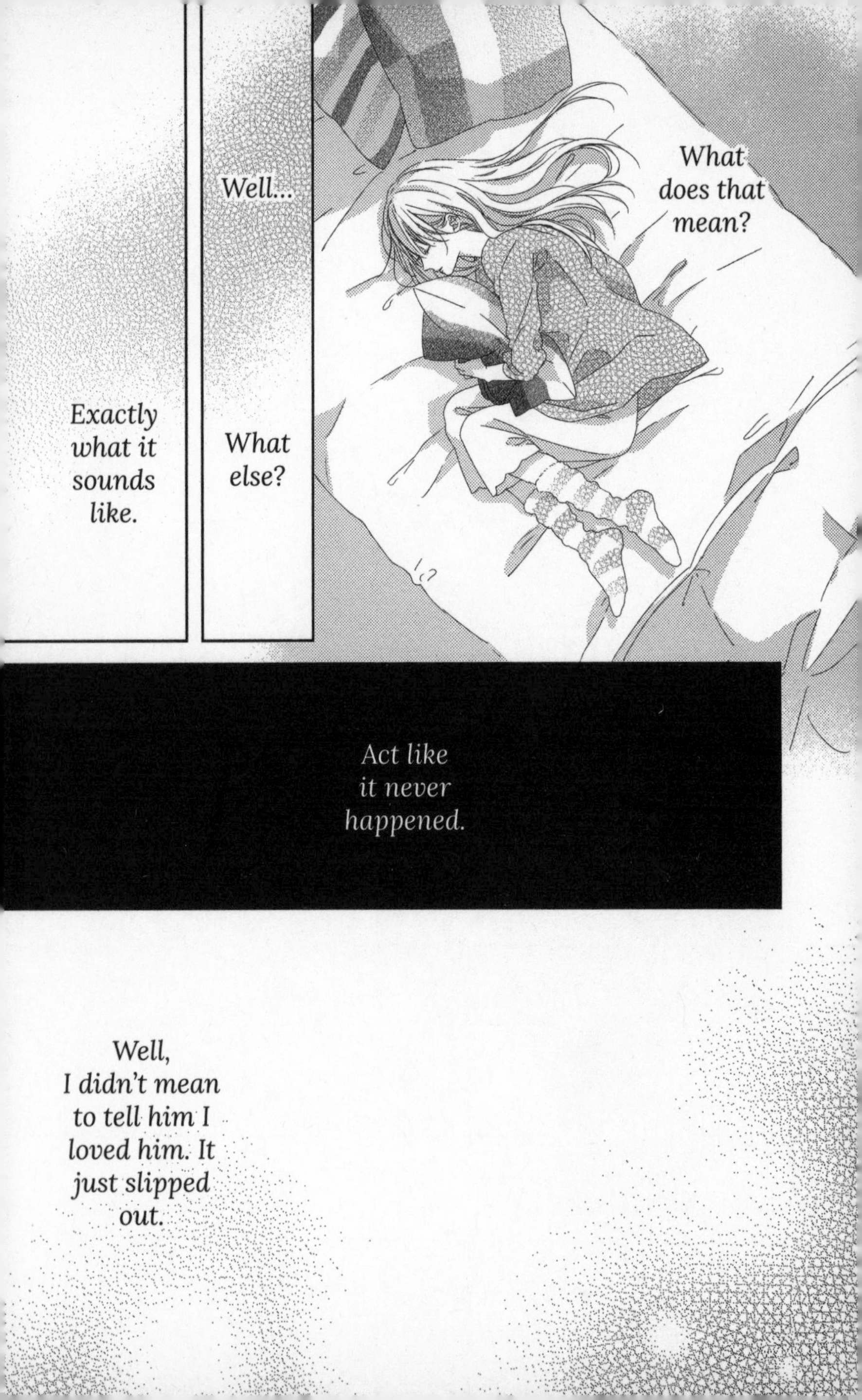

What does that mean?
Well...
What else?
Exactly what it sounds like.
Act like it never happened.
Well, I didn't mean to tell him I loved him. It just slipped out.

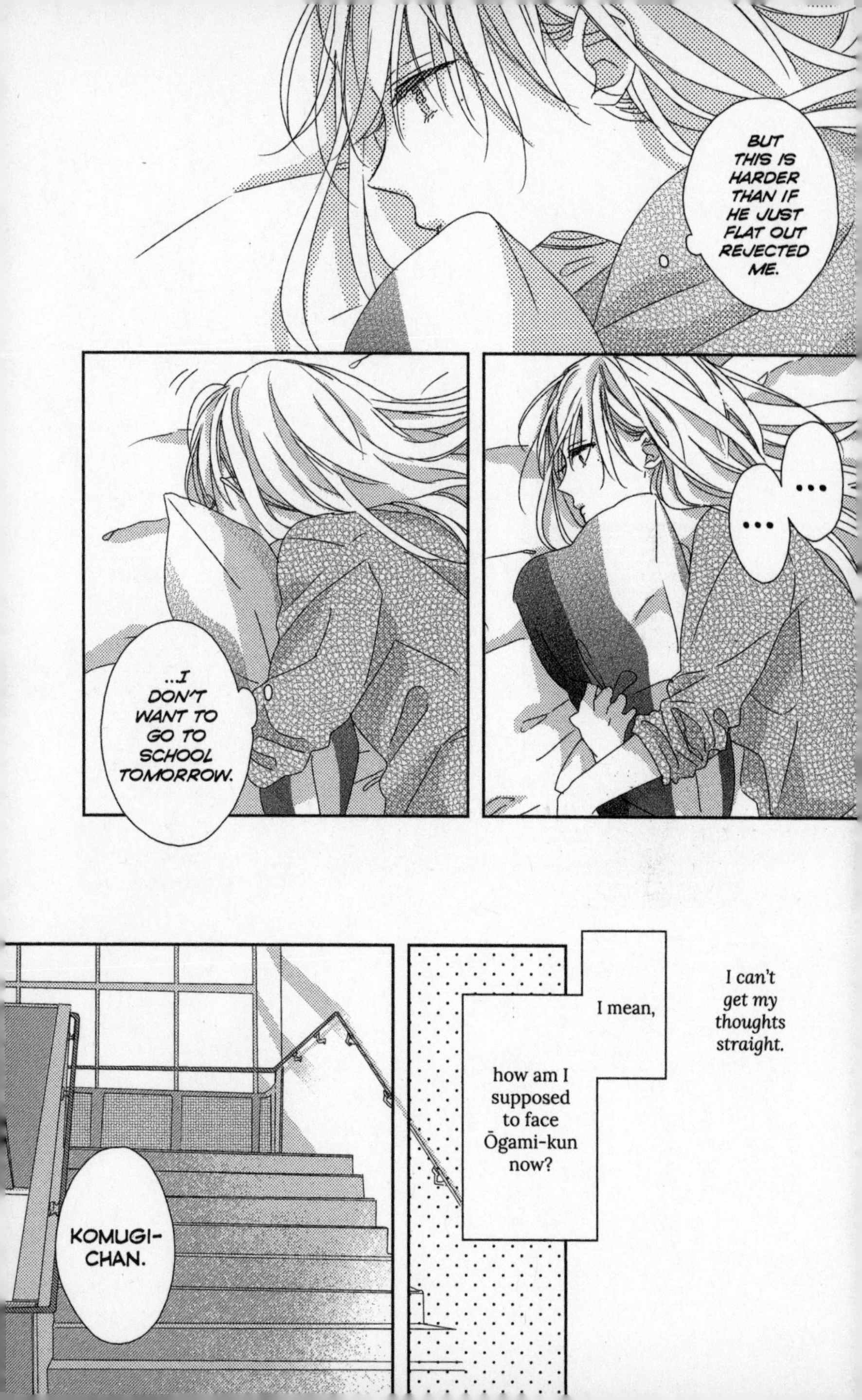
BUT THIS IS HARDER THAN IF HE JUST FLAT OUT REJECTED ME.
... ...
...I DON'T WANT TO GO TO SCHOOL TOMORROW.
I can't get my thoughts straight.
I mean,
how am I supposed to face Ōgami-kun now?
KOMUGI-CHAN.

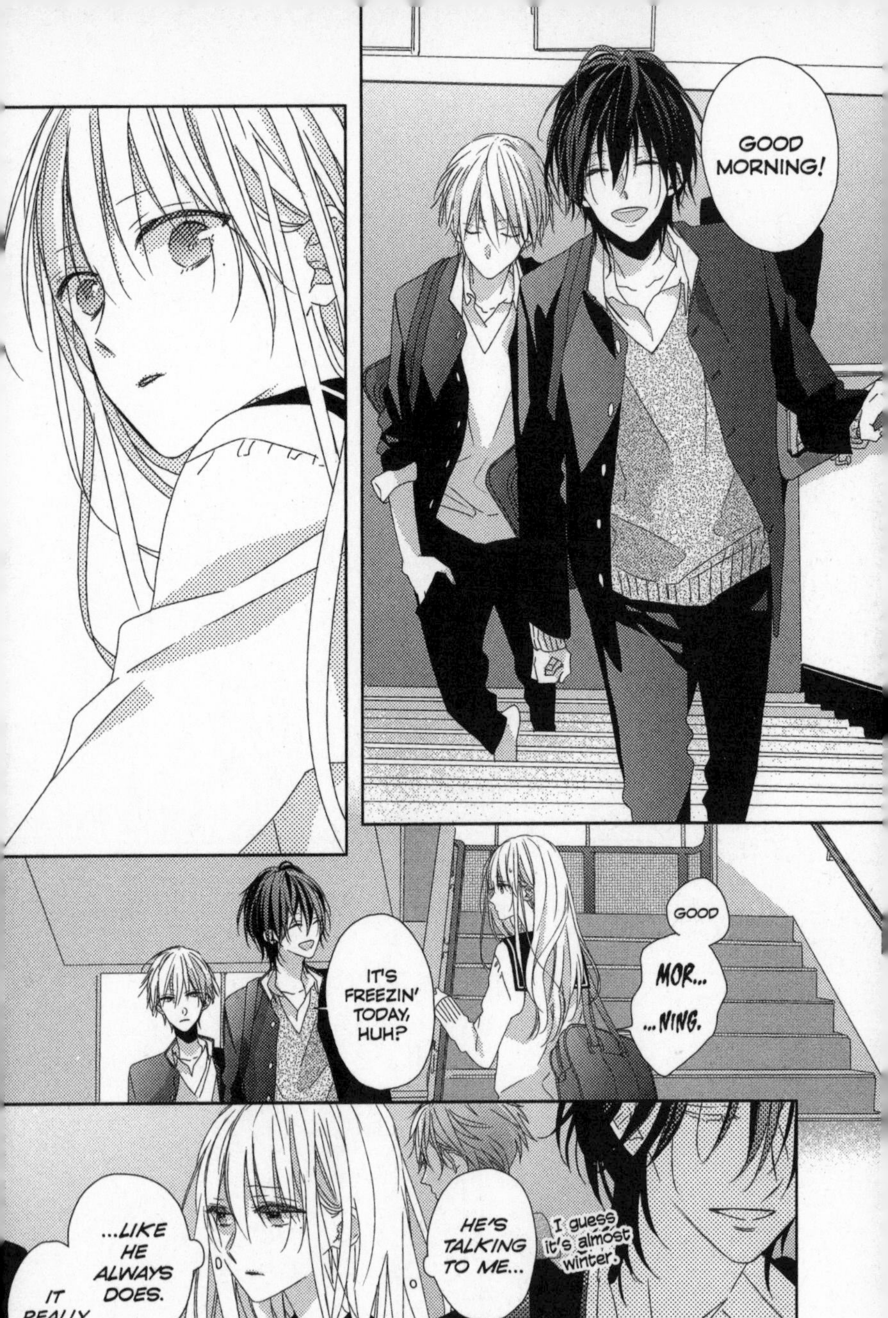
GOOD MORNING!
GOOD
MOR...
...NING.
IT'S FREEZIN' TODAY, HUH?
I guess it's almost winter.
HE'S TALKING TO ME...
...LIKE HE ALWAYS DOES.
IT REALLY IS...

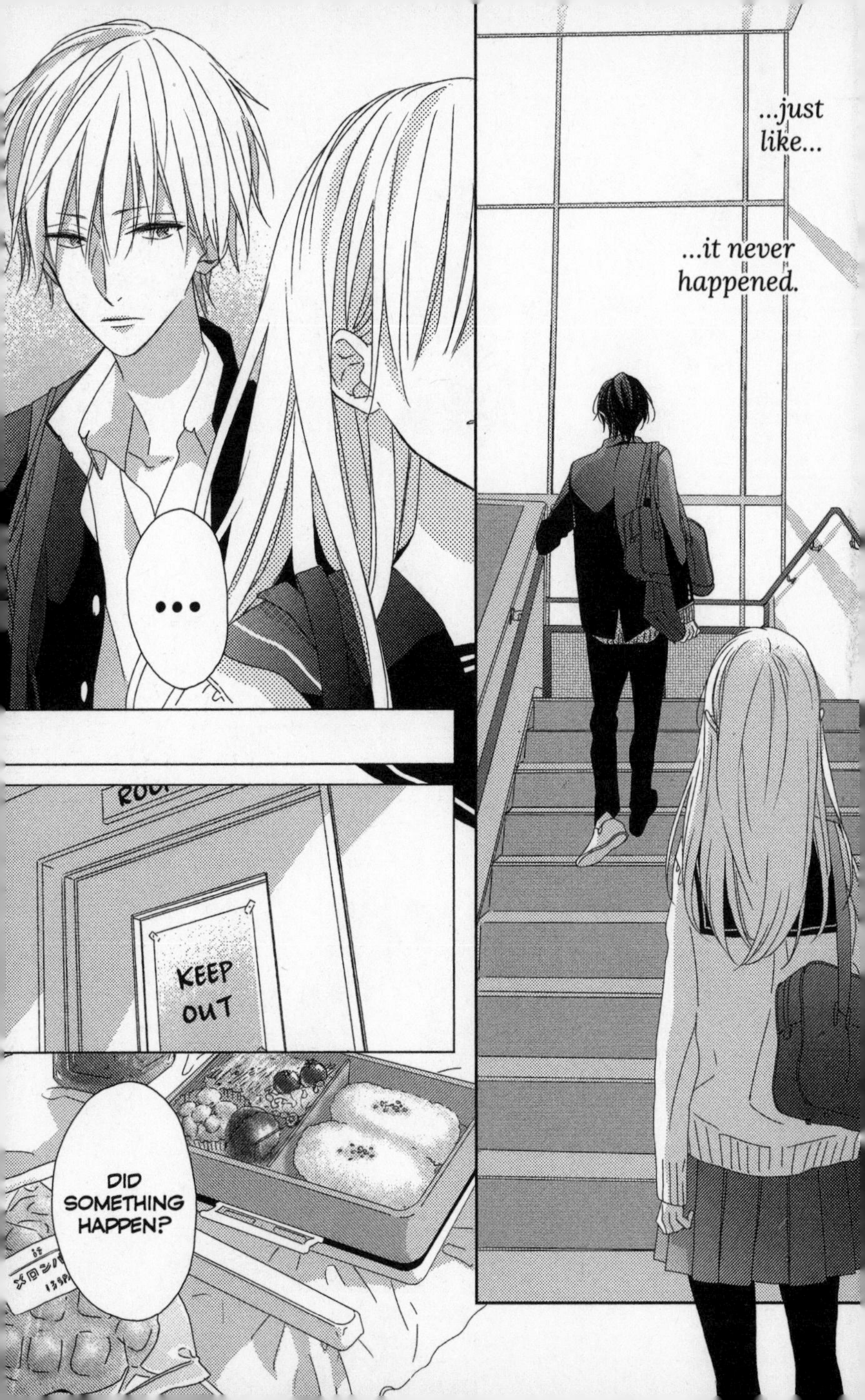
...just like...
...it never happened.
...
KEEP OUT
DID SOMETHING HAPPEN?

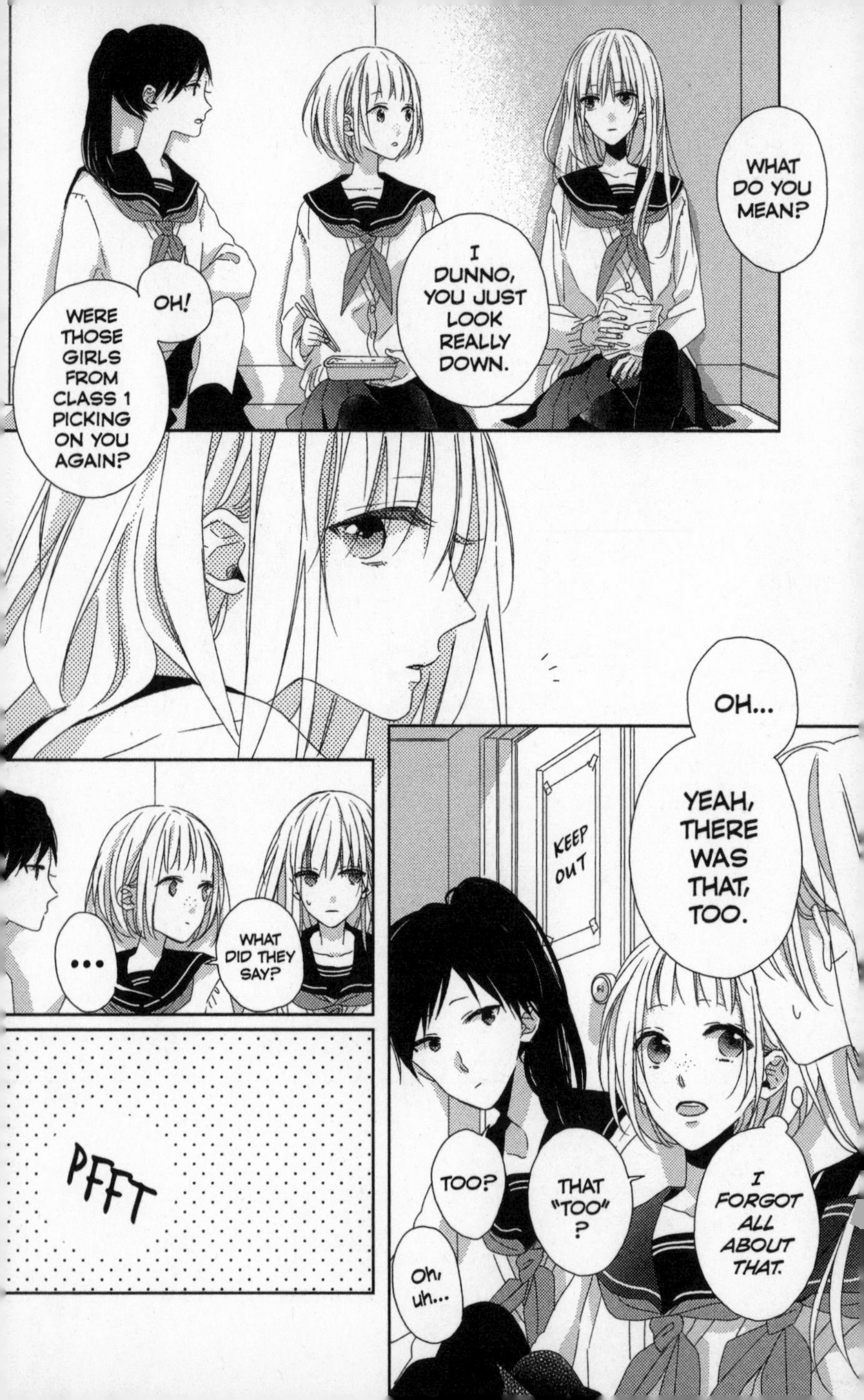
WHAT DO YOU MEAN?
I DUNNO, YOU JUST LOOK REALLY DOWN.
OH!
WERE THOSE GIRLS FROM CLASS 1 PICKING ON YOU AGAIN?
OH...
YEAH, THERE WAS THAT, TOO.
KEEP OUT
I FORGOT ALL ABOUT THAT.
THAT "TOO"?
TOO?
Oh, uh...
WHAT DID THEY SAY?
...
PFFT

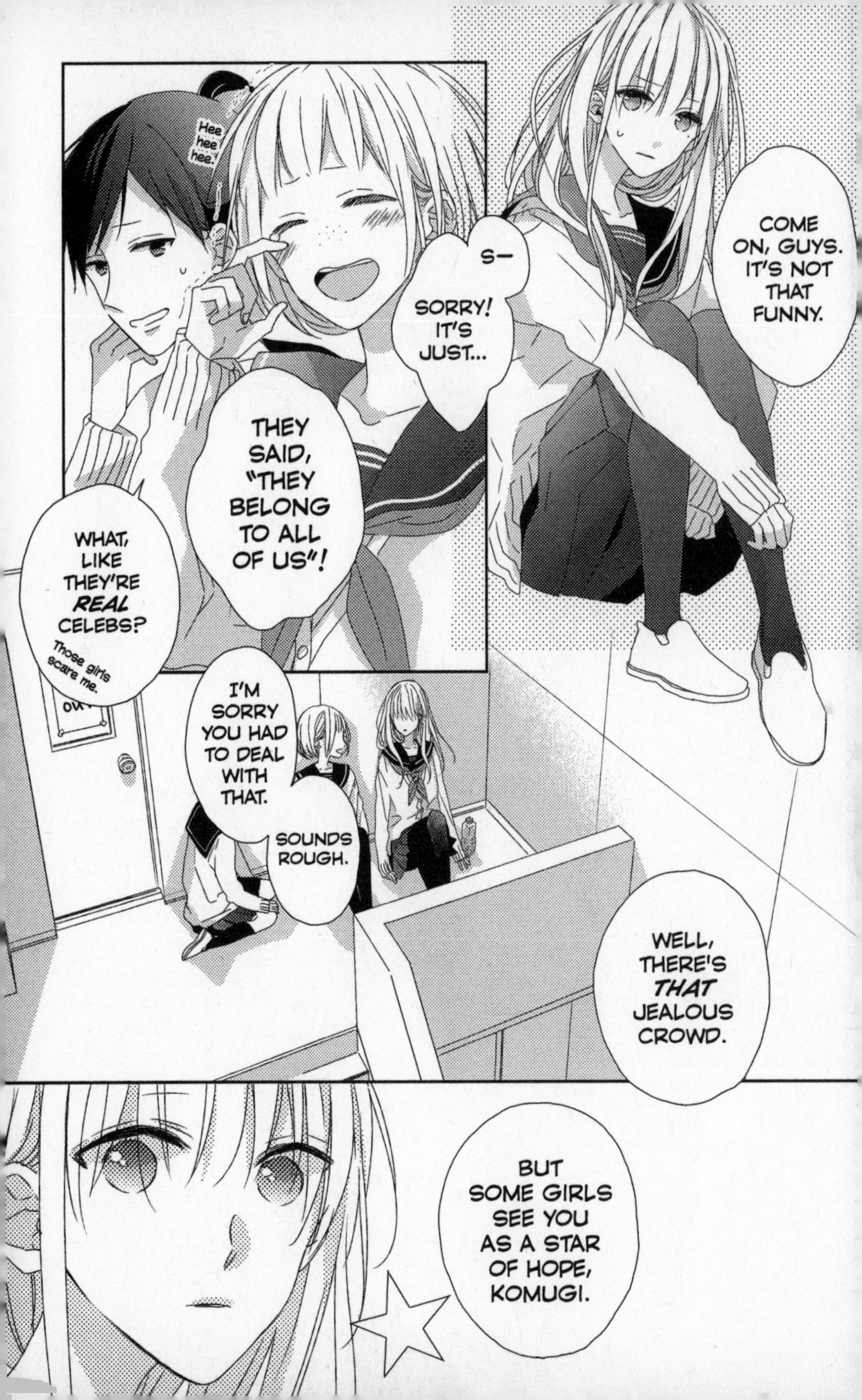
COME ON, GUYS. IT'S NOT THAT FUNNY.
S—
SORRY! IT'S JUST...
Hee hee hee.
THEY SAID, "THEY BELONG TO ALL OF US"!
WHAT, LIKE THEY'RE *REAL* CELEBS?
Those girls scare me.
I'M SORRY YOU HAD TO DEAL WITH THAT.
SOUNDS ROUGH.
WELL, THERE'S *THAT* JEALOUS CROWD.
BUT SOME GIRLS SEE YOU AS A STAR OF HOPE, KOMUGI.

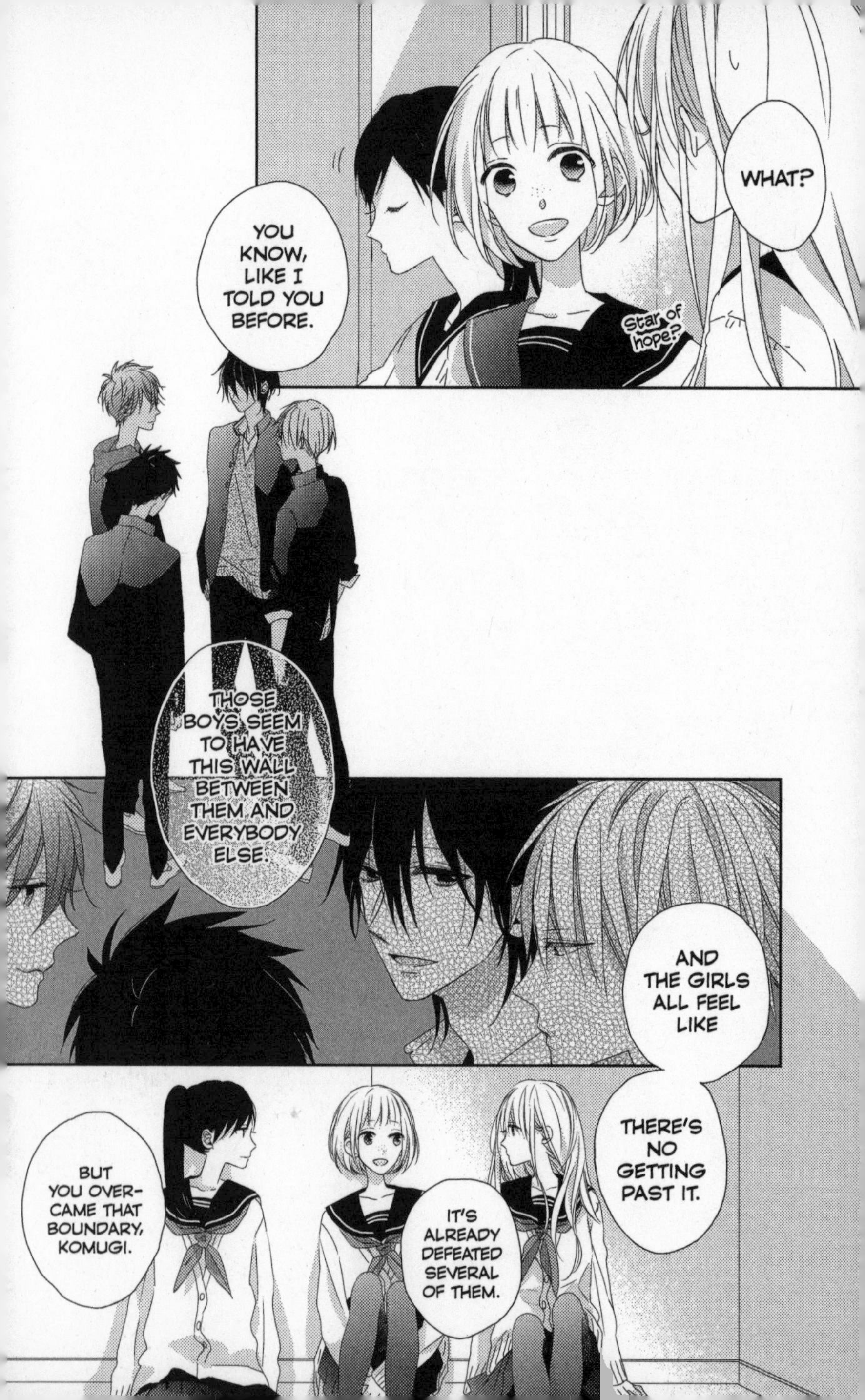
WHAT?
Star of hope?
YOU KNOW, LIKE I TOLD YOU BEFORE.
THOSE BOYS SEEM TO HAVE THIS WALL BETWEEN THEM AND EVERYBODY ELSE.
AND THE GIRLS ALL FEEL LIKE
THERE'S NO GETTING PAST IT.
IT'S ALREADY DEFEATED SEVERAL OF THEM.
BUT YOU OVER-CAME THAT BOUNDARY, KOMUGI.

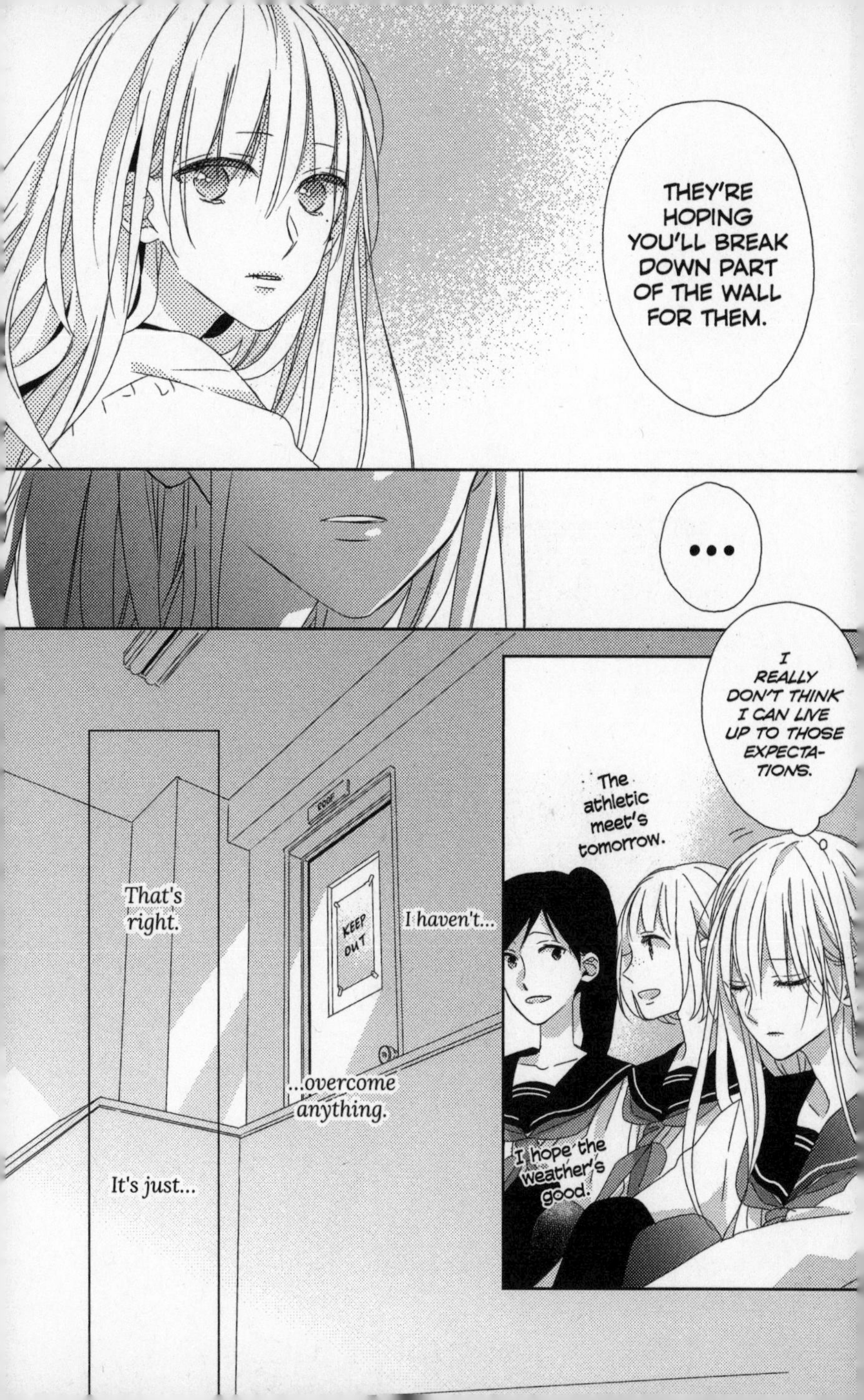
THEY'RE HOPING YOU'LL BREAK DOWN PART OF THE WALL FOR THEM.
...
I REALLY DON'T THINK I CAN LIVE UP TO THOSE EXPECTA-TIONS.
The athletic meet's tomorrow.
I hope the weather's good.
That's right.
I haven't...
KEEP OUT
...overcome anything.
It's just...

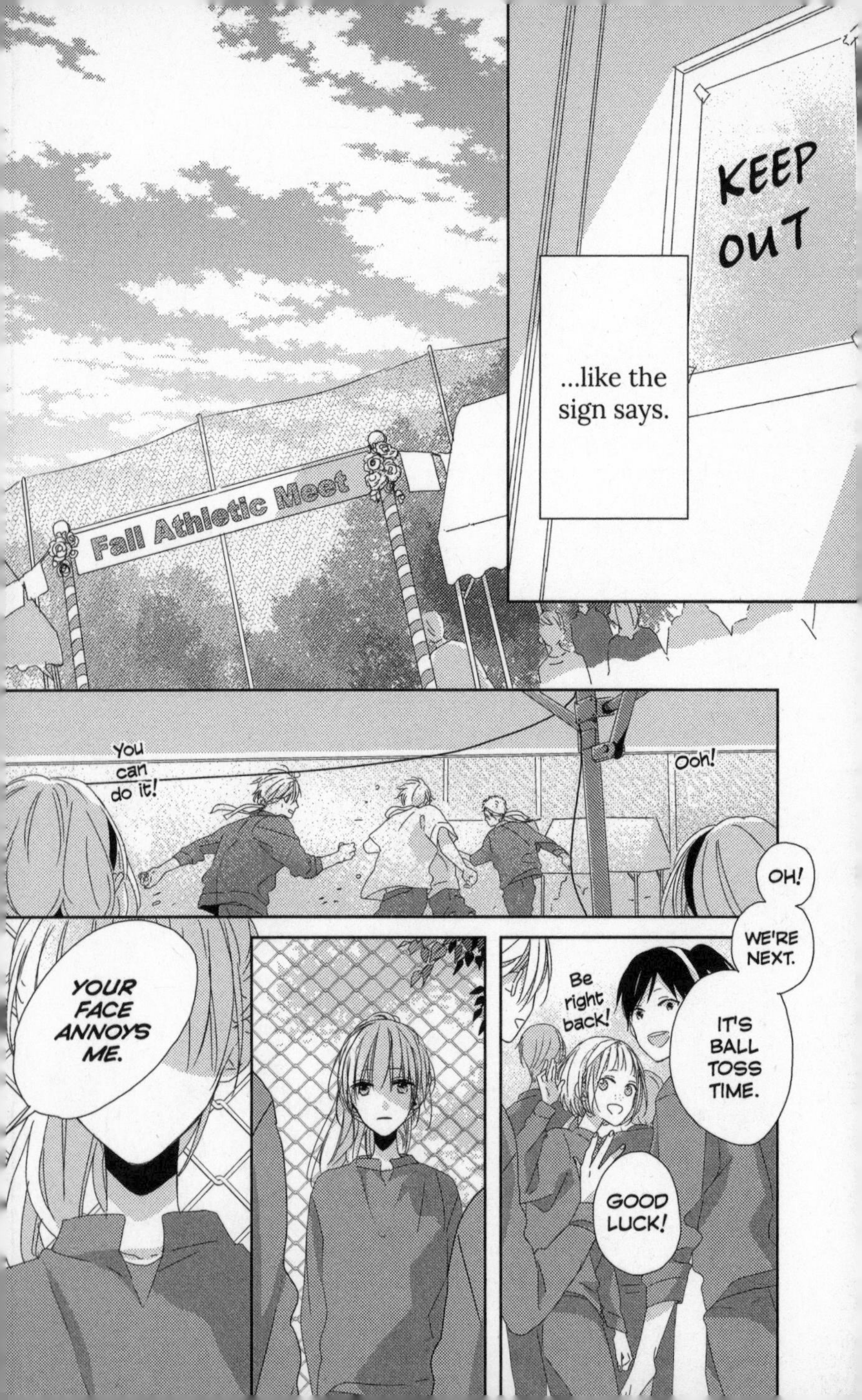
KEEP OUT
...like the sign says.
Fall Athletic Meet
Ooh!
You can do it!
OH!
WE'RE NEXT.
IT'S BALL TOSS TIME.
Be right back!
GOOD LUCK!
YOUR FACE ANNOYS ME.

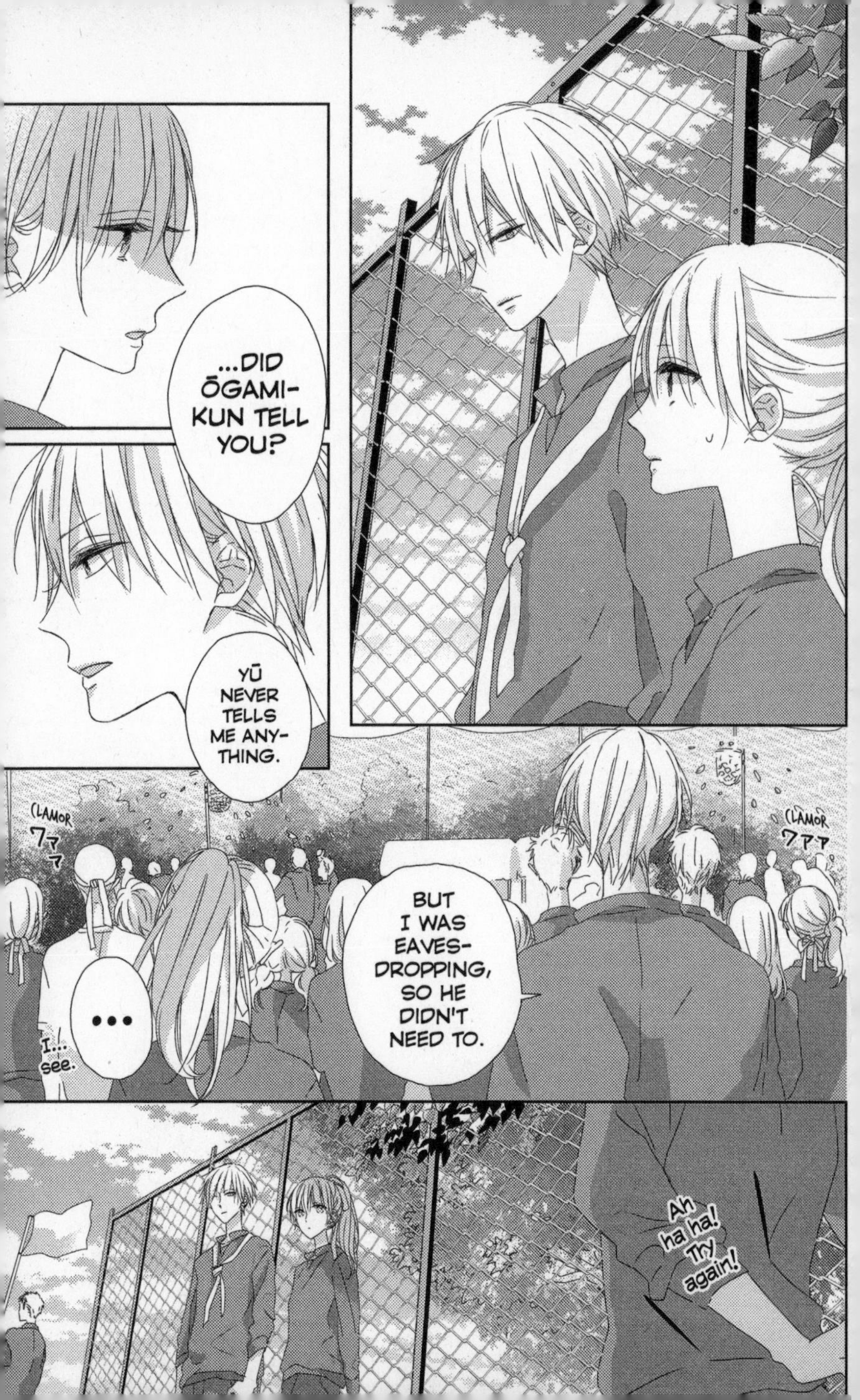
...DID ŌGAMI-KUN TELL YOU?
YŪ NEVER TELLS ME ANY-THING.
CLAMOR ワァァ
BUT I WAS EAVES-DROPPING, SO HE DIDN'T NEED TO.
...
I... see.
CLAMOR ワァァ
Ah ha ha! Try again!

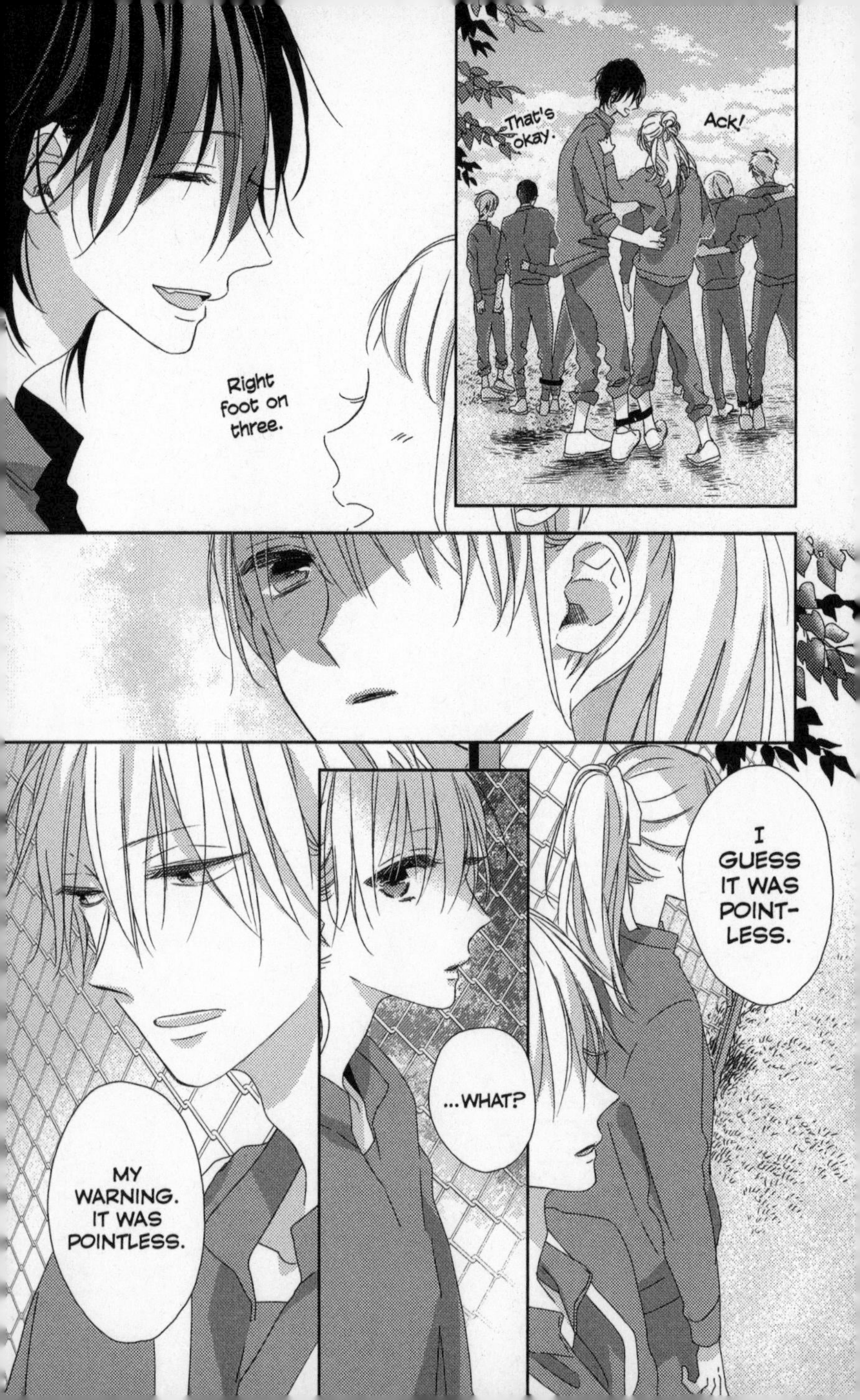
Ack!
That's okay.
Right foot on three.
I GUESS IT WAS POINT-LESS.
...WHAT?
MY WARNING. IT WAS POINTLESS.

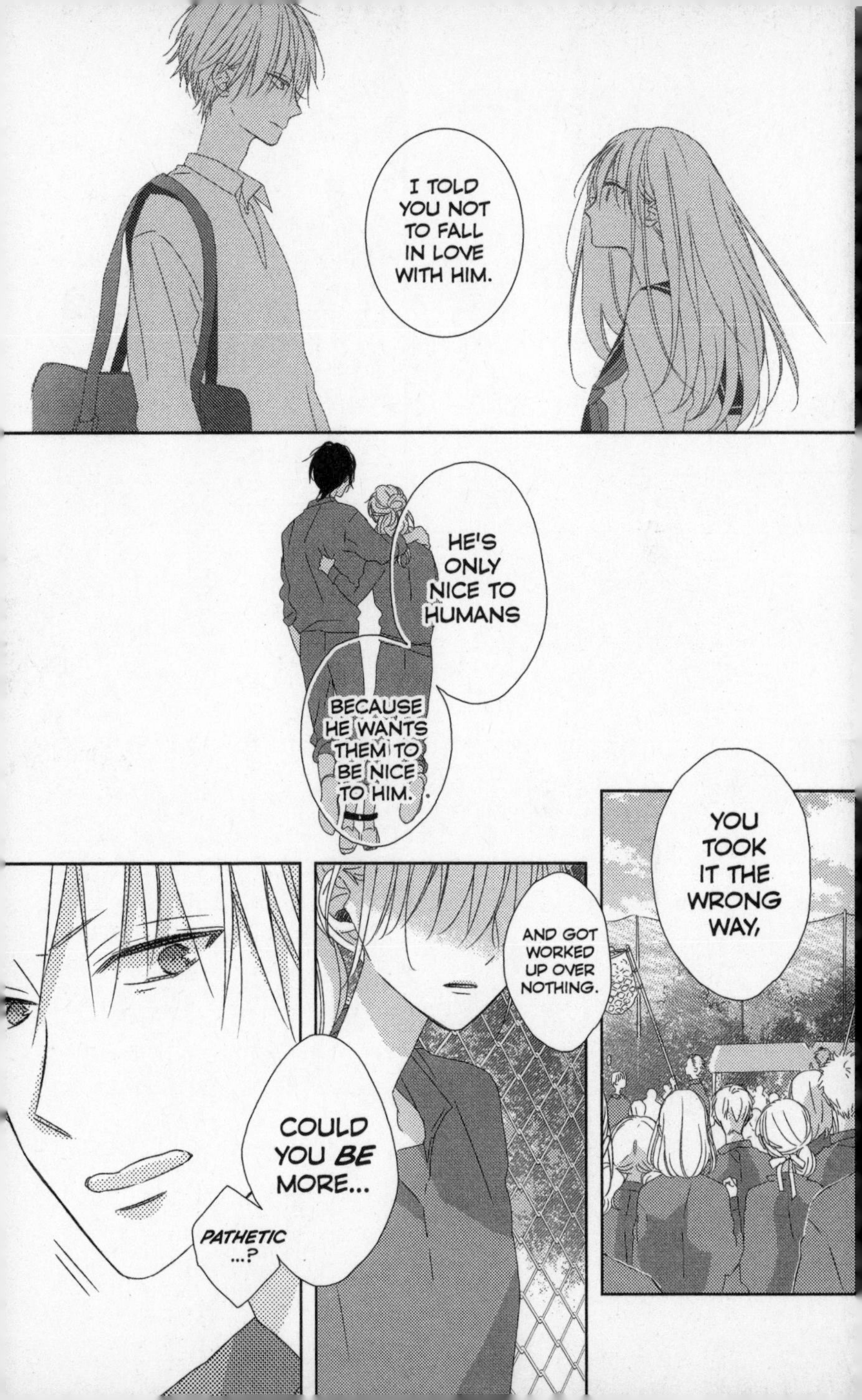
I TOLD YOU NOT TO FALL IN LOVE WITH HIM.
HE'S ONLY NICE TO HUMANS
BECAUSE HE WANTS THEM TO BE NICE TO HIM.
YOU TOOK IT THE WRONG WAY,
AND GOT WORKED UP OVER NOTHING.
COULD YOU *BE* MORE...
PATHETIC ...?

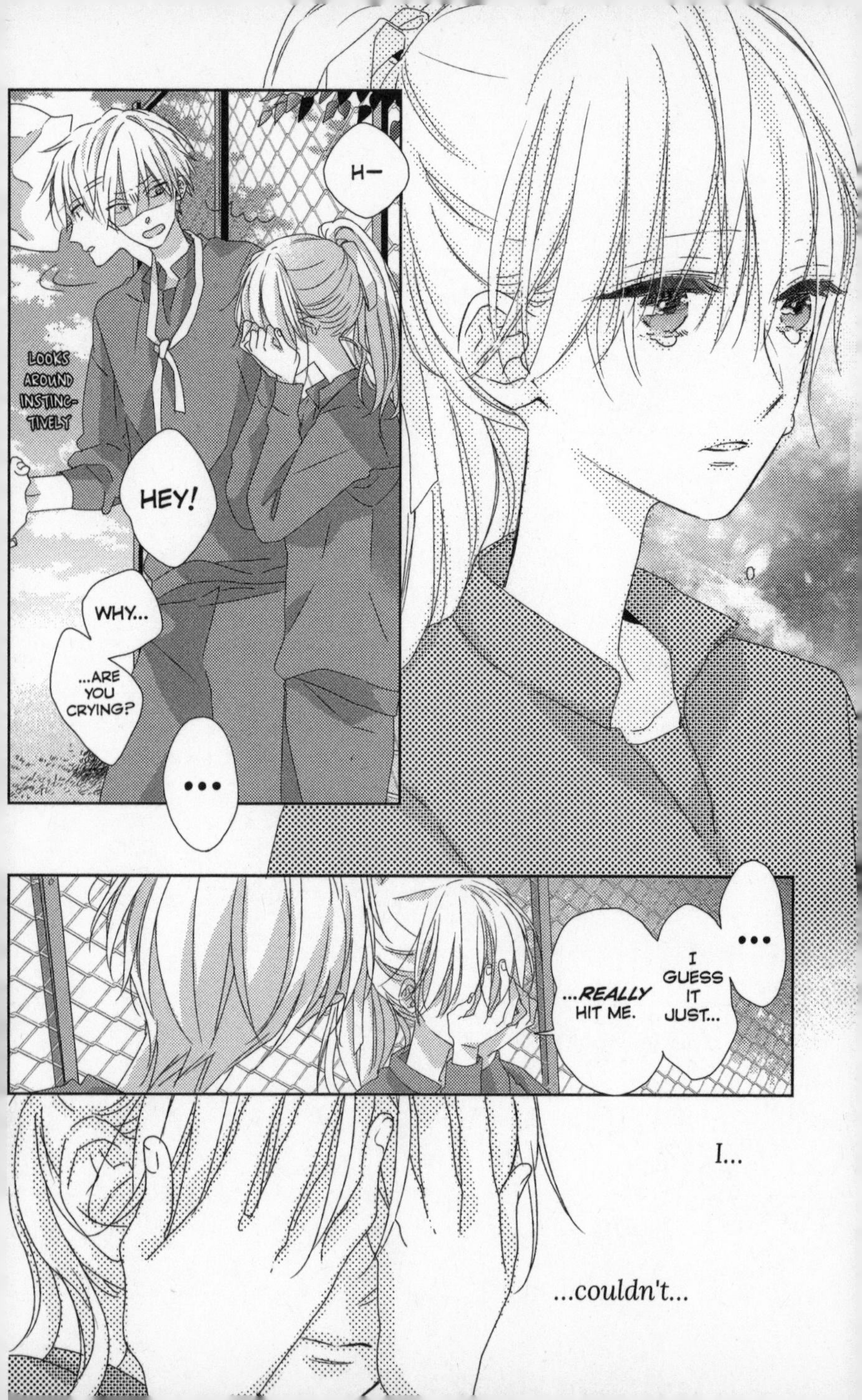
H—
LOOKS AROUND INSTINC-TIVELY
HEY!
WHY...
...ARE YOU CRYING?
...
...
I GUESS IT JUST...
...REALLY HIT ME.
I...
...couldn't...

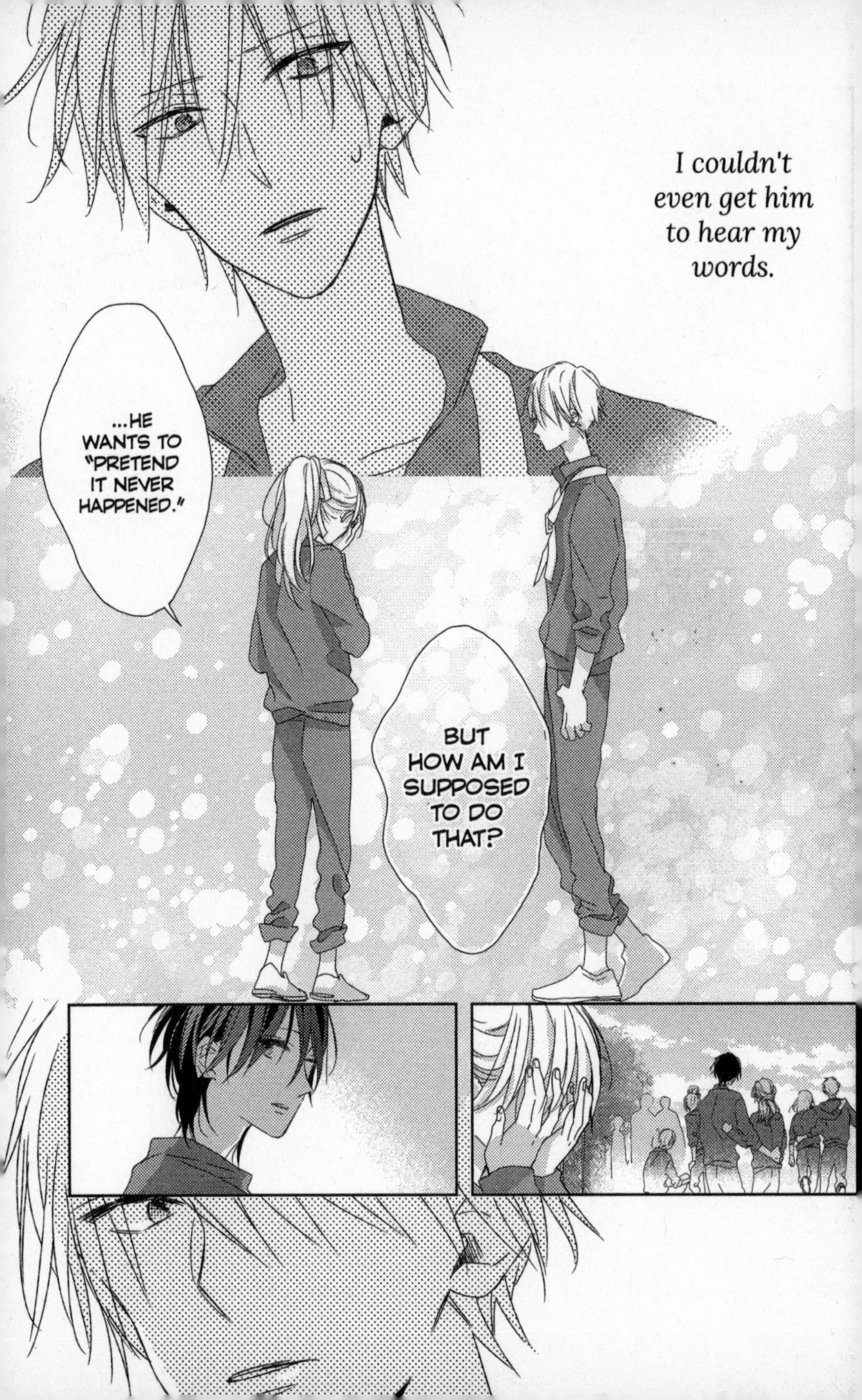
I couldn't even get him to hear my words.
...HE WANTS TO "PRETEND IT NEVER HAPPENED."
BUT HOW AM I SUPPOSED TO DO THAT?

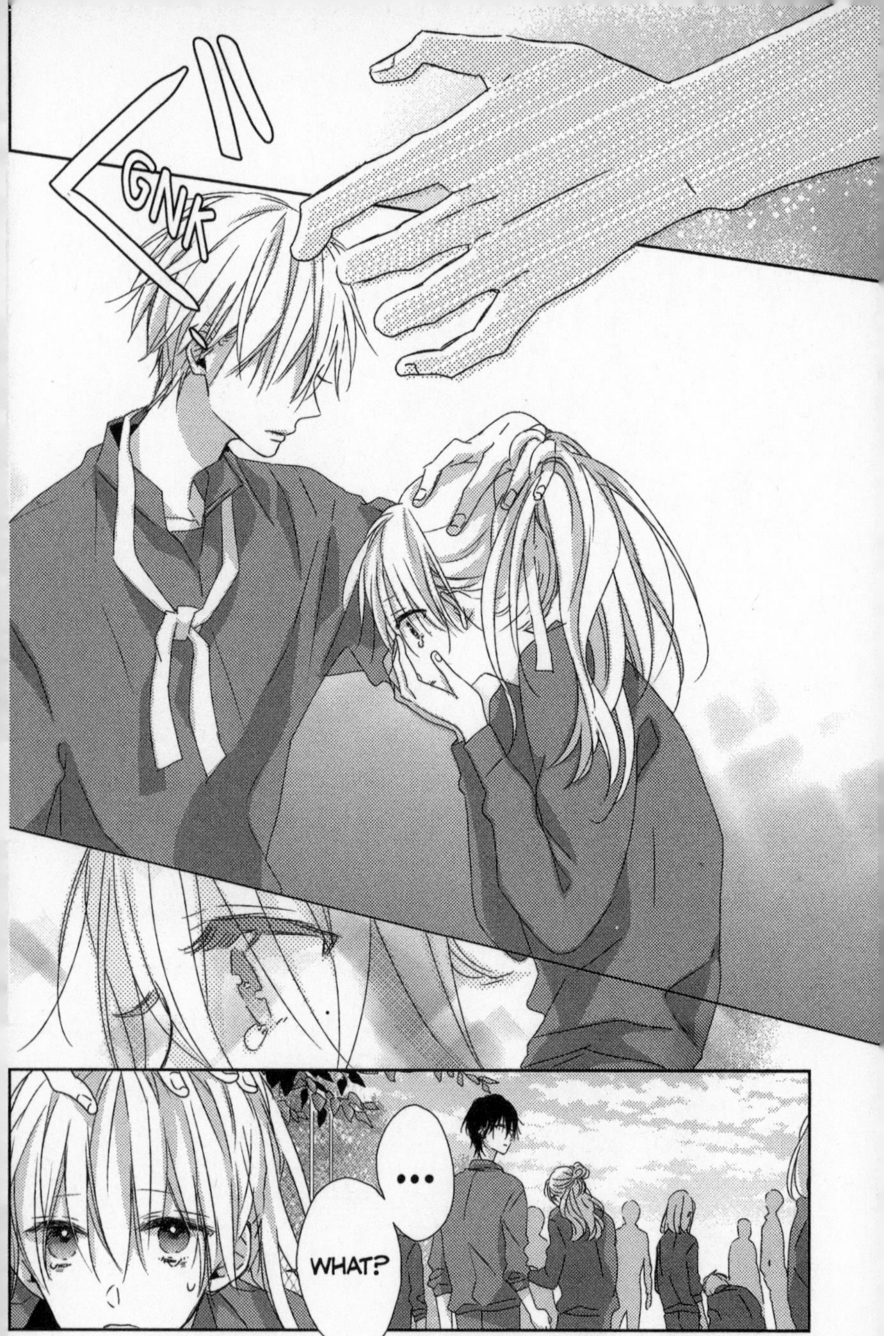
GNK
...
WHAT?

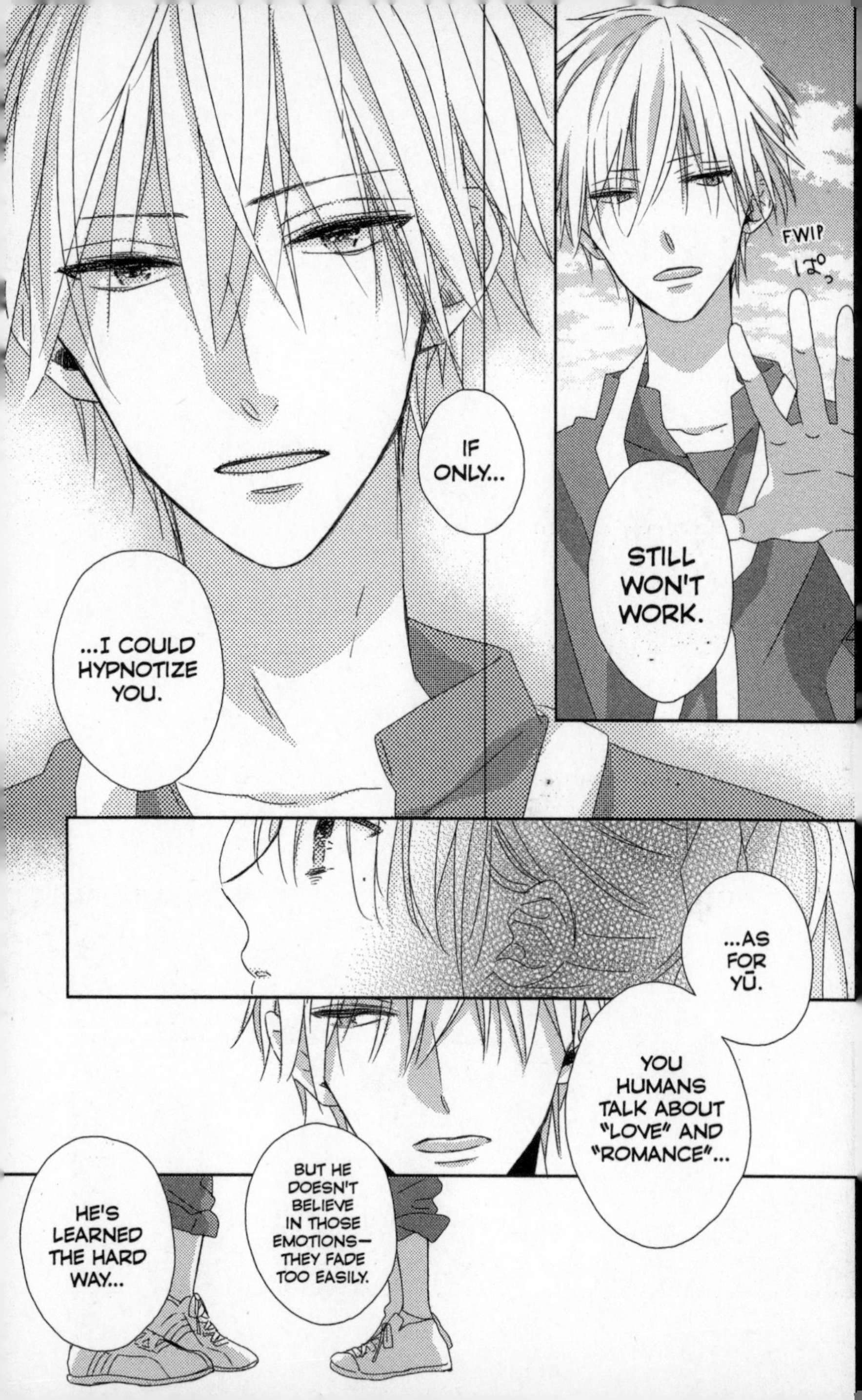
FWIP
ぱっ
STILL WON'T WORK.
IF ONLY...
...I COULD HYPNOTIZE YOU.
...AS FOR YŪ.
YOU HUMANS TALK ABOUT "LOVE" AND "ROMANCE"...
BUT HE DOESN'T BELIEVE IN THOSE EMOTIONS—THEY FADE TOO EASILY.
HE'S LEARNED THE HARD WAY...

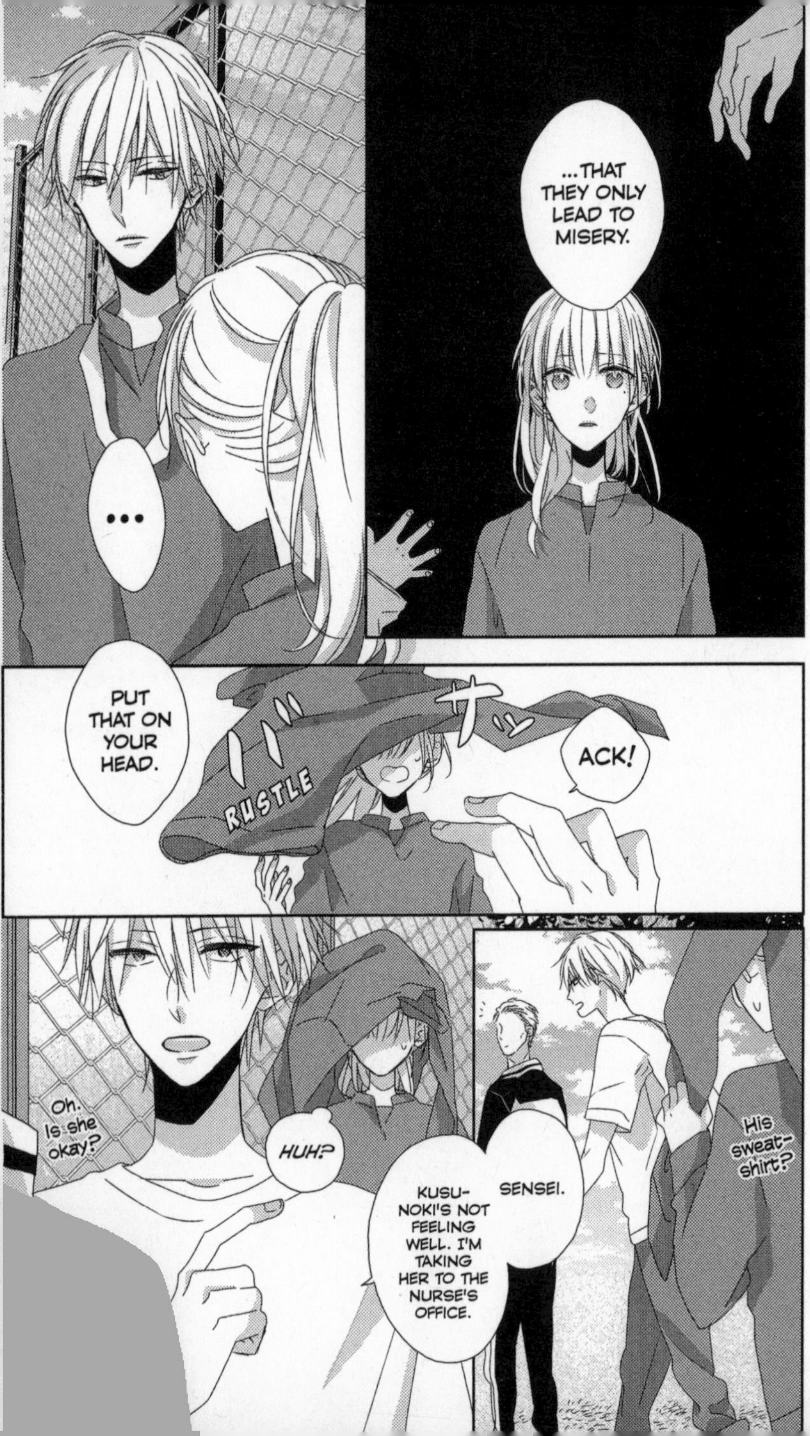
...THAT THEY ONLY LEAD TO MISERY.
...
ACK!
ザッ
RUSTLE
PUT THAT ON YOUR HEAD.
His sweat-shirt?
SENSEI.
KUSU-NOKI'S NOT FEELING WELL. I'M TAKING HER TO THE NURSE'S OFFICE.
HUH?
Oh. Is she okay?

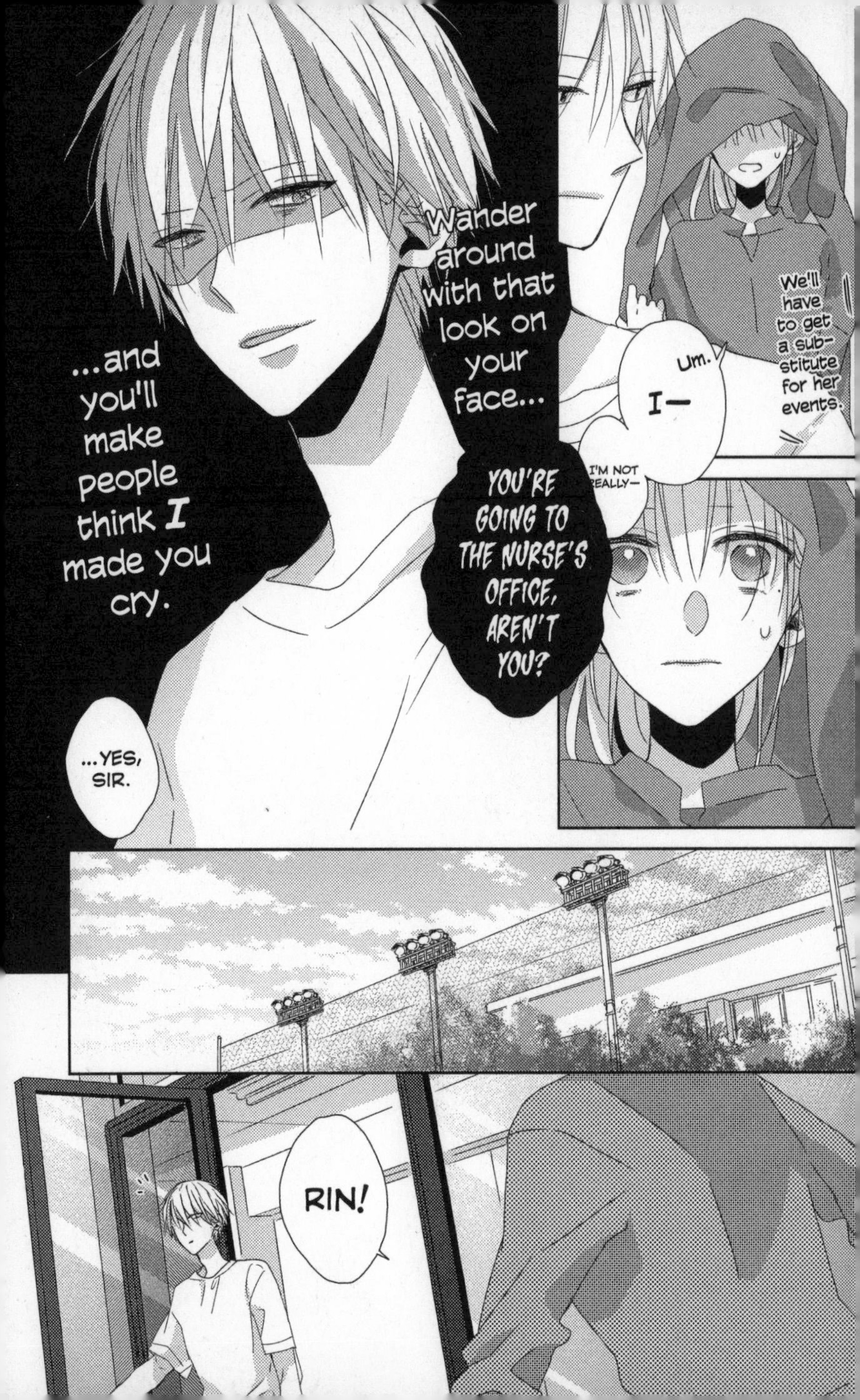
We'll have to get a sub-stitute for her events.
Um. I—
I'M NOT REALLY—
Wander around with that look on your face...
...and you'll make people think I made you cry.
YOU'RE GOING TO THE NURSE'S OFFICE, AREN'T YOU?
...YES, SIR.
RIN!

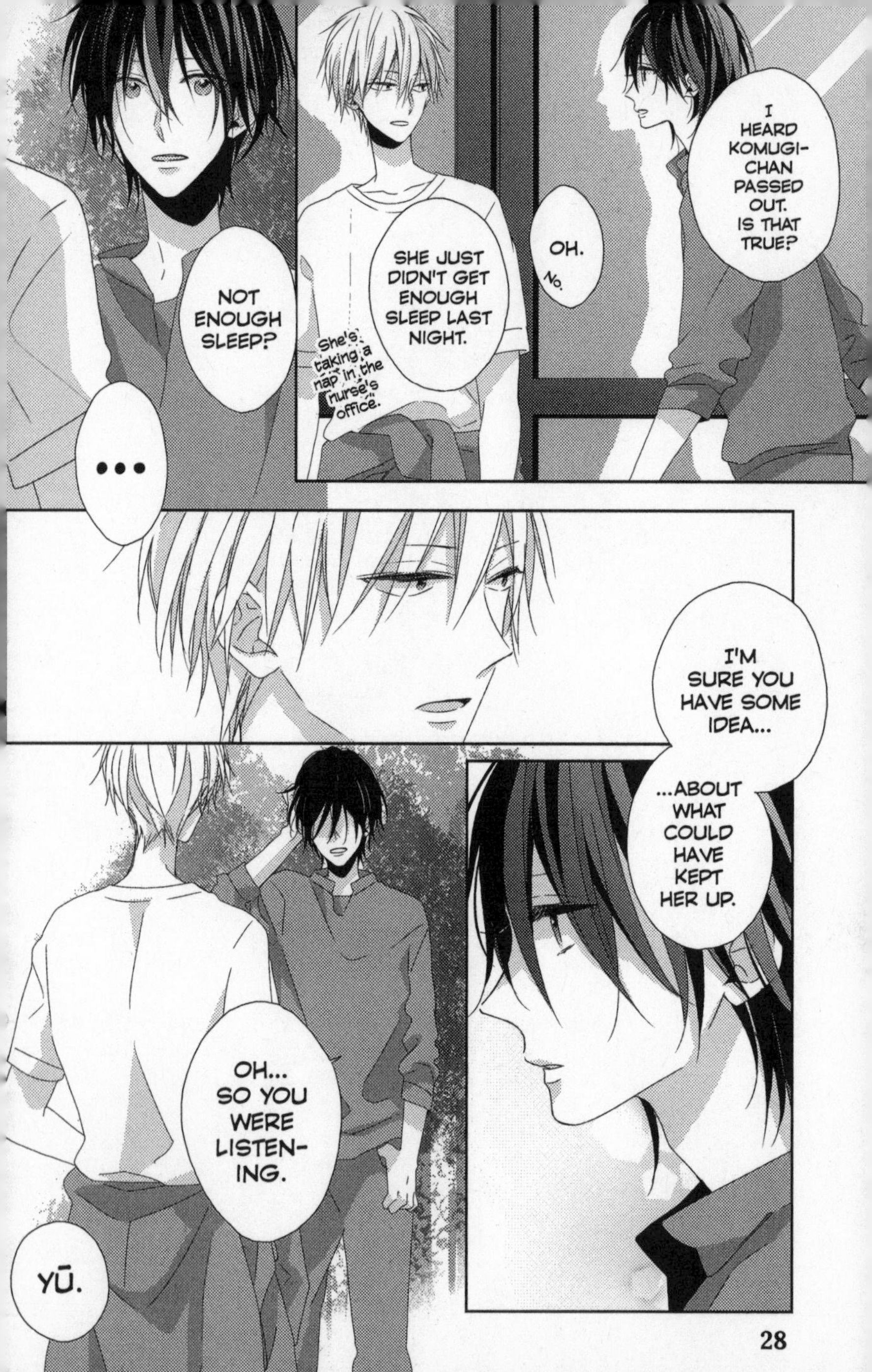
I HEARD KOMUGI-CHAN PASSED OUT. IS THAT TRUE?
OH.
No.
SHE JUST DIDN'T GET ENOUGH SLEEP LAST NIGHT.
She's taking a nap in the nurse's office.
NOT ENOUGH SLEEP?
...
I'M SURE YOU HAVE SOME IDEA...
...ABOUT WHAT COULD HAVE KEPT HER UP.
OH... SO YOU WERE LISTENING.
YŪ.

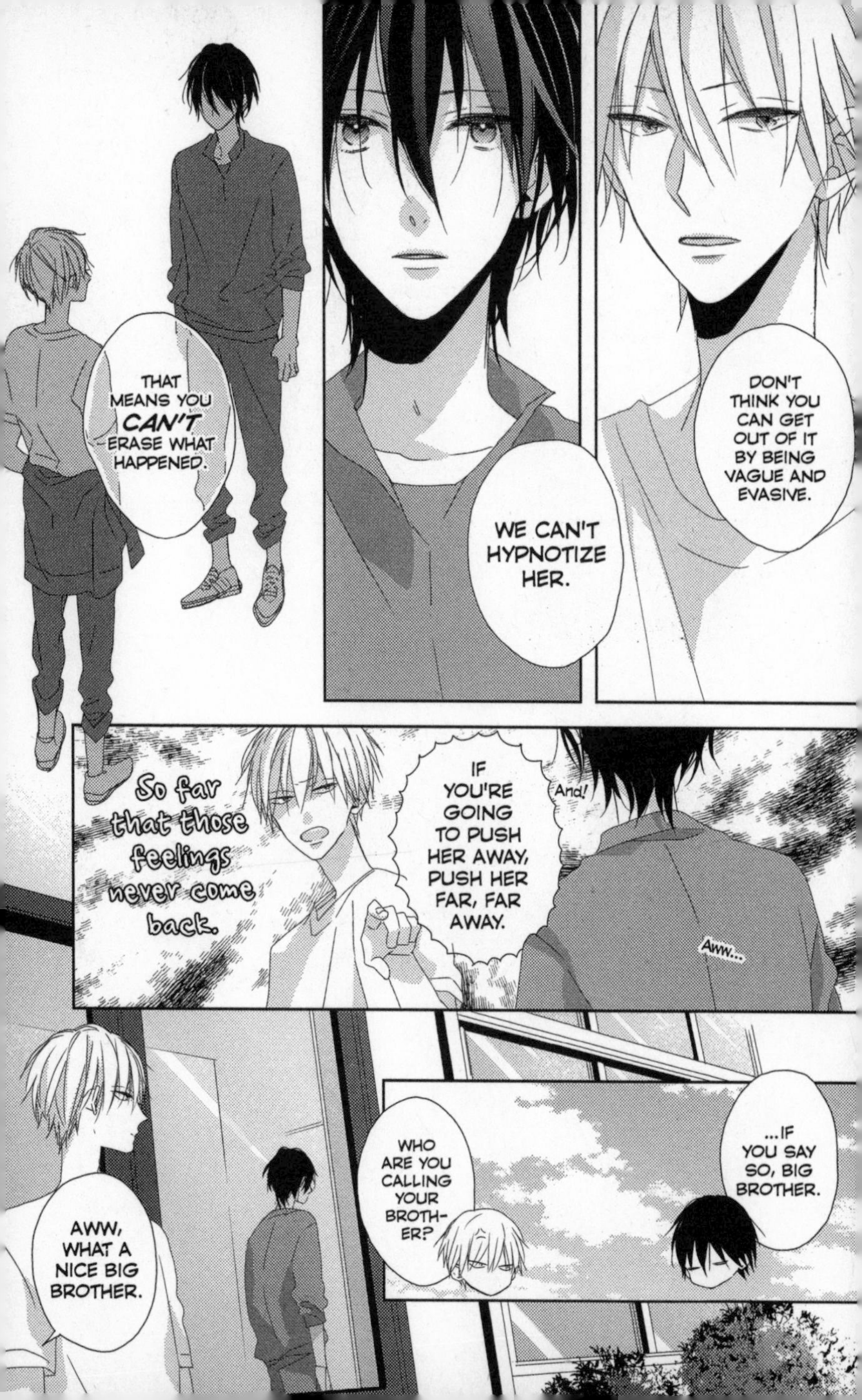
DON'T THINK YOU CAN GET OUT OF IT BY BEING VAGUE AND EVASIVE.
WE CAN'T HYPNOTIZE HER.
THAT MEANS YOU CAN'T ERASE WHAT HAPPENED.
And!
IF YOU'RE GOING TO PUSH HER AWAY, PUSH HER FAR, FAR AWAY.
So far that those feelings never come back.
Aww...
...IF YOU SAY SO, BIG BROTHER.
WHO ARE YOU CALLING YOUR BROTH-ER?
AWW, WHAT A NICE BIG BROTHER.

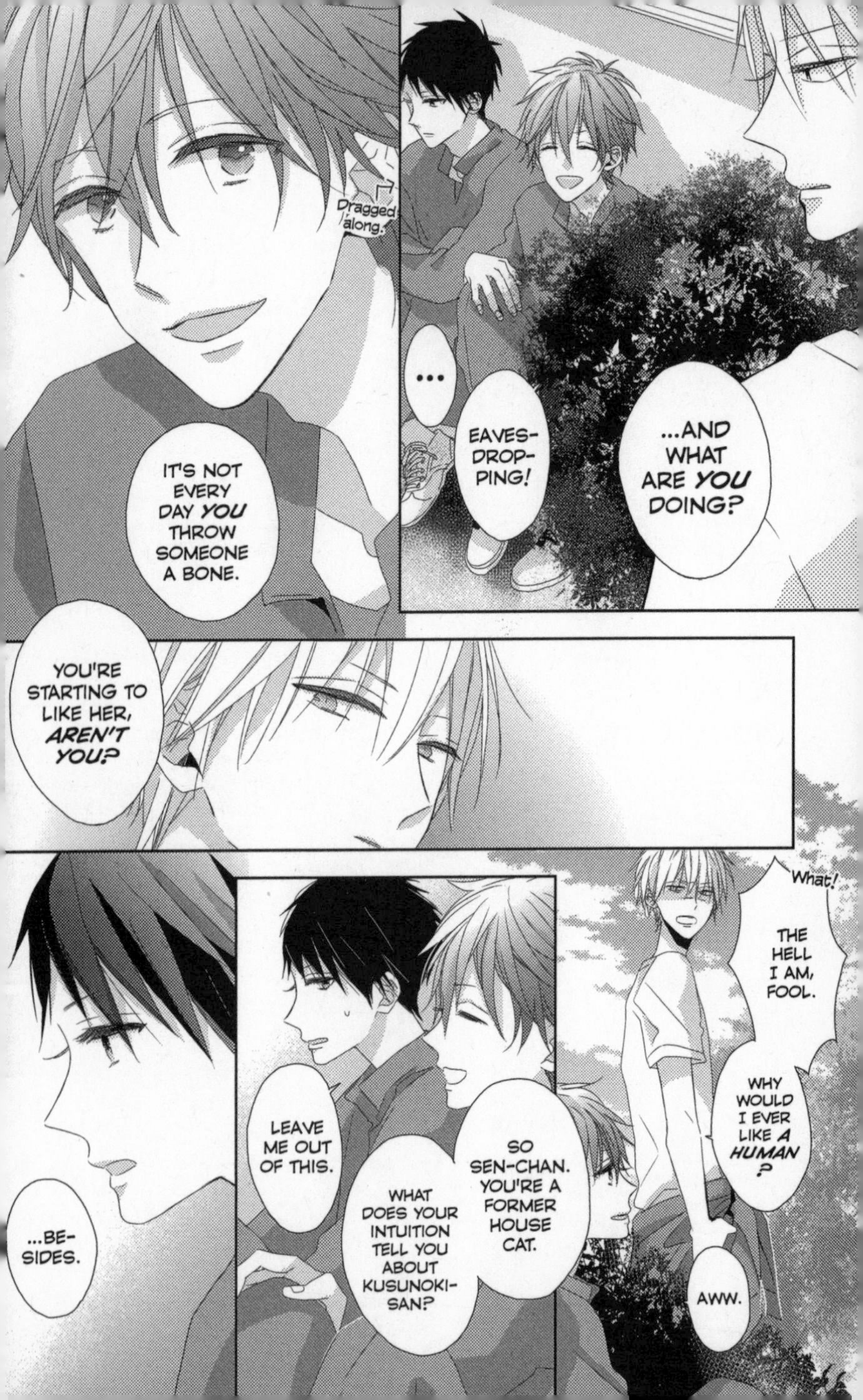
...AND WHAT ARE YOU DOING?
EAVES-DROPPING!
...
Dragged along.
IT'S NOT EVERY DAY YOU THROW SOMEONE A BONE.
YOU'RE STARTING TO LIKE HER, AREN'T YOU?
What!
THE HELL I AM, FOOL.
WHY WOULD I EVER LIKE A HUMAN?
AWW.
SO SEN-CHAN. YOU'RE A FORMER HOUSE CAT.
LEAVE ME OUT OF THIS.
WHAT DOES YOUR INTUITION TELL YOU ABOUT KUSUNOKI-SAN?
...BE-SIDES.

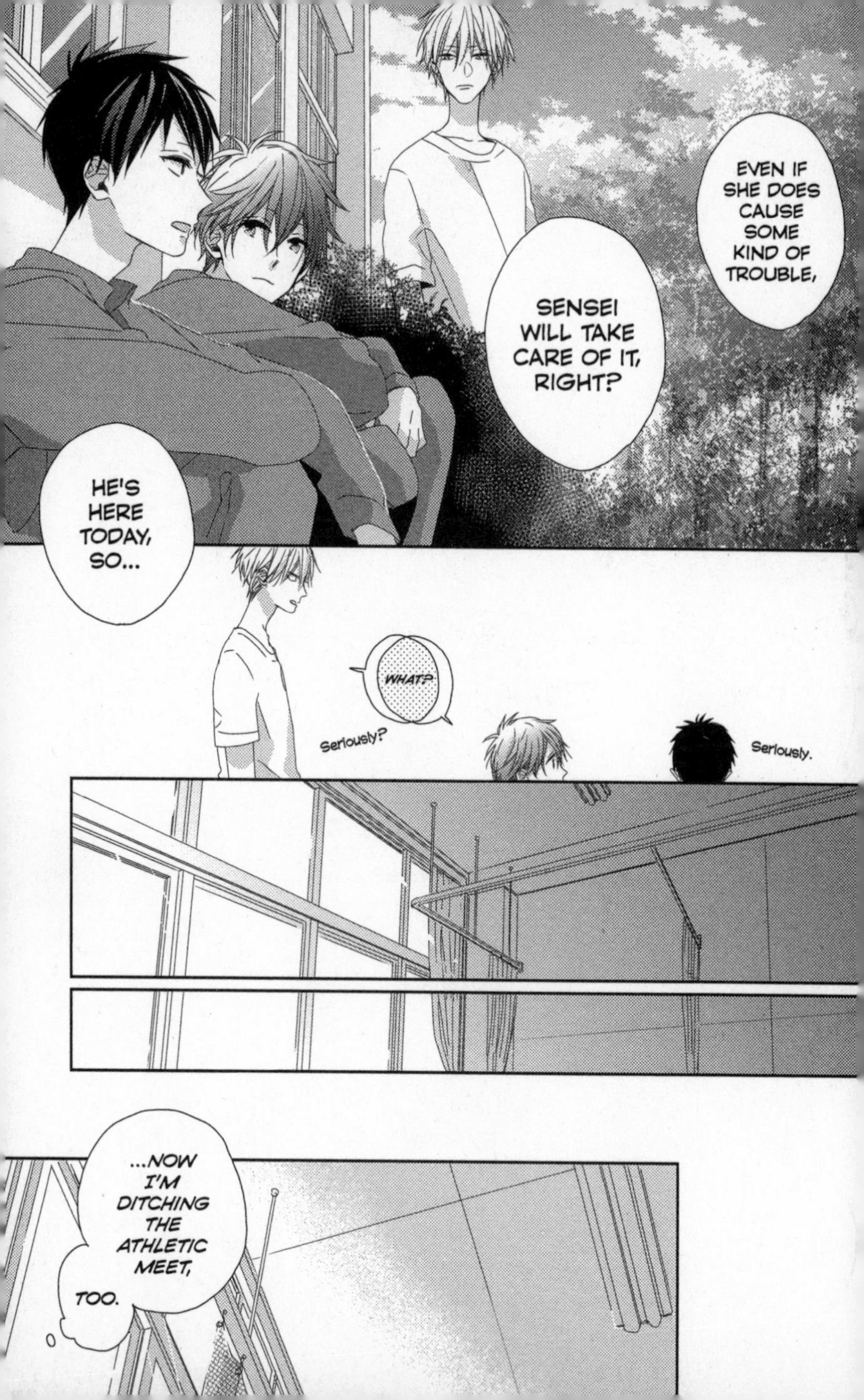
EVEN IF SHE DOES CAUSE SOME KIND OF TROUBLE,
SENSEI WILL TAKE CARE OF IT, RIGHT?
HE'S HERE TODAY, SO...
WHAT?
Seriously?
Seriously.
...NOW I'M DITCHING THE ATHLETIC MEET,
TOO.

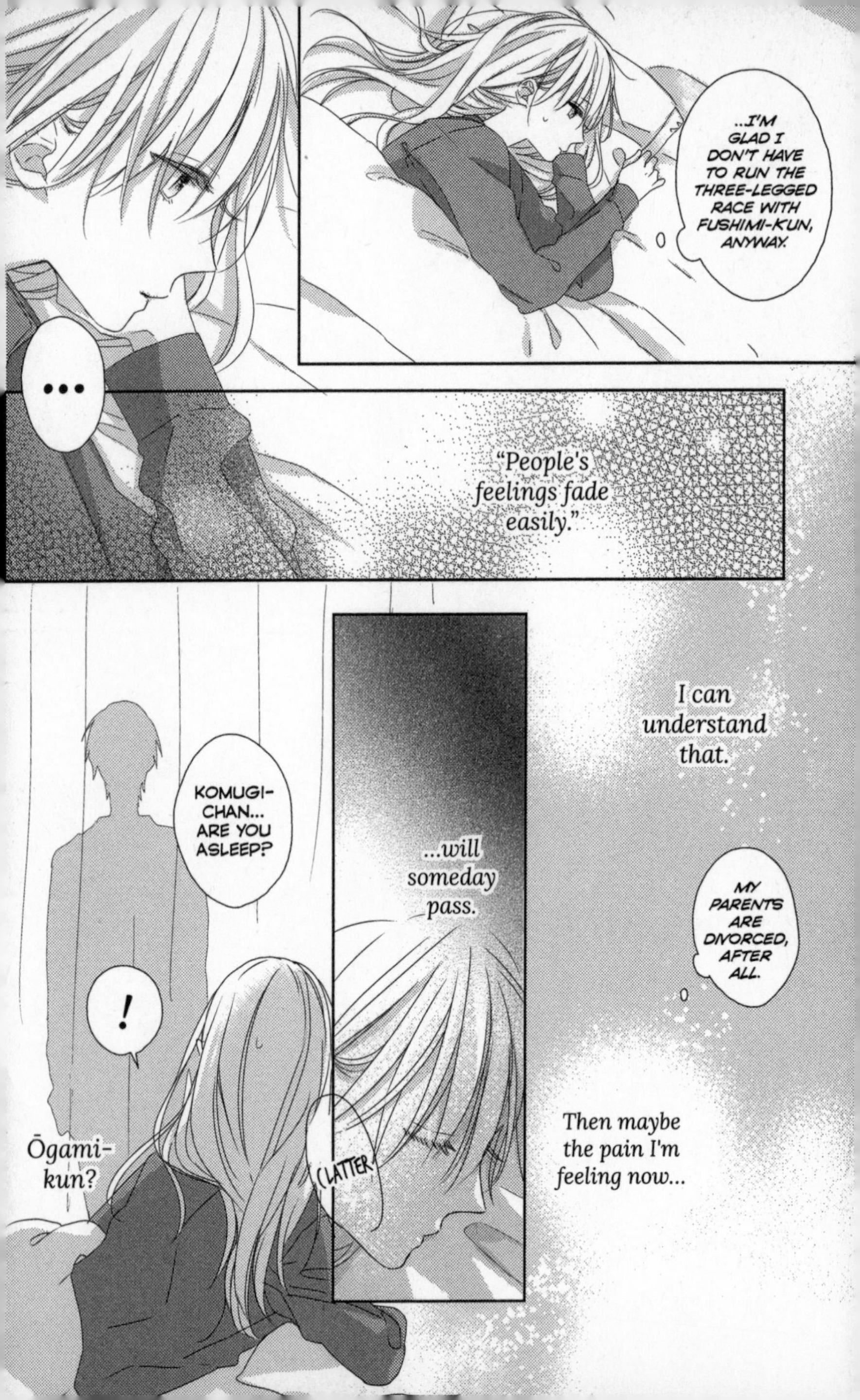
...I'M GLAD I DON'T HAVE TO RUN THE THREE-LEGGED RACE WITH FUSHIMI-KUN, ANYWAY.
...
"People's feelings fade easily."
I can understand that.
MY PARENTS ARE DIVORCED, AFTER ALL.
Then maybe the pain I'm feeling now...
...will someday pass.
CLATTER
KOMUGI-CHAN... ARE YOU ASLEEP?
!
Ōgami-kun?

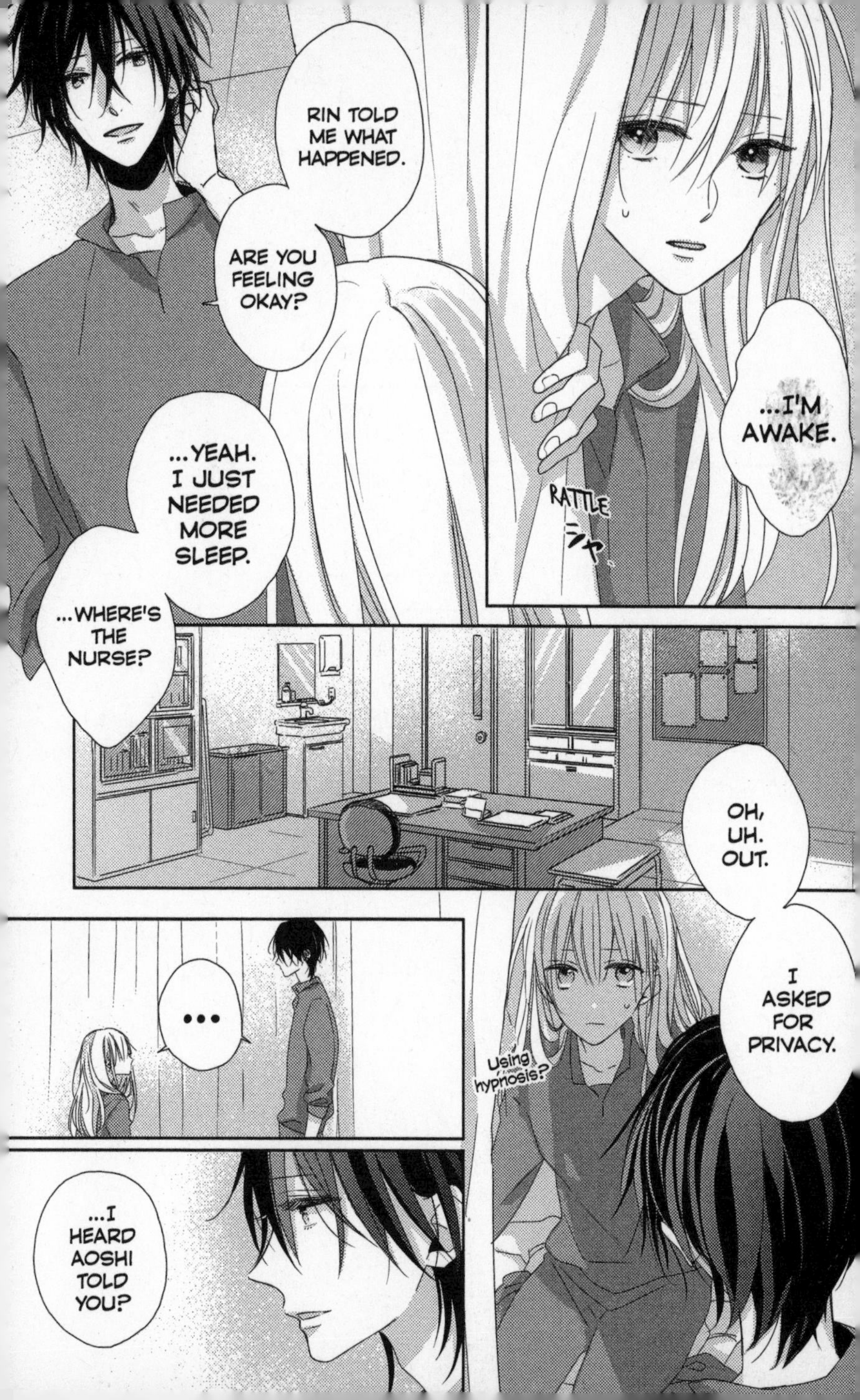
...I'M AWAKE.
RATTLE
シャ
RIN TOLD ME WHAT HAPPENED.
ARE YOU FEELING OKAY?
...YEAH. I JUST NEEDED MORE SLEEP.
...WHERE'S THE NURSE?
OH, UH. OUT.
I ASKED FOR PRIVACY.
Using hypnosis?
...
...I HEARD AOSHI TOLD YOU?

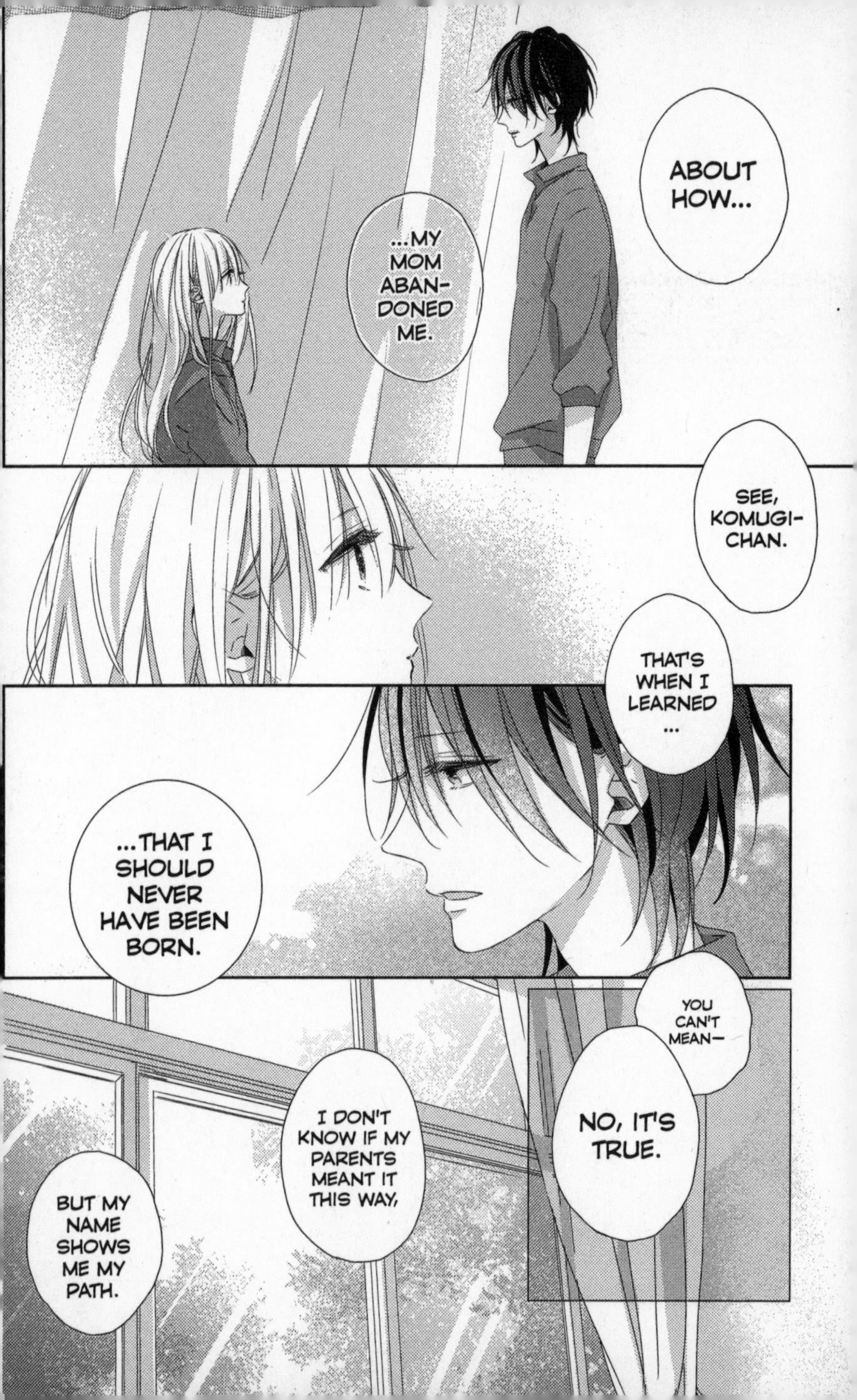
ABOUT HOW...
...MY MOM ABAN-DONED ME.
SEE, KOMUGI-CHAN.
THAT'S WHEN I LEARNED ...
...THAT I SHOULD NEVER HAVE BEEN BORN.
YOU CAN'T MEAN—
NO, IT'S TRUE.
I DON'T KNOW IF MY PARENTS MEANT IT THIS WAY,
BUT MY NAME SHOWS ME MY PATH.

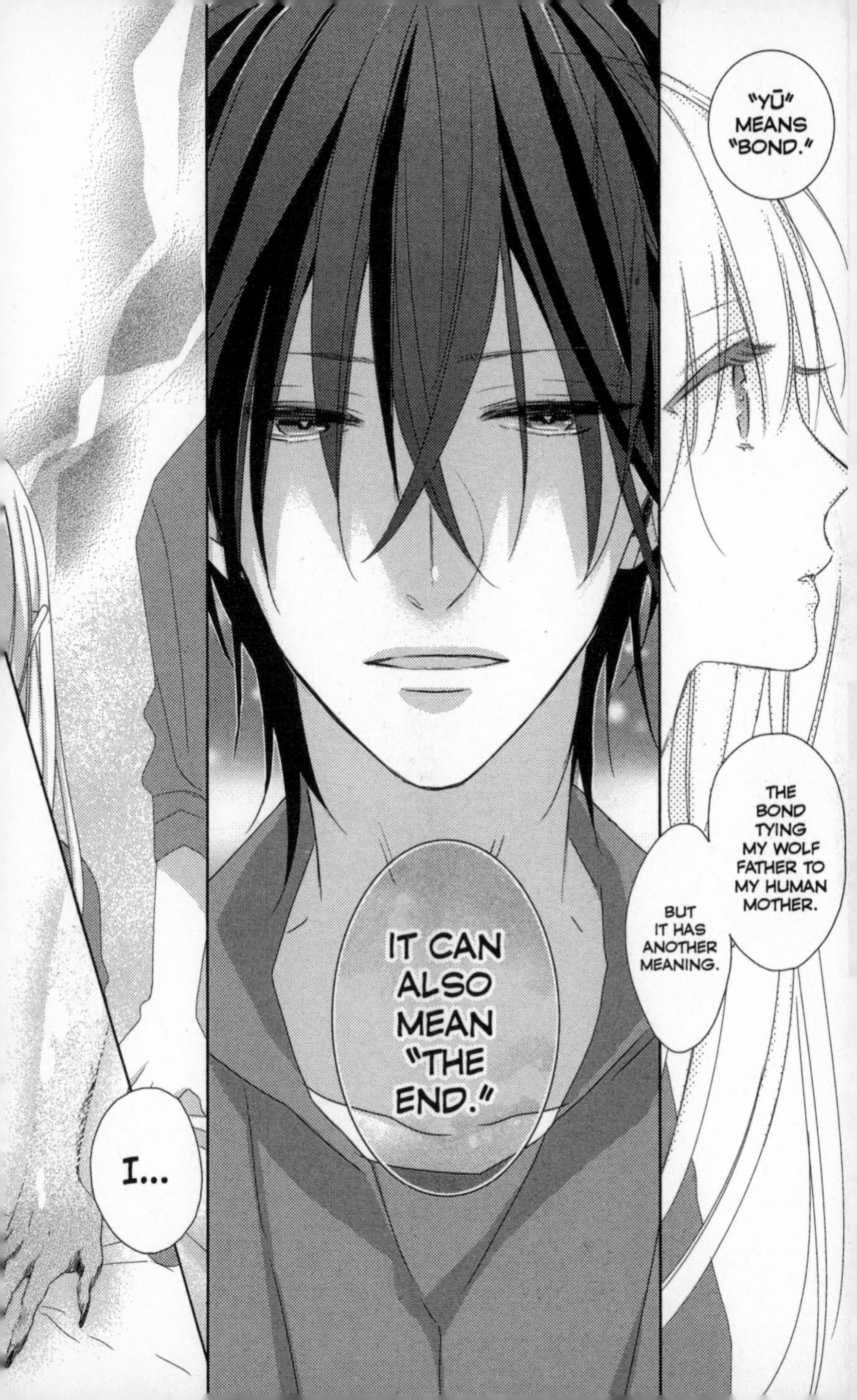
"YŪ" MEANS "BOND."
THE BOND TYING MY WOLF FATHER TO MY HUMAN MOTHER.
BUT IT HAS ANOTHER MEANING.
IT CAN ALSO MEAN "THE END."
I...

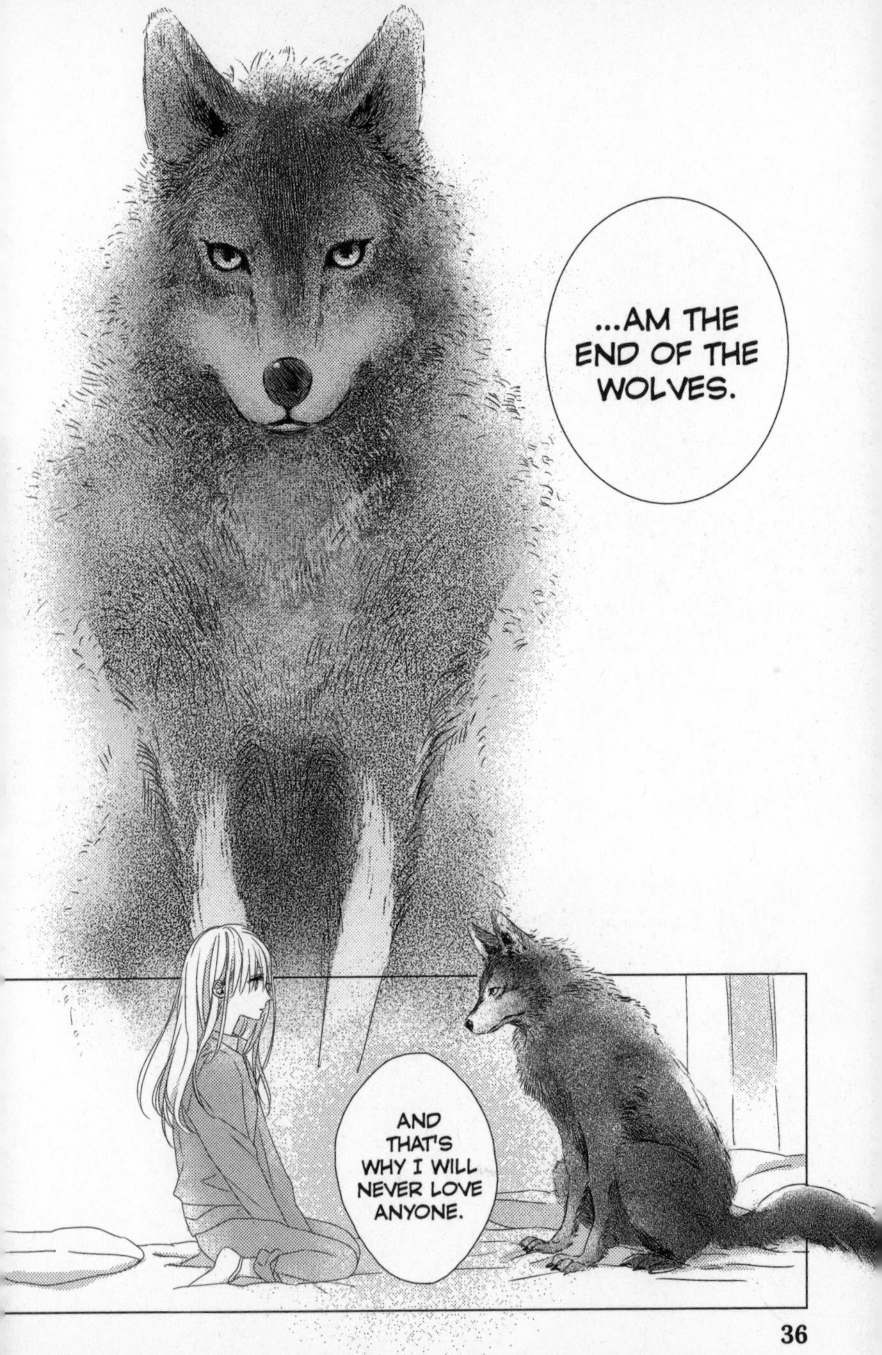
...AM THE END OF THE WOLVES.
AND THAT'S WHY I WILL NEVER LOVE ANYONE.

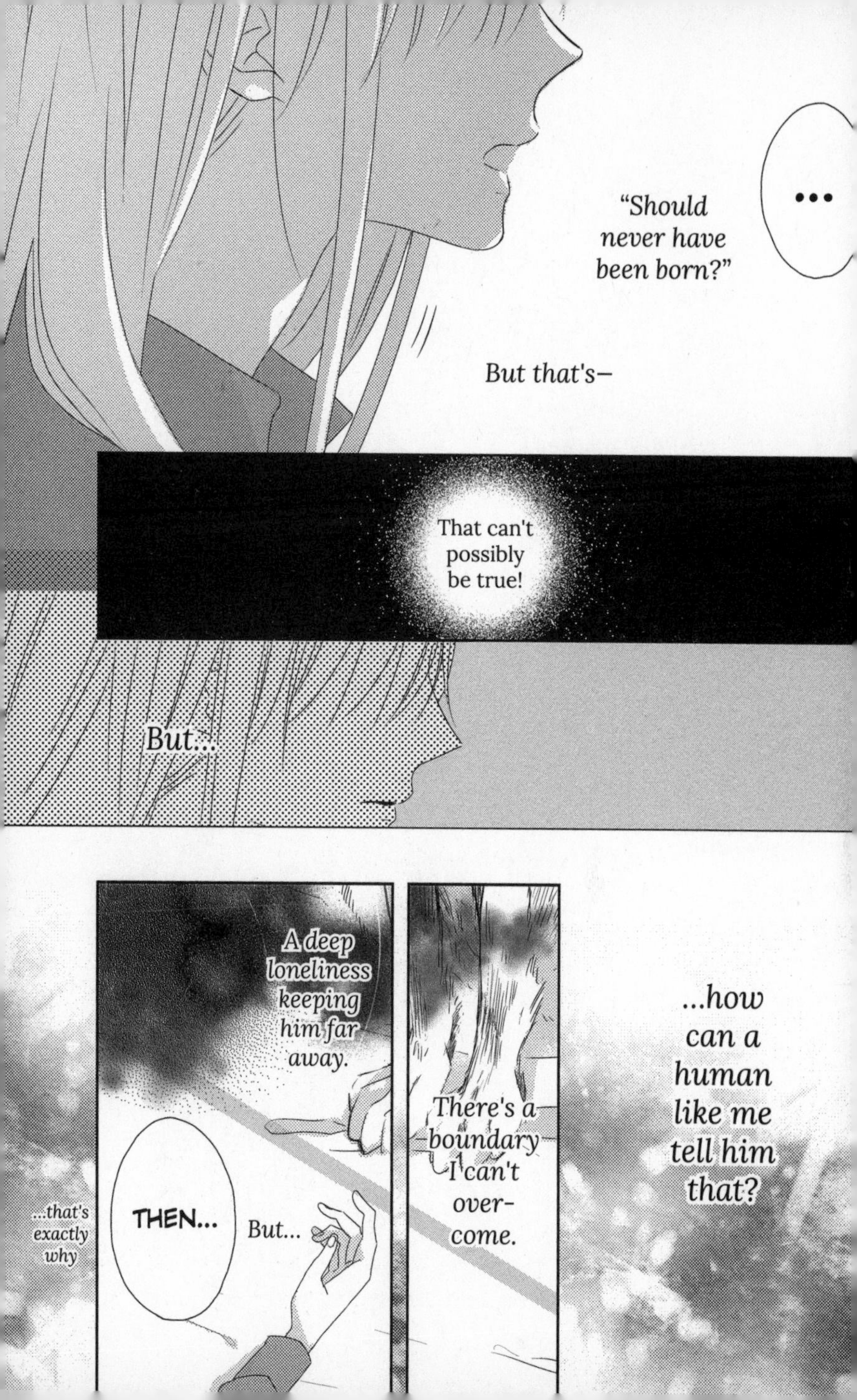

...
"Should never have been born?"
But that's–
That can't possibly be true!
But...
...how can a human like me tell him that?
There's a boundary I can't overcome.
A deep loneliness keeping him far away.
But...
THEN...
...that's exactly why

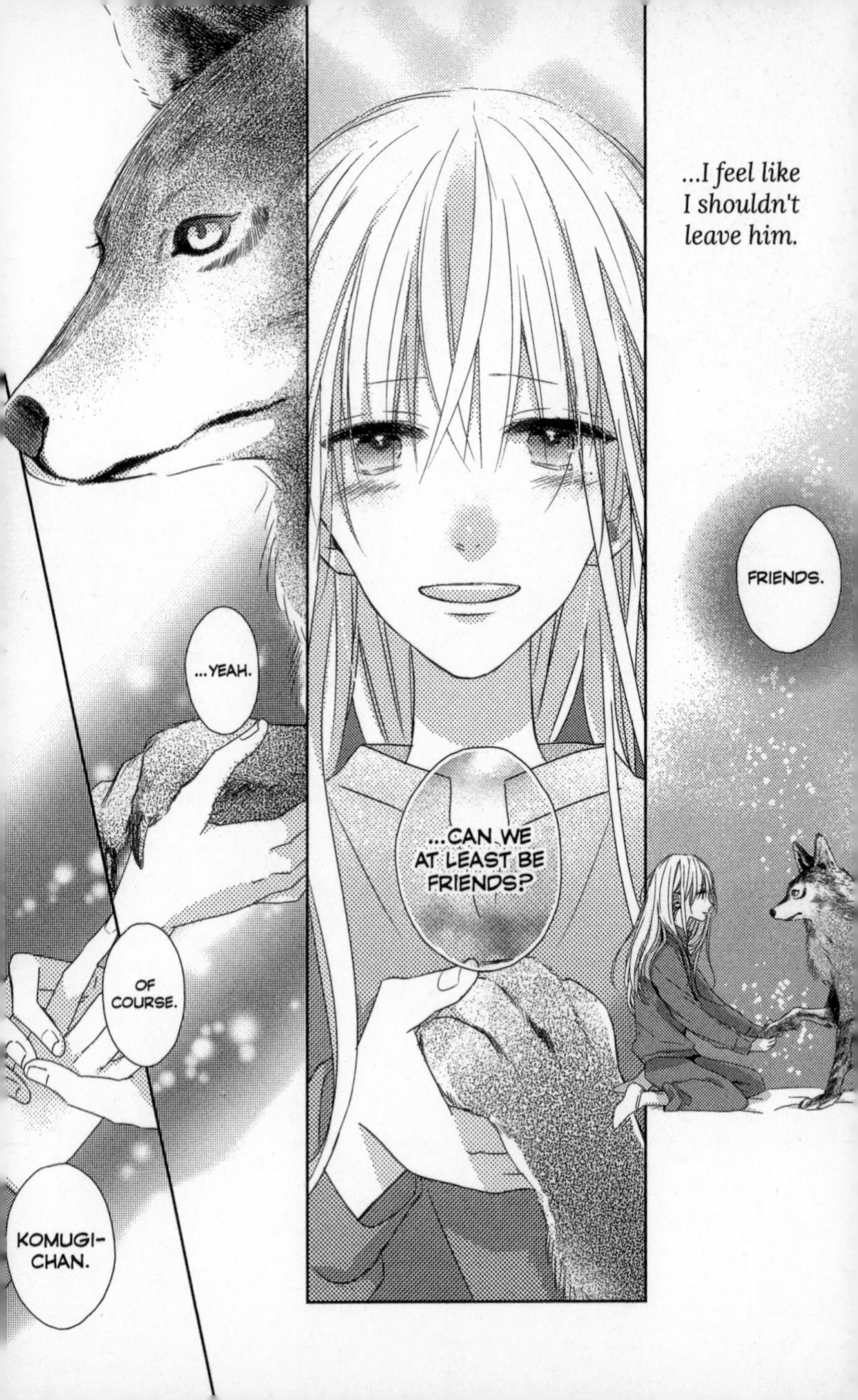
...I feel like I shouldn't leave him.
FRIENDS.
...CAN WE AT LEAST BE FRIENDS?
...YEAH.
OF COURSE.
KOMUGI-CHAN.

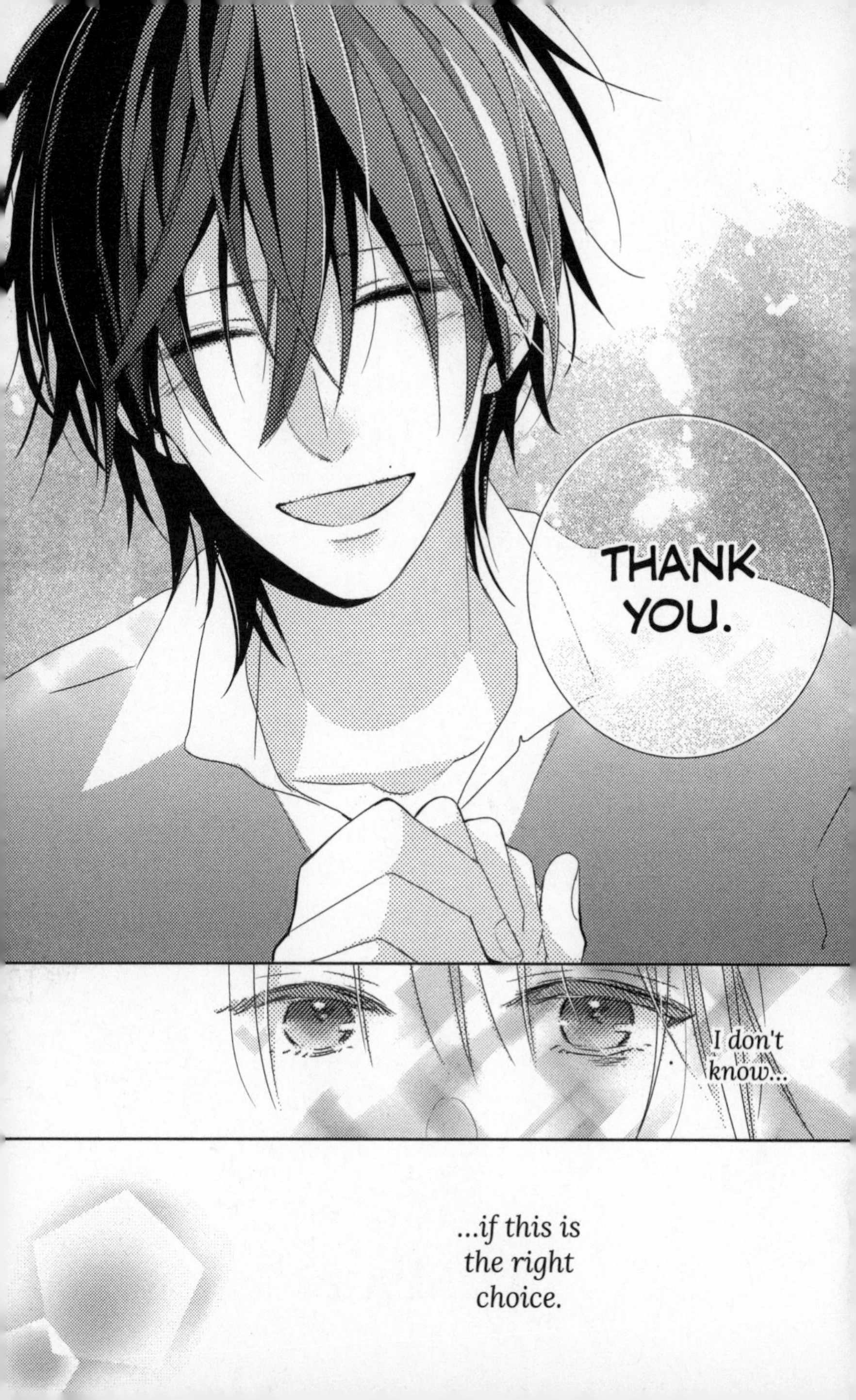
THANK YOU.
I don't know...
...if this is the right choice.

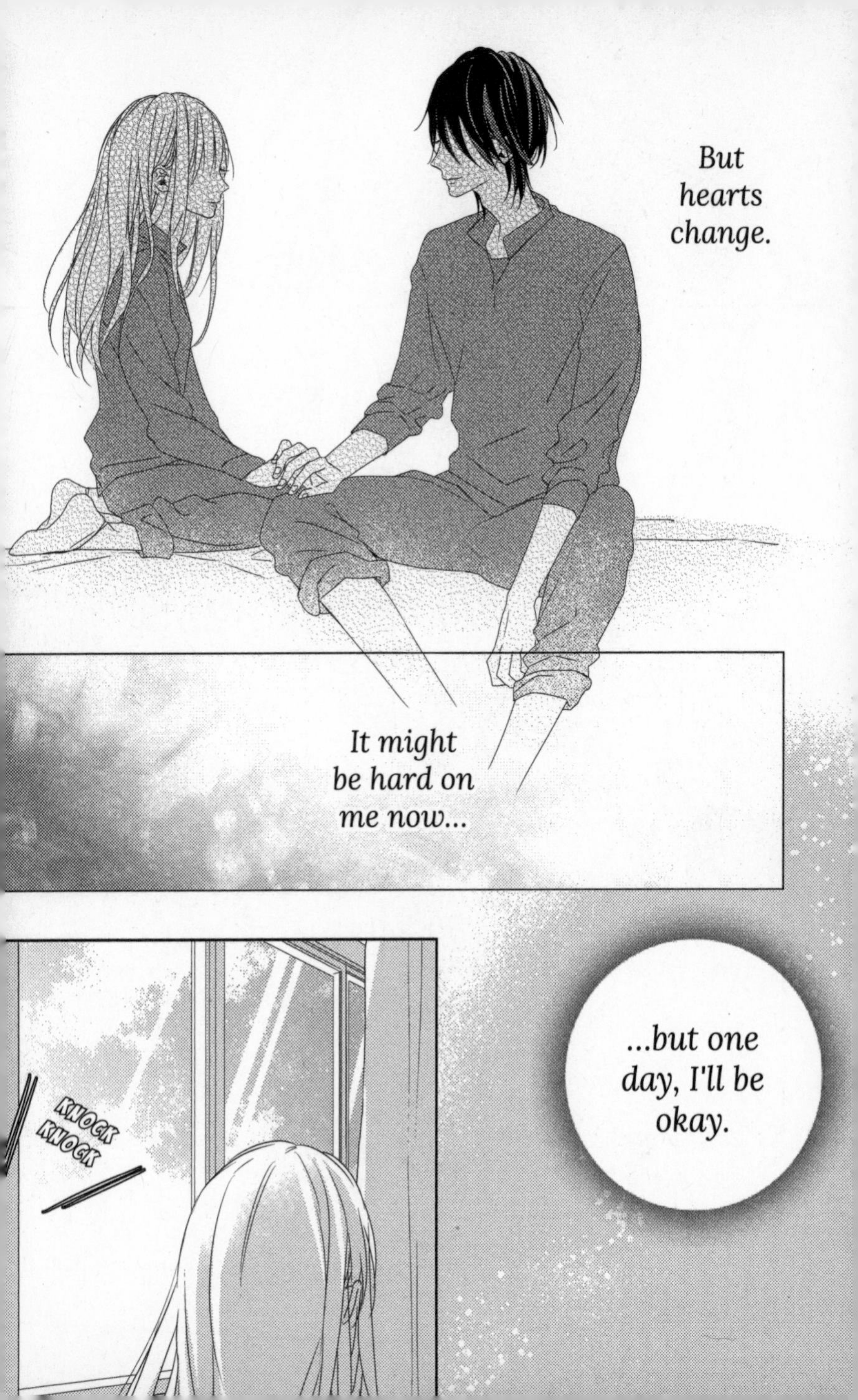
But hearts change.
It might be hard on me now...
...but one day, I'll be okay.
KNOCK KNOCK

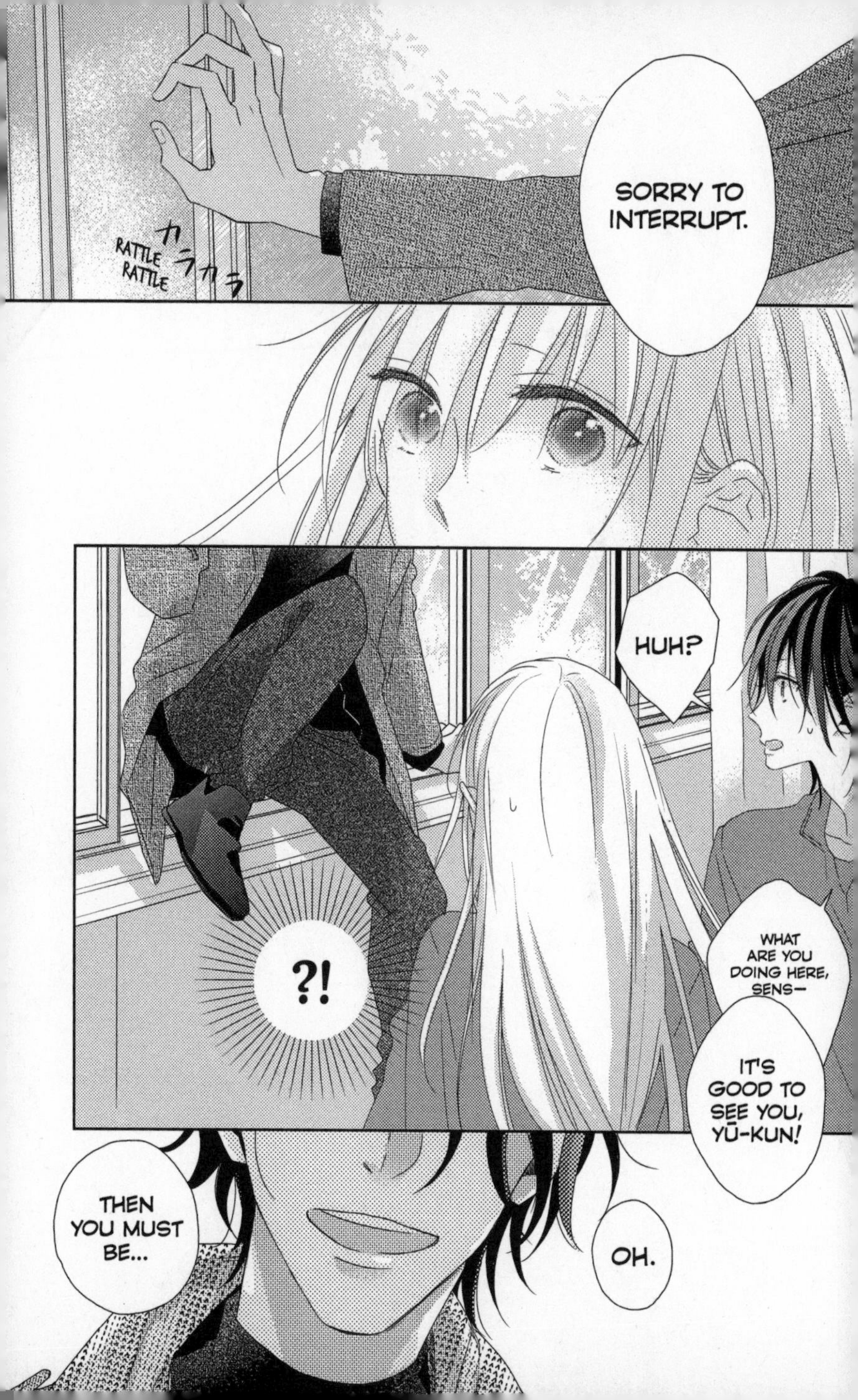
SORRY TO INTERRUPT.
RATTLE RATTLE
カラカラ
HUH?
WHAT ARE YOU DOING HERE, SENS—
IT'S GOOD TO SEE YOU, YŪ-KUN!
?!
OH.
THEN YOU MUST BE...

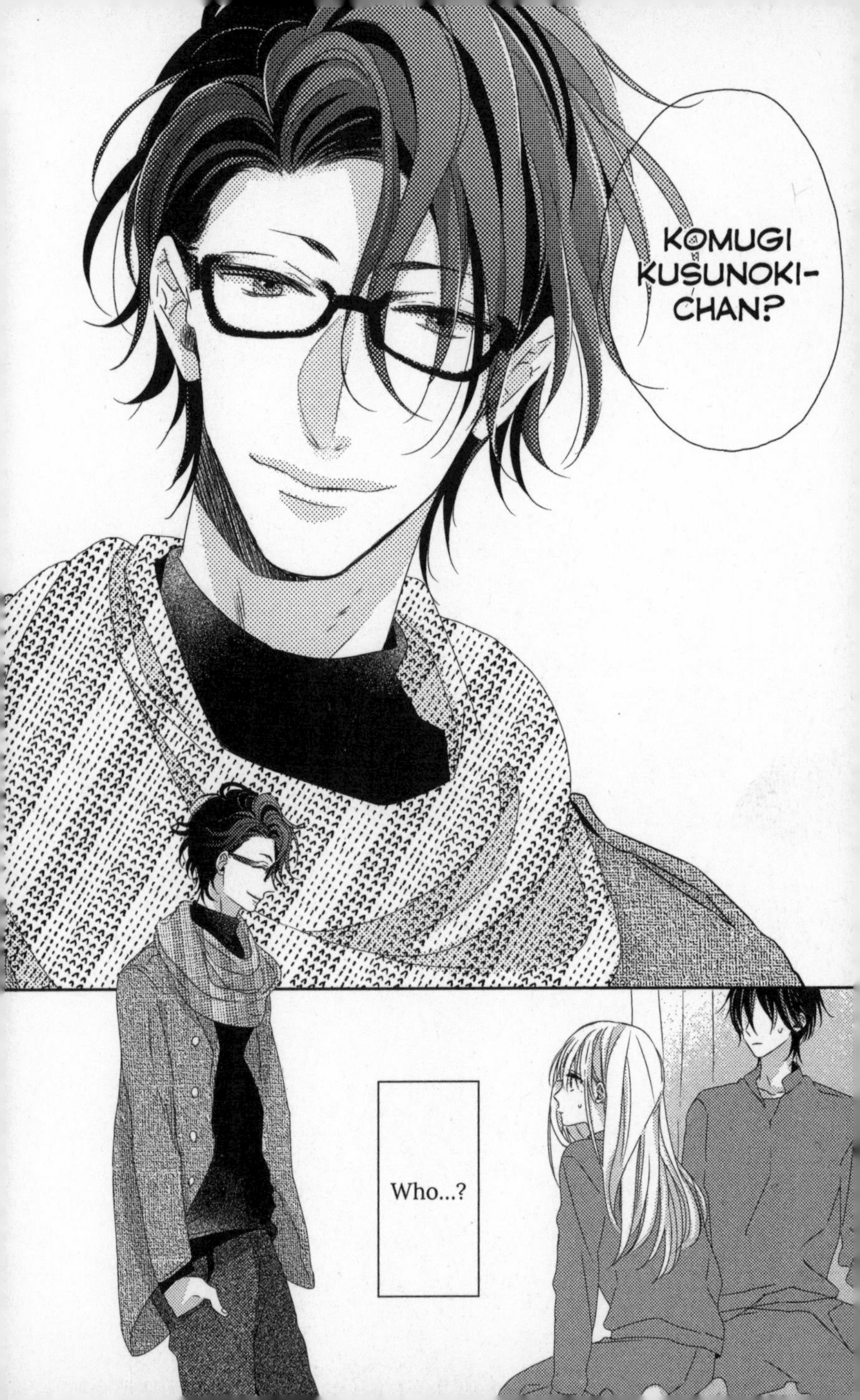
KOMUGI KUSUNOKI-CHAN?
Who...?

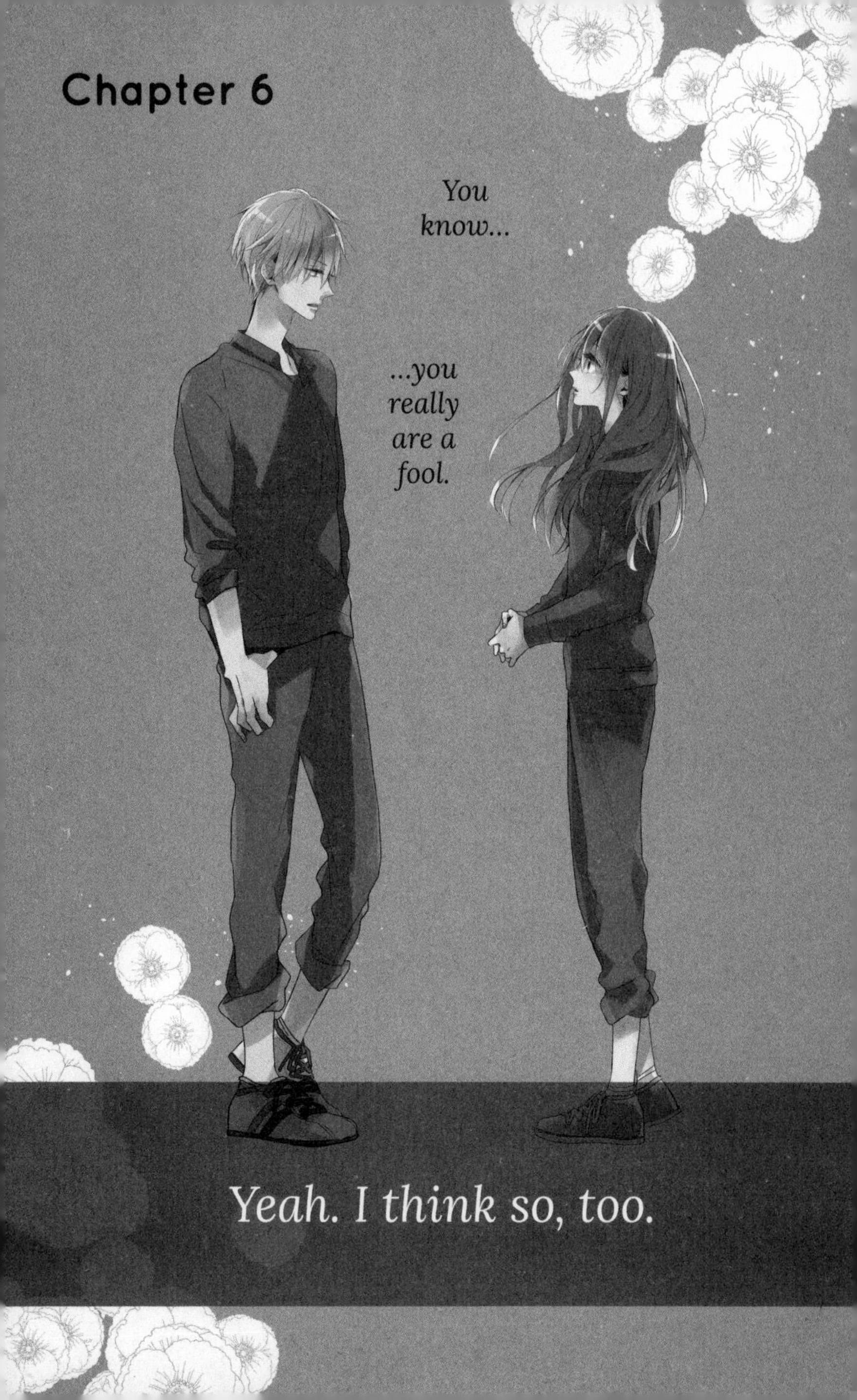
Chapter 6
You know...
...you really are a fool.
Yeah. I think so, too.

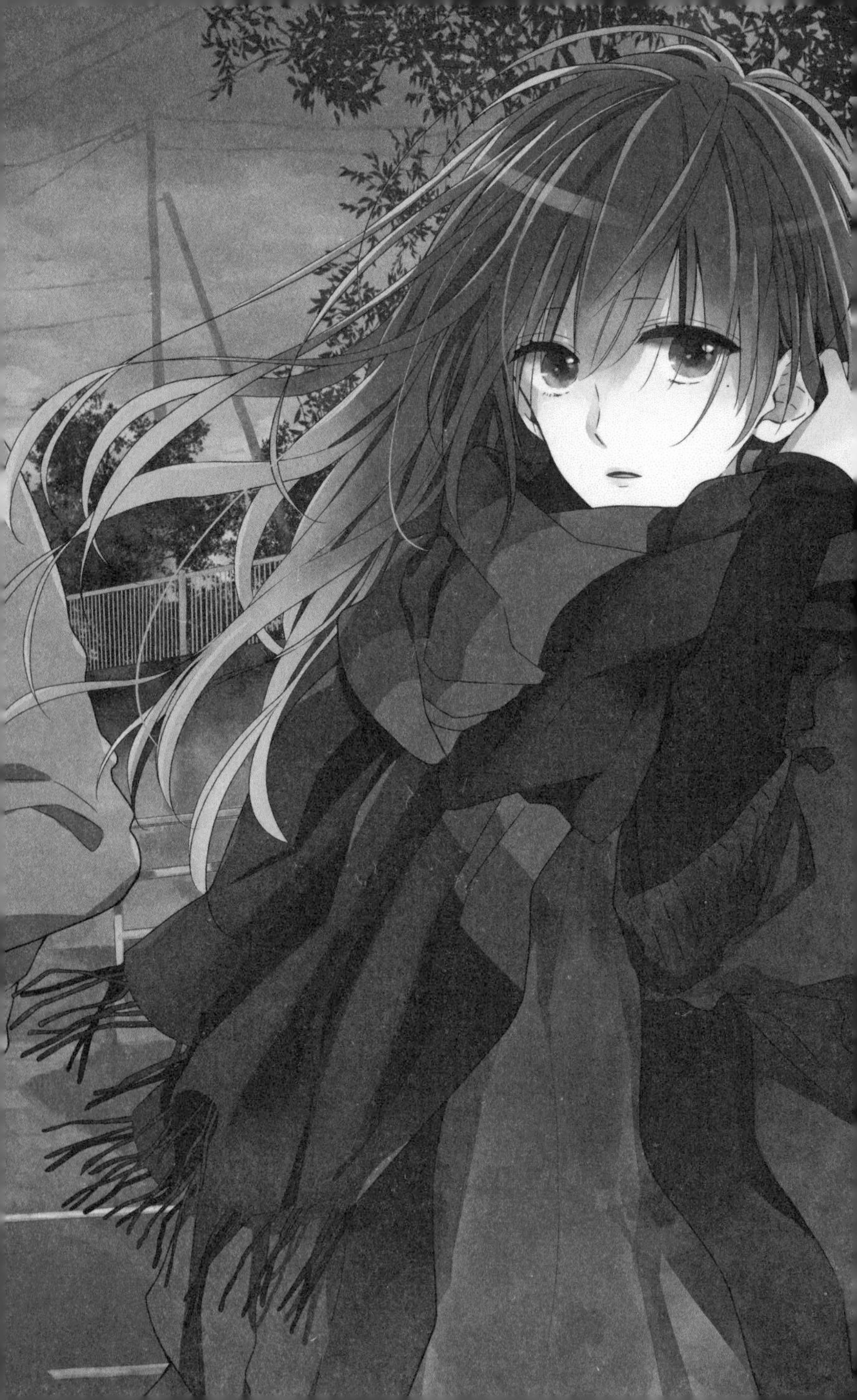

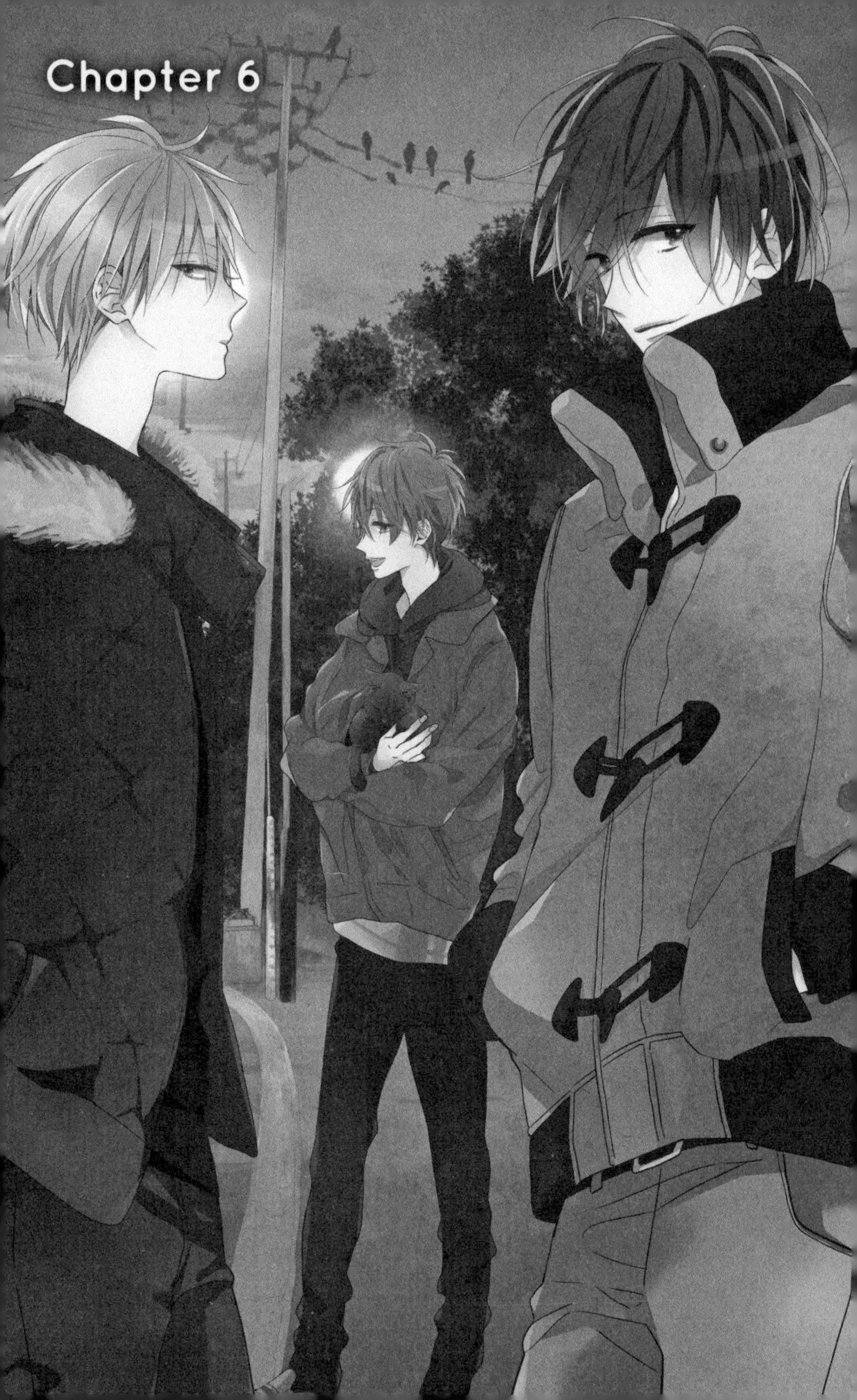
Chapter 6

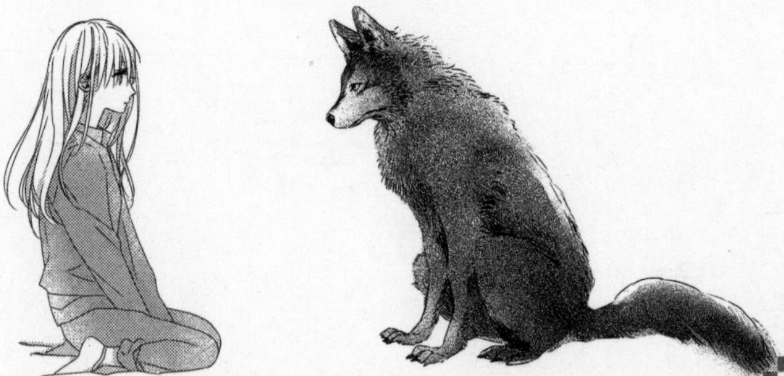

That Wolf-Boy is Mine!

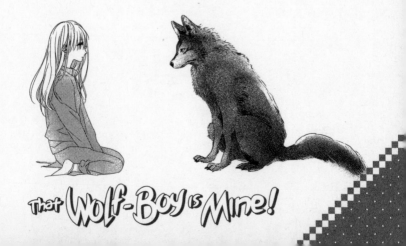

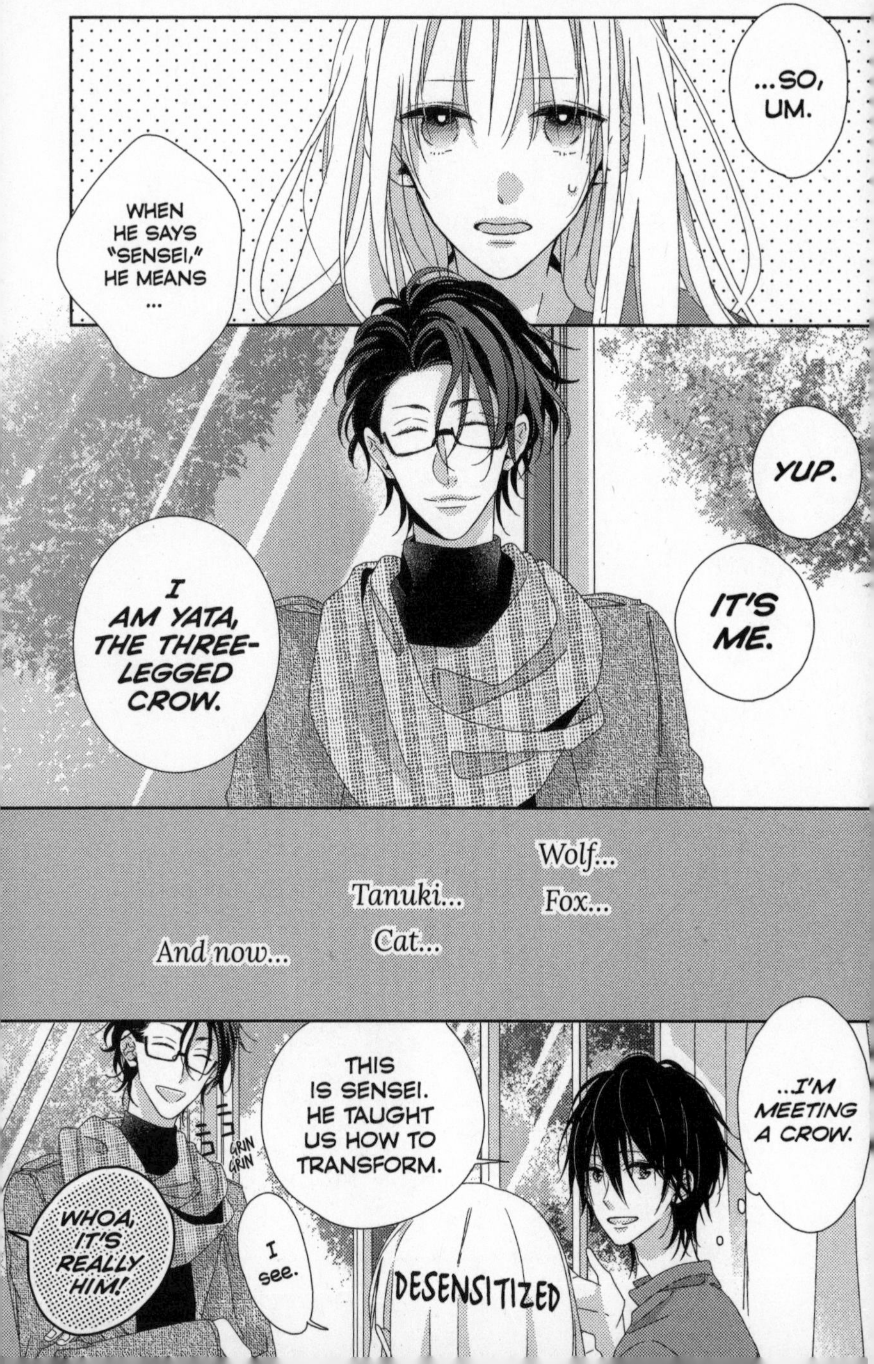
...SO, UM.
WHEN HE SAYS "SENSEI," HE MEANS ...
YUP.
IT'S ME.
I AM YATA, THE THREE-LEGGED CROW.
Wolf...
Fox...
Tanuki...
Cat...
And now...
...I'M MEETING A CROW.
THIS IS SENSEI. HE TAUGHT US HOW TO TRANSFORM.
DESENSITIZED
I see.
GRIN GRIN
WHOA, IT'S REALLY HIM!

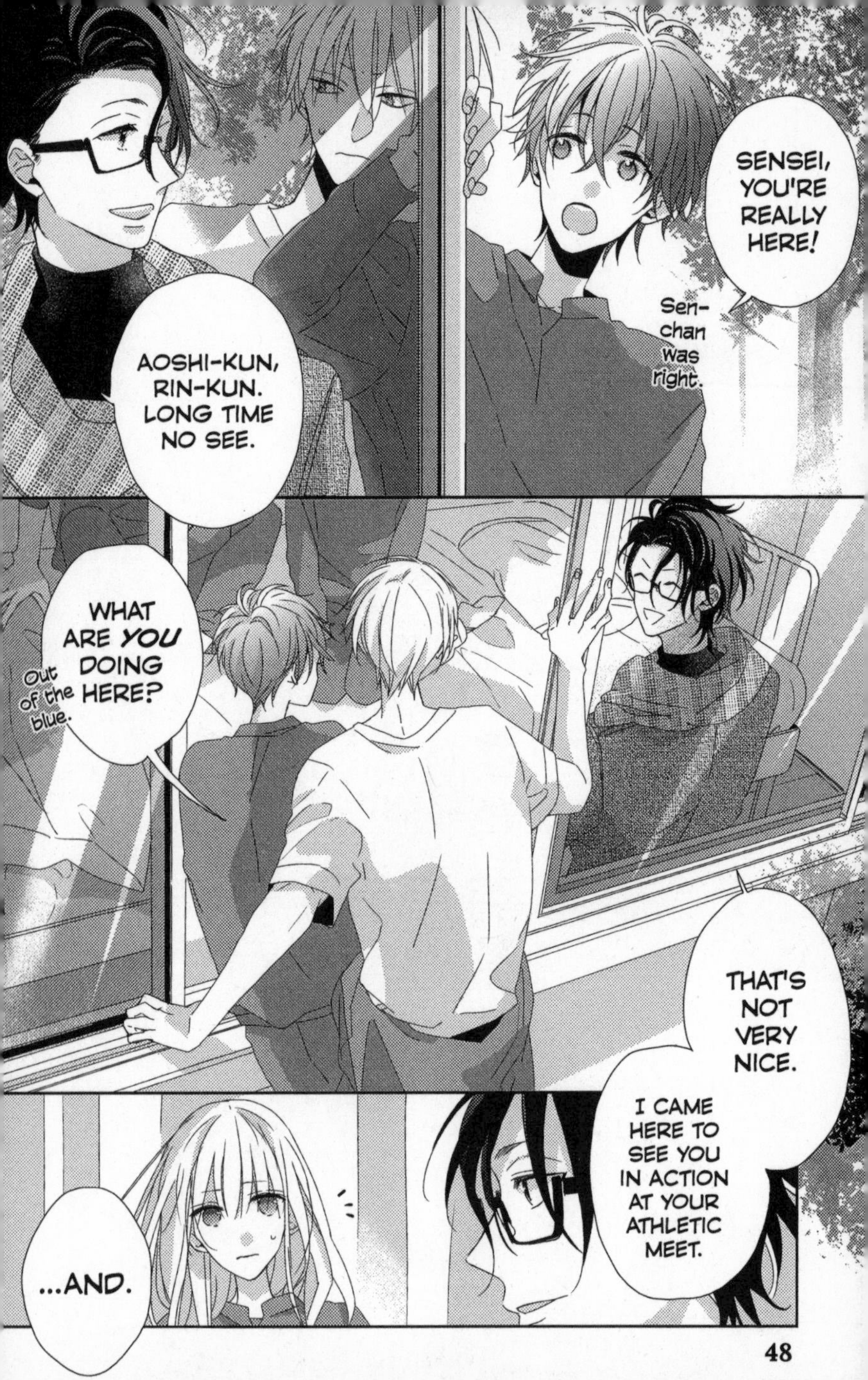
SENSEI, YOU'RE REALLY HERE!
Sen-chan was right.
AOSHI-KUN, RIN-KUN. LONG TIME NO SEE.
WHAT ARE *YOU* DOING HERE?
Out of the blue.
THAT'S NOT VERY NICE.
I CAME HERE TO SEE YOU IN ACTION AT YOUR ATHLETIC MEET.
...AND.

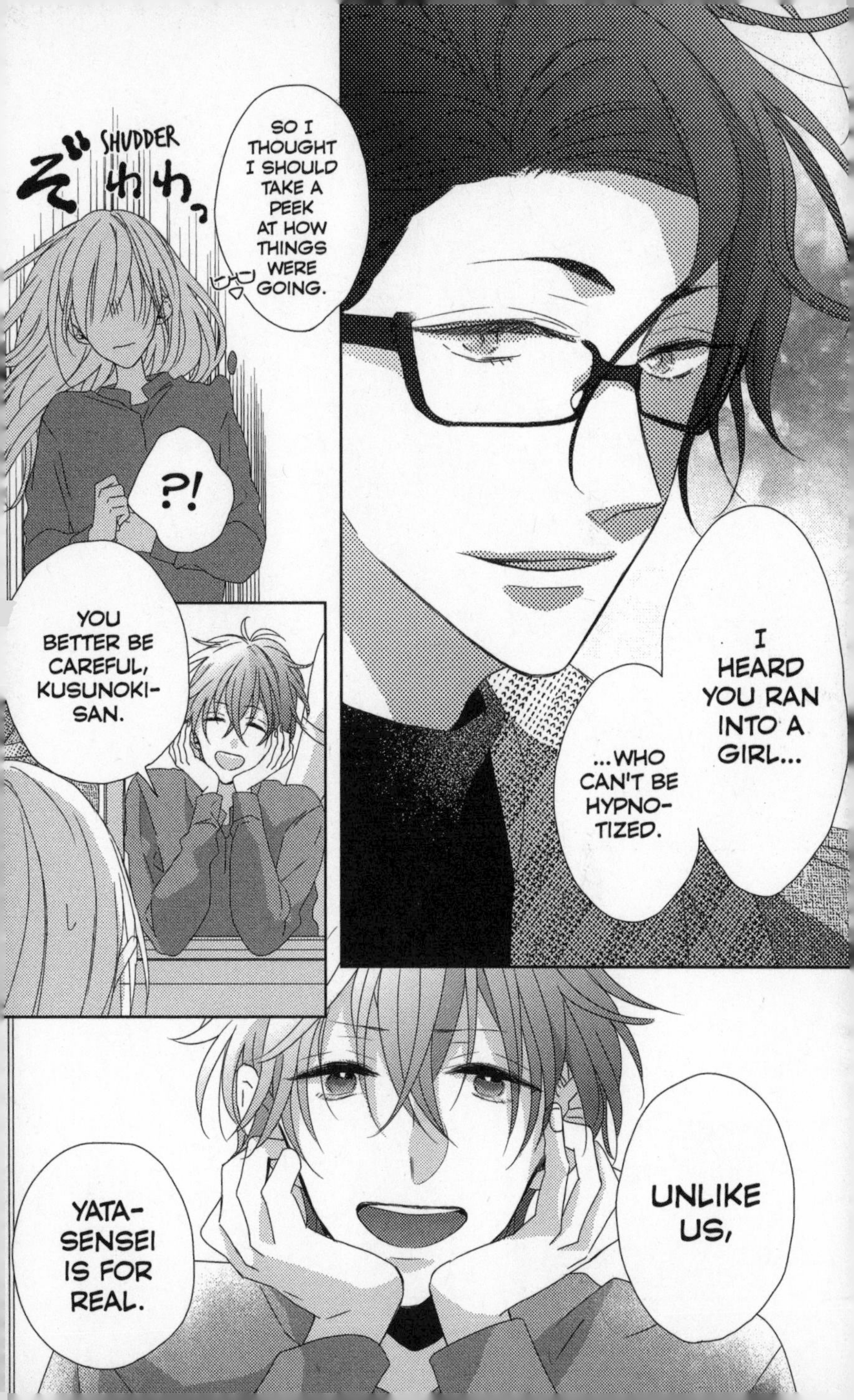
I HEARD YOU RAN INTO A GIRL...
...WHO CAN'T BE HYPNOTIZED.
SO I THOUGHT I SHOULD TAKE A PEEK AT HOW THINGS WERE GOING.
ざわわっ
SHUDDER
?!
YOU BETTER BE CAREFUL, KUSUNOKI-SAN.
UNLIKE US,
YATA-SENSEI IS FOR REAL.

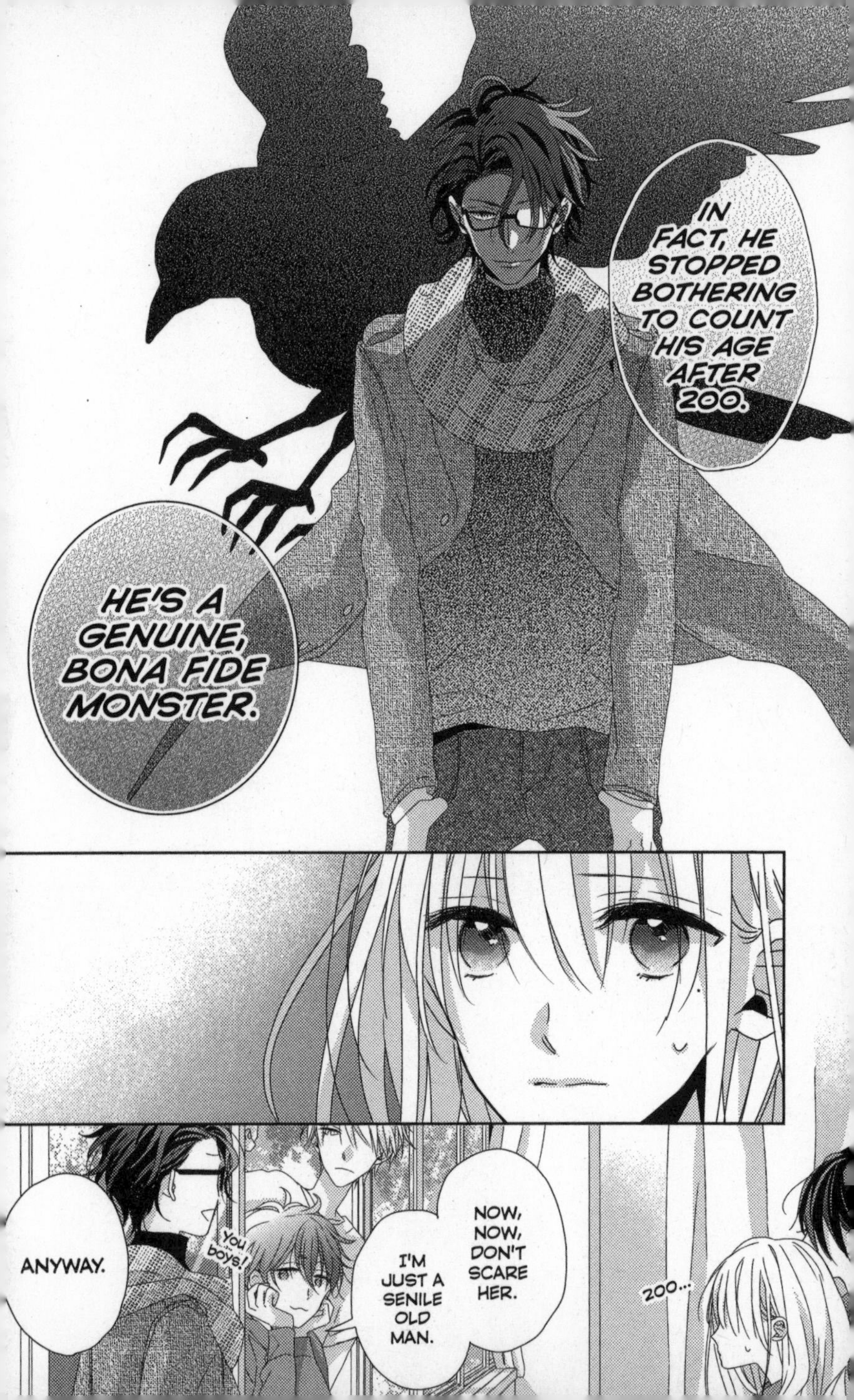

IN FACT, HE STOPPED BOTHERING TO COUNT HIS AGE AFTER 200.
HE'S A GENUINE, BONA FIDE MONSTER.
200...
NOW, NOW, DON'T SCARE HER.
I'M JUST A SENILE OLD MAN.
You boys!
ANYWAY.

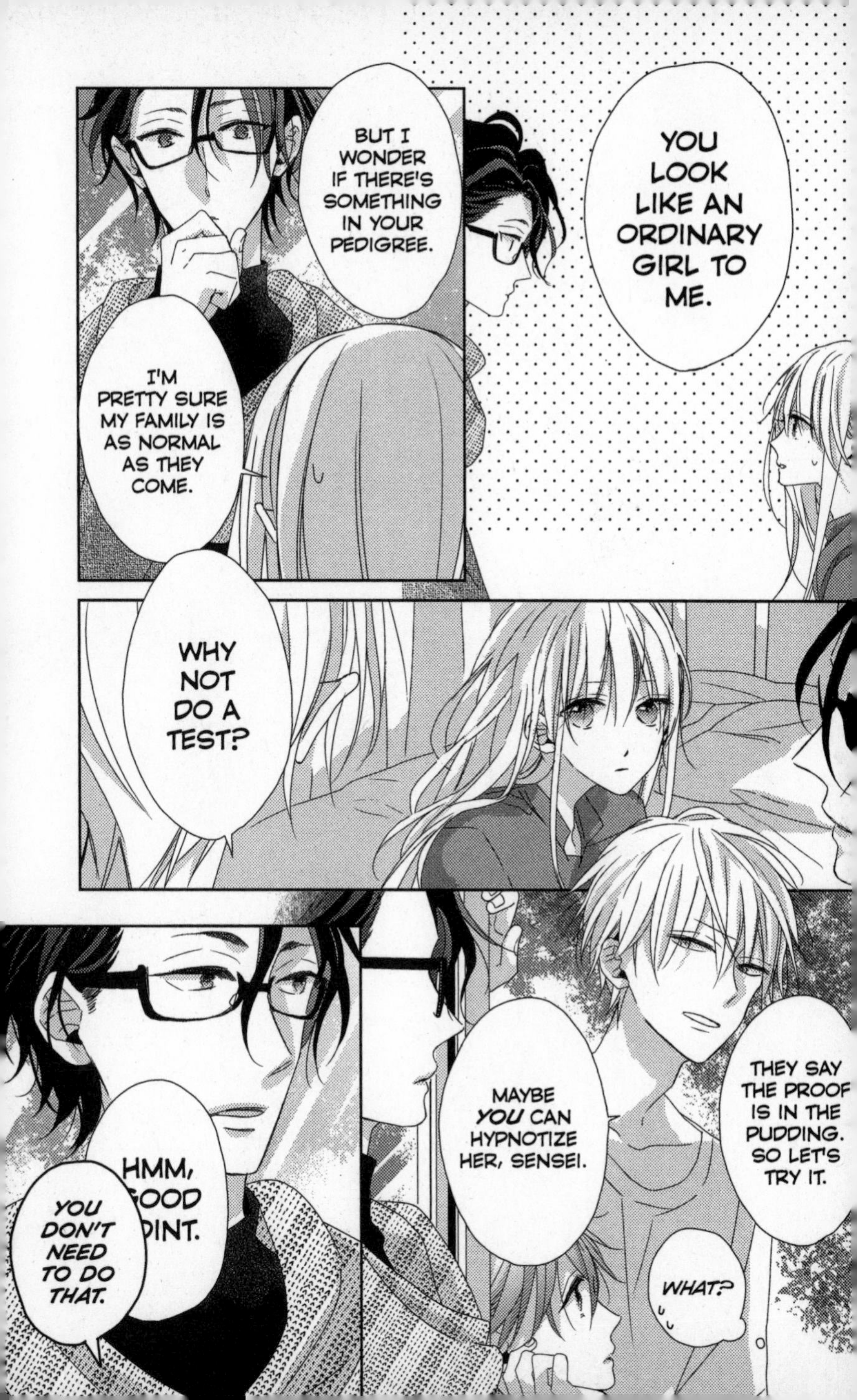
YOU LOOK LIKE AN ORDINARY GIRL TO ME.
BUT I WONDER IF THERE'S SOMETHING IN YOUR PEDIGREE.
I'M PRETTY SURE MY FAMILY IS AS NORMAL AS THEY COME.
WHY NOT DO A TEST?
THEY SAY THE PROOF IS IN THE PUDDING. SO LET'S TRY IT.
MAYBE *YOU* CAN HYPNOTIZE HER, SENSEI.
WHAT?
HMM,
YOU DON'T NEED TO DO THAT.

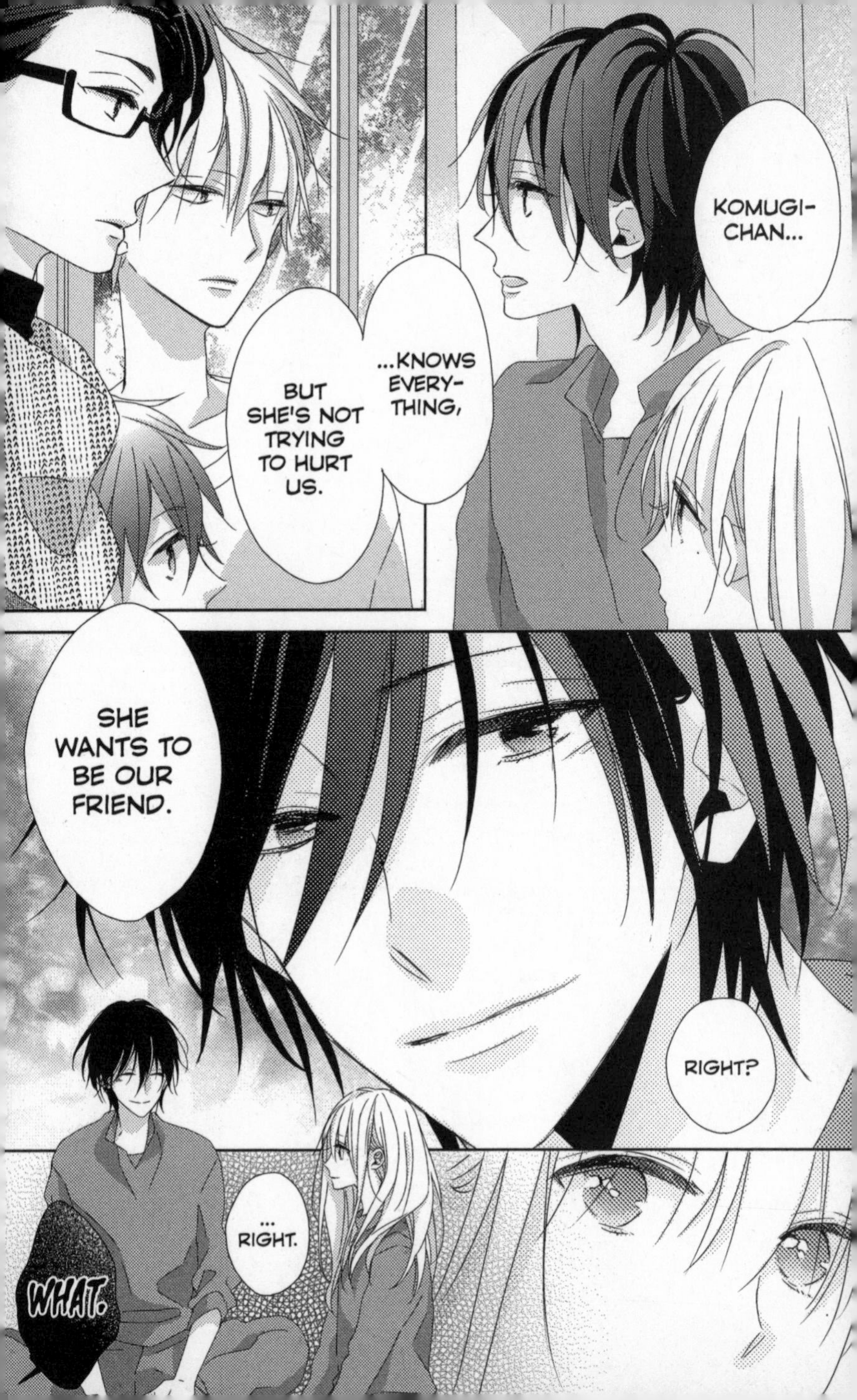
KOMUGI-CHAN...
...KNOWS EVERY-THING,
BUT SHE'S NOT TRYING TO HURT US.
SHE WANTS TO BE OUR FRIEND.
RIGHT?
...RIGHT.
WHAT.

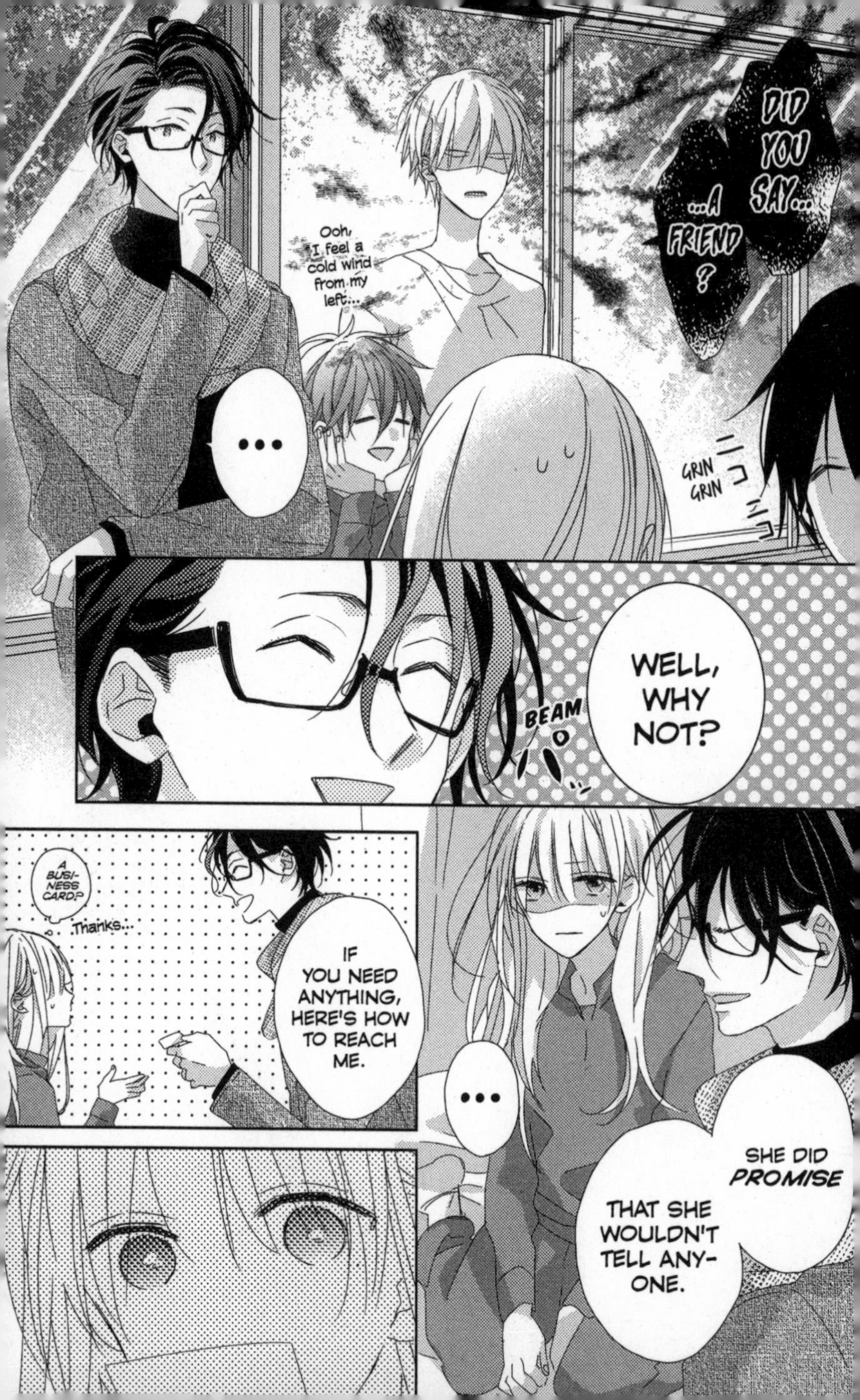

DID YOU SAY...
...A FRIEND?
GRIN GRIN
Ooh, I feel a cold wind from my left...
...
WELL, WHY NOT?
BEAM
...
SHE DID PROMISE
THAT SHE WOULDN'T TELL ANY-ONE.
IF YOU NEED ANYTHING, HERE'S HOW TO REACH ME.
A BUSI-NESS CARD?
Thanks...

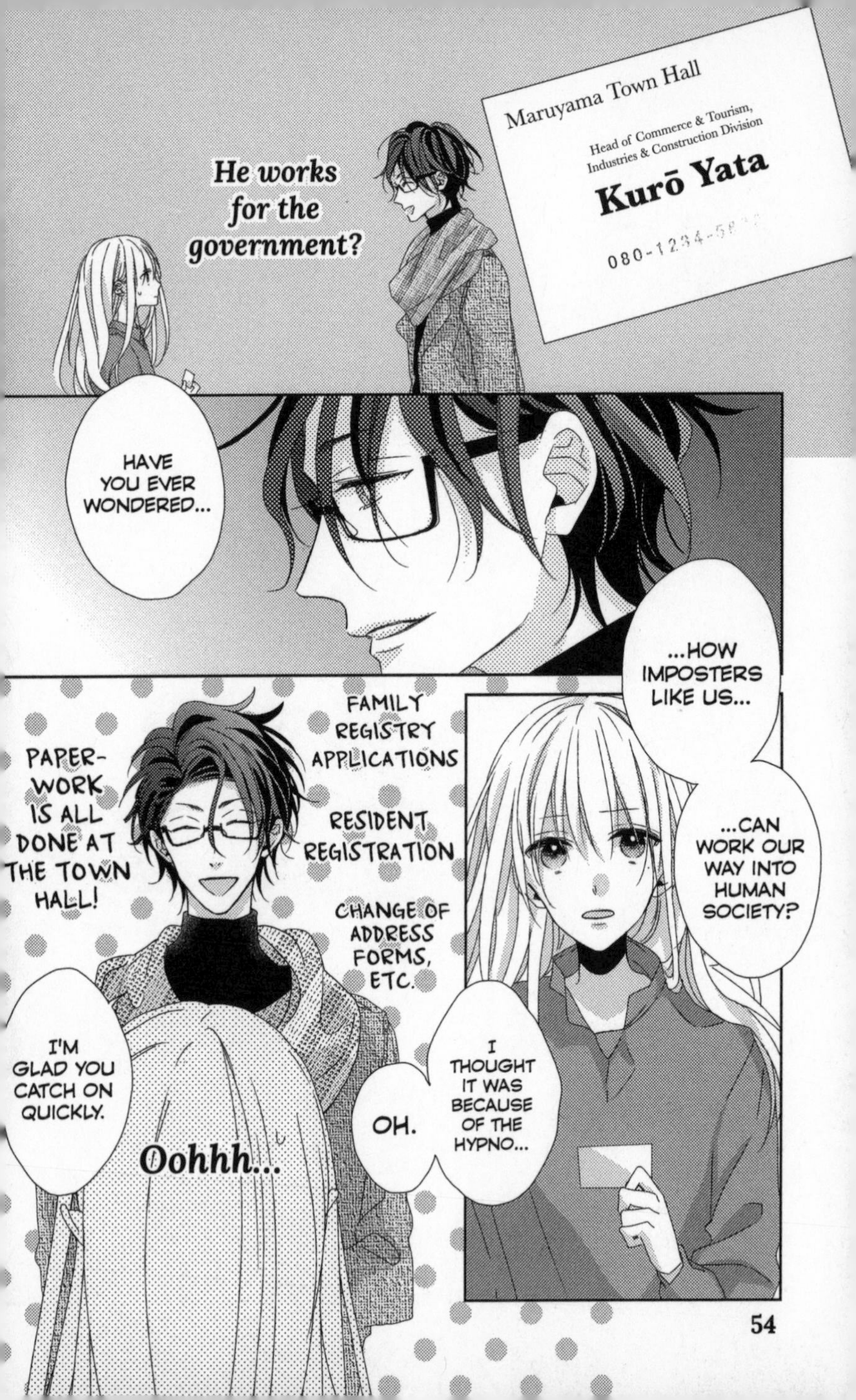
Maruyama Town Hall
Head of Commerce & Tourism, Industries & Construction Division
Kurō Yata
080-1234-5
He works for the government?
HAVE YOU EVER WONDERED...
...HOW IMPOSTERS LIKE US...
...CAN WORK OUR WAY INTO HUMAN SOCIETY?
I THOUGHT IT WAS BECAUSE OF THE HYPNO...
OH.
FAMILY REGISTRY APPLICATIONS
RESIDENT REGISTRATION
CHANGE OF ADDRESS FORMS, ETC.
PAPER-WORK IS ALL DONE AT THE TOWN HALL!
I'M GLAD YOU CATCH ON QUICKLY.
Oohhh...

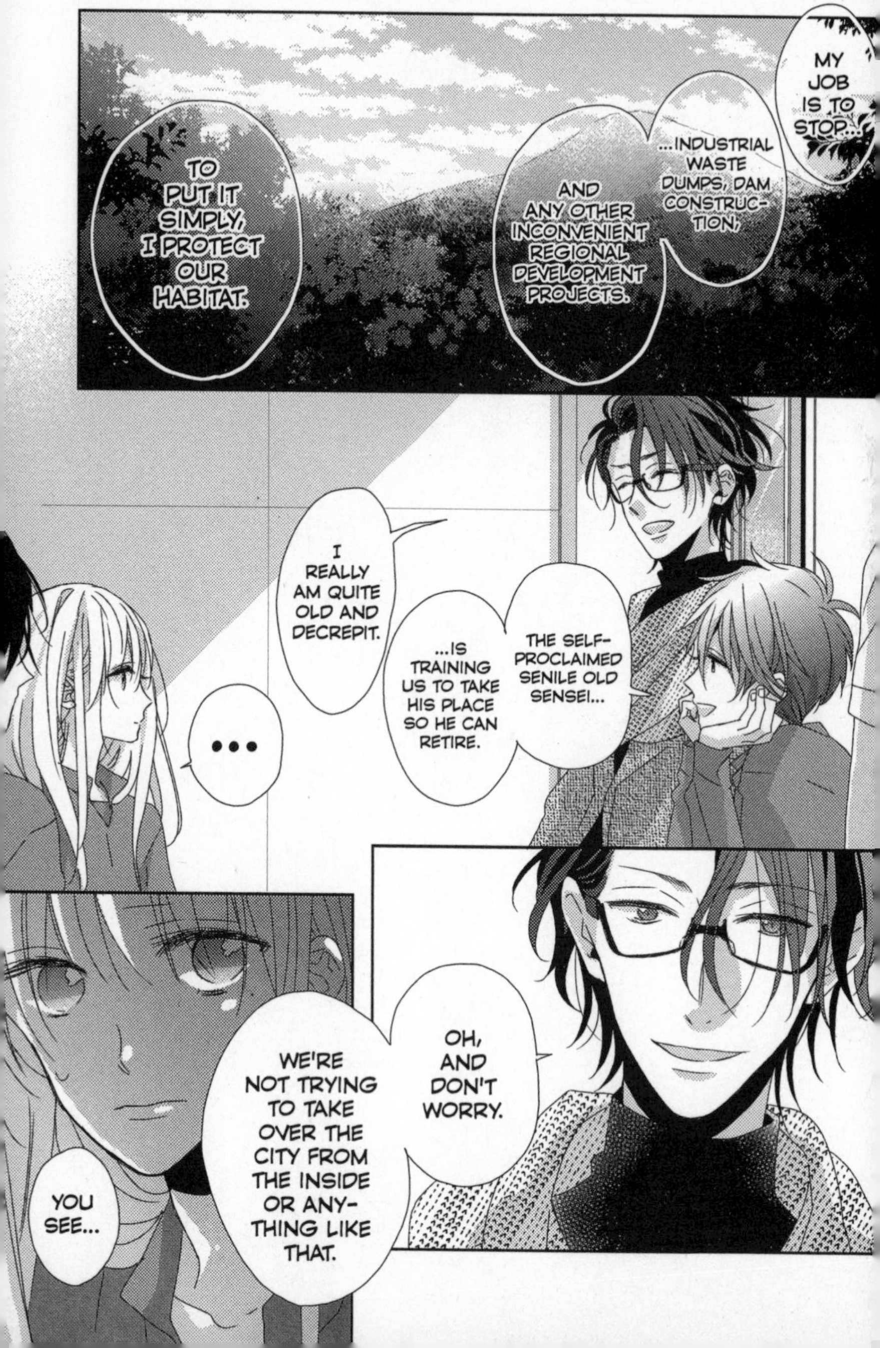
MY JOB IS TO STOP...
...INDUSTRIAL WASTE DUMPS, DAM CONSTRUC-TION,
AND ANY OTHER INCONVENIENT REGIONAL DEVELOPMENT PROJECTS.
TO PUT IT SIMPLY, I PROTECT OUR HABITAT.
THE SELF-PROCLAIMED SENILE OLD SENSEI...
...IS TRAINING US TO TAKE HIS PLACE SO HE CAN RETIRE.
I REALLY AM QUITE OLD AND DECREPIT.
...
OH, AND DON'T WORRY.
WE'RE NOT TRYING TO TAKE OVER THE CITY FROM THE INSIDE OR ANY-THING LIKE THAT.
YOU SEE...

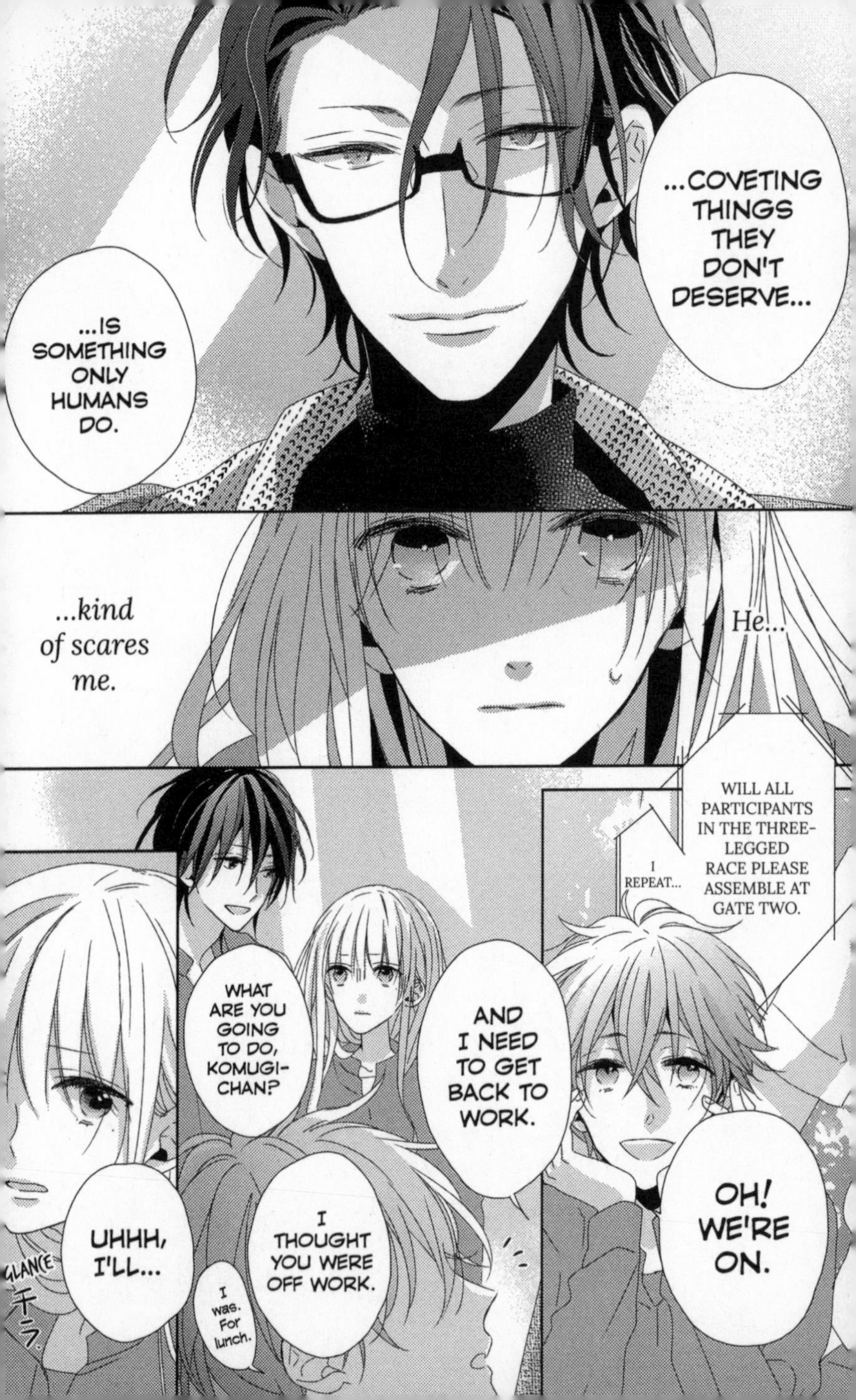
...COVETING THINGS THEY DON'T DESERVE...
...IS SOMETHING ONLY HUMANS DO.
He...
...kind of scares me.
WILL ALL PARTICIPANTS IN THE THREE-LEGGED RACE PLEASE ASSEMBLE AT GATE TWO.
I REPEAT...
OH! WE'RE ON.
AND I NEED TO GET BACK TO WORK.
I THOUGHT YOU WERE OFF WORK.
I was. For lunch.
WHAT ARE YOU GOING TO DO, KOMUGI-CHAN?
UHHH, I'LL...
GLANCE
チラ

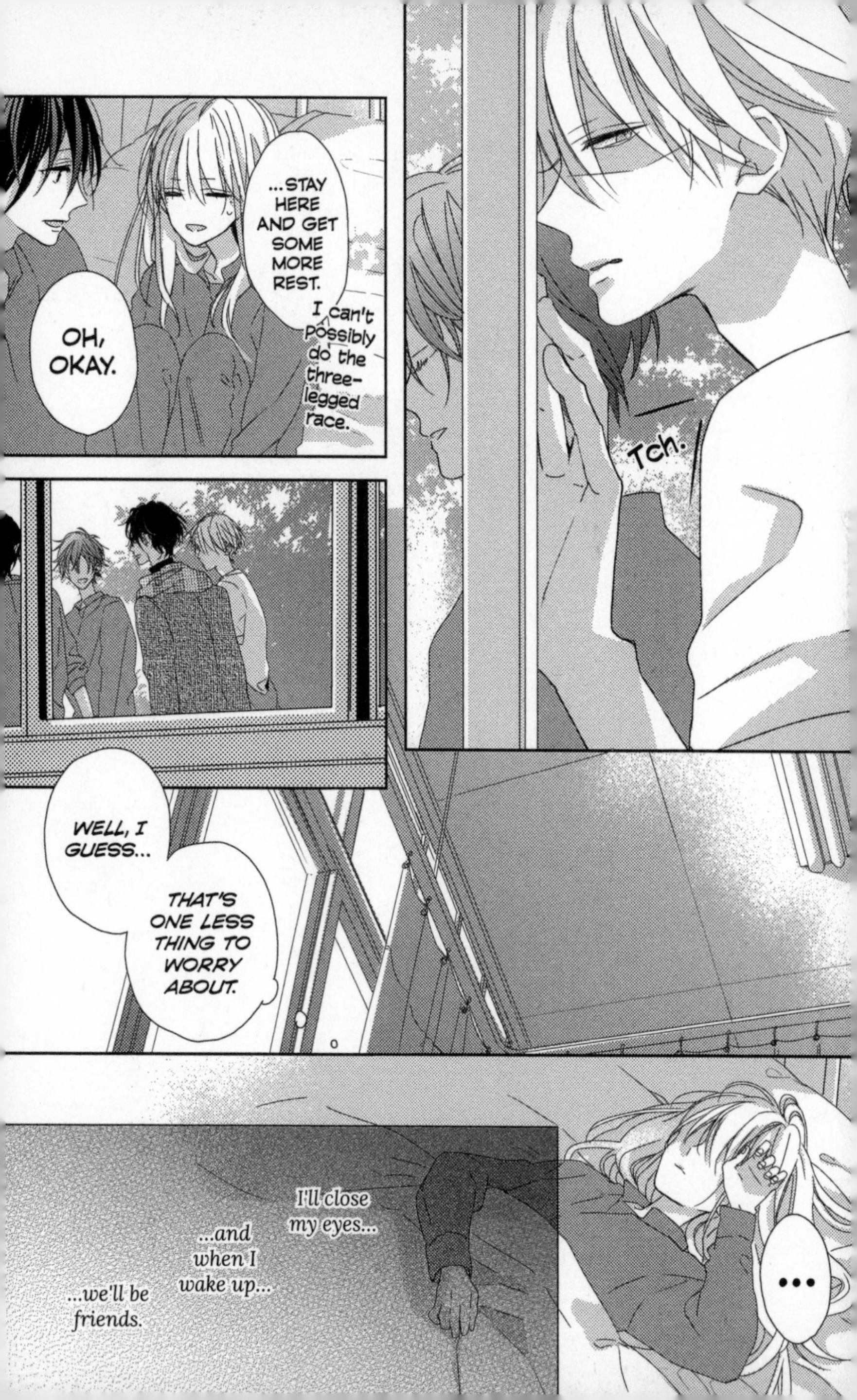
Tch.
...STAY HERE AND GET SOME MORE REST.
I can't possibly do the three-legged race.
OH, OKAY.
WELL, I GUESS...
THAT'S ONE LESS THING TO WORRY ABOUT.
...
I'll close my eyes...
...and when I wake up...
...we'll be friends.

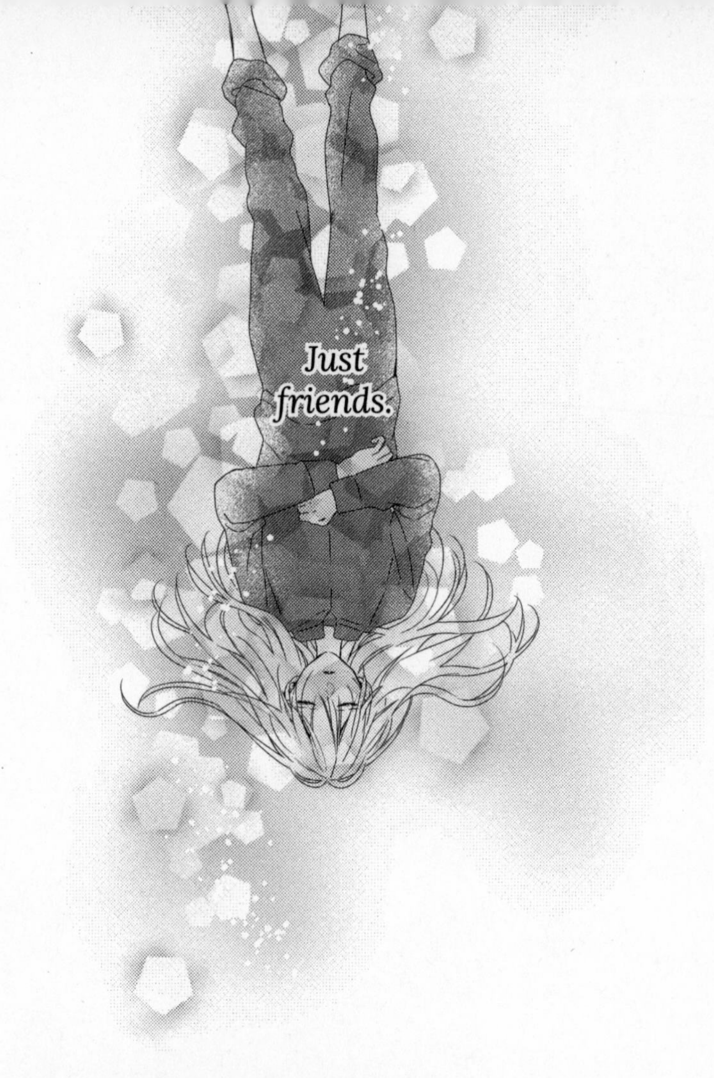
Just friends.

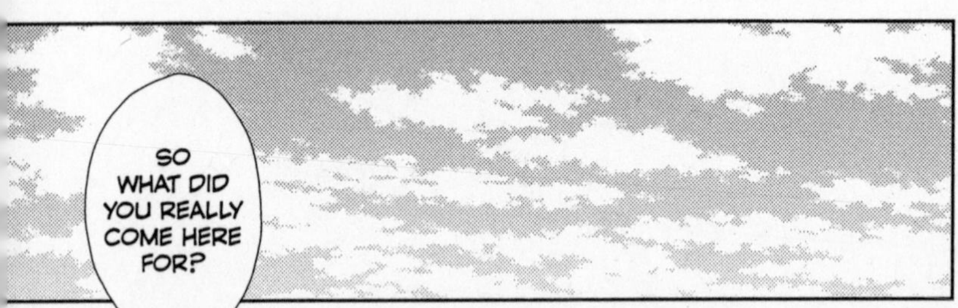
SO WHAT DID YOU REALLY COME HERE FOR?

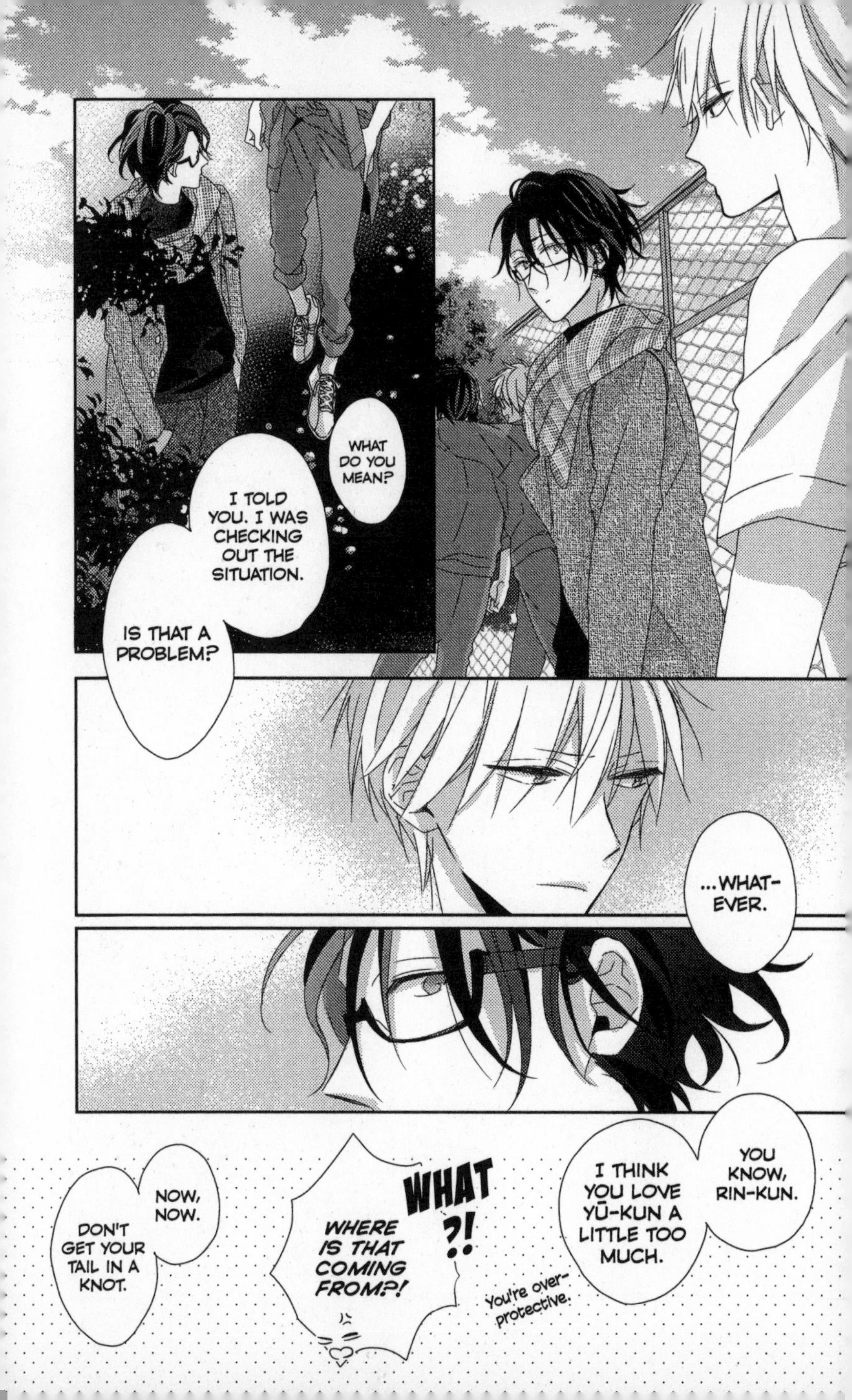
WHAT DO YOU MEAN?
I TOLD YOU. I WAS CHECKING OUT THE SITUATION.
IS THAT A PROBLEM?
...WHATEVER.
YOU KNOW, RIN-KUN.
I THINK YOU LOVE YŪ-KUN A LITTLE TOO MUCH.
You're over-protective.
WHAT ?!
WHERE IS THAT COMING FROM?!
NOW, NOW.
DON'T GET YOUR TAIL IN A KNOT.

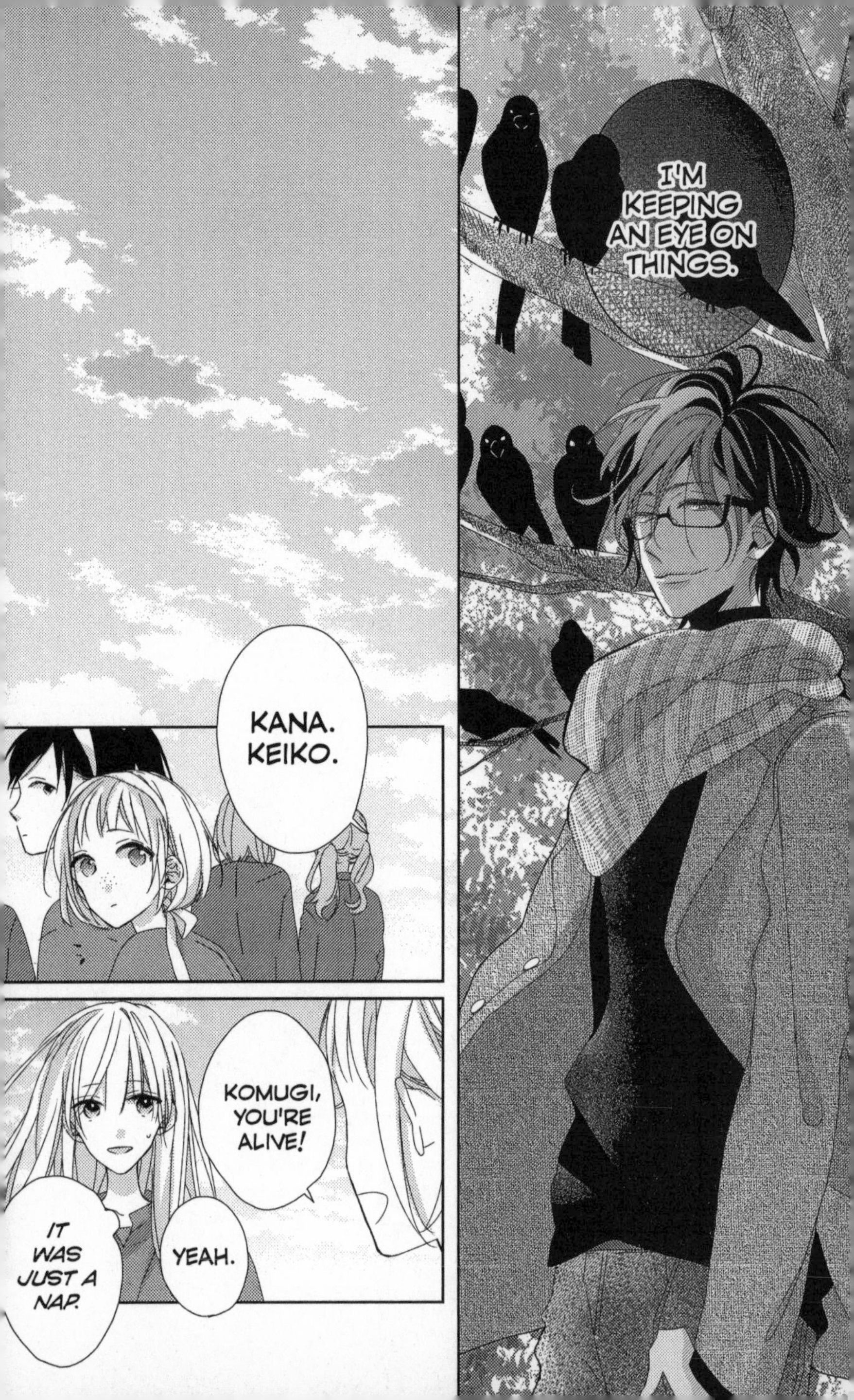
I'M KEEPING AN EYE ON THINGS.
KANA. KEIKO.
KOMUGI, YOU'RE ALIVE!
YEAH.
IT WAS JUST A NAP.

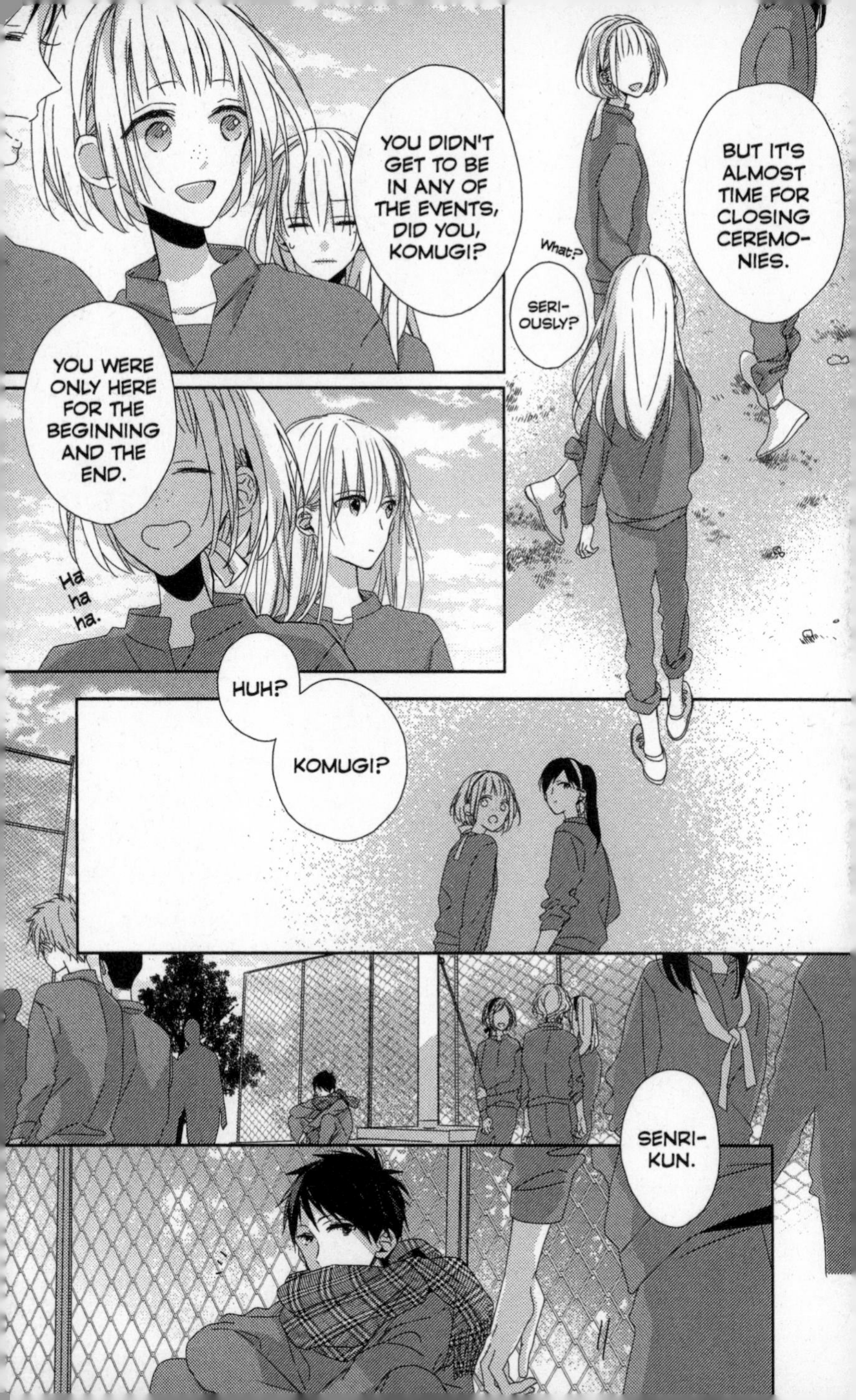
BUT IT'S ALMOST TIME FOR CLOSING CEREMONIES.
What?
SERIOUSLY?
YOU DIDN'T GET TO BE IN ANY OF THE EVENTS, DID YOU, KOMUGI?
YOU WERE ONLY HERE FOR THE BEGINNING AND THE END.
Ha ha ha.
HUH?
KOMUGI?
SENRI-KUN.

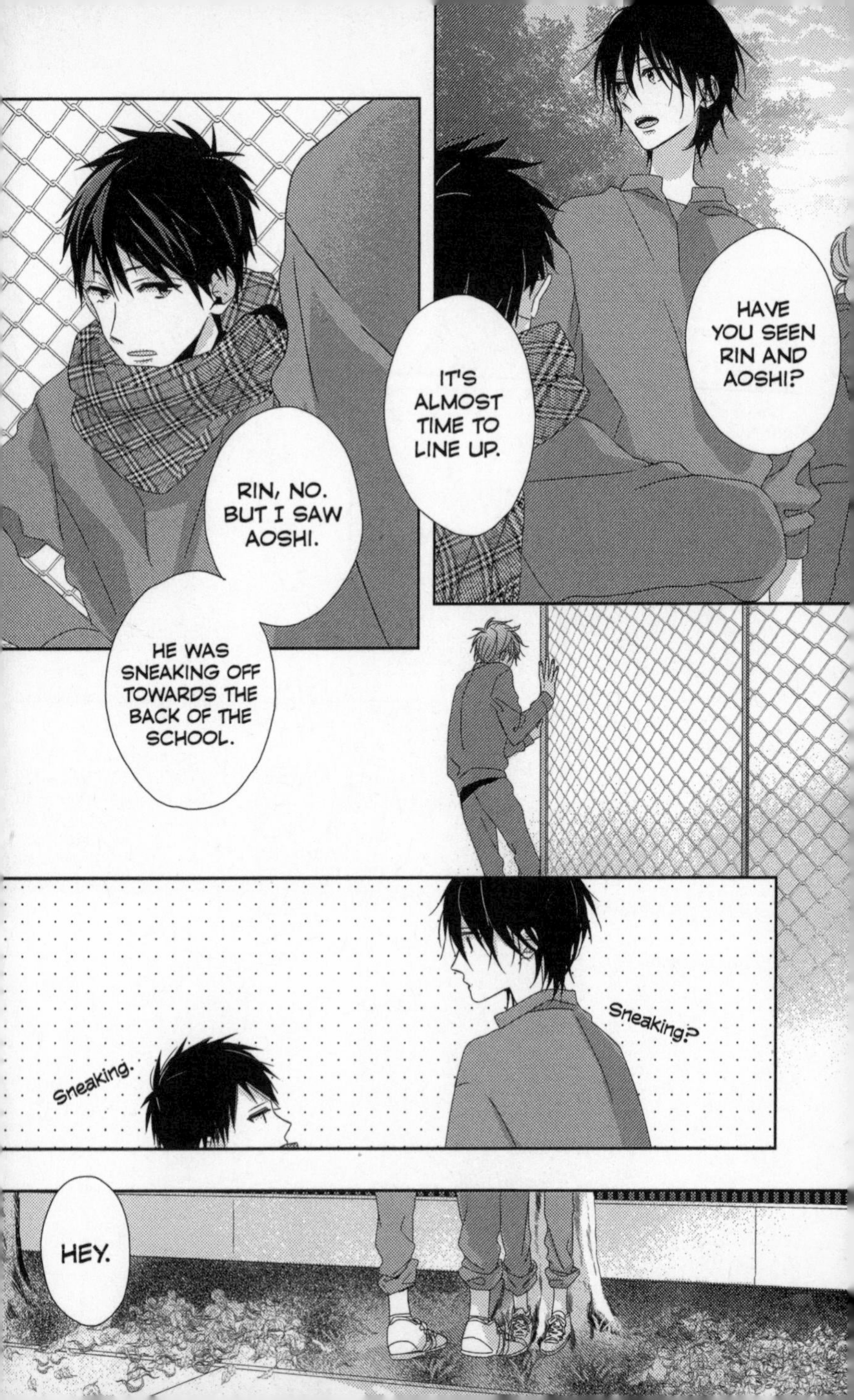
HAVE YOU SEEN RIN AND AOSHI?
IT'S ALMOST TIME TO LINE UP.
RIN, NO. BUT I SAW AOSHI.
HE WAS SNEAKING OFF TOWARDS THE BACK OF THE SCHOOL.
Sneaking?
Sneaking.
HEY.

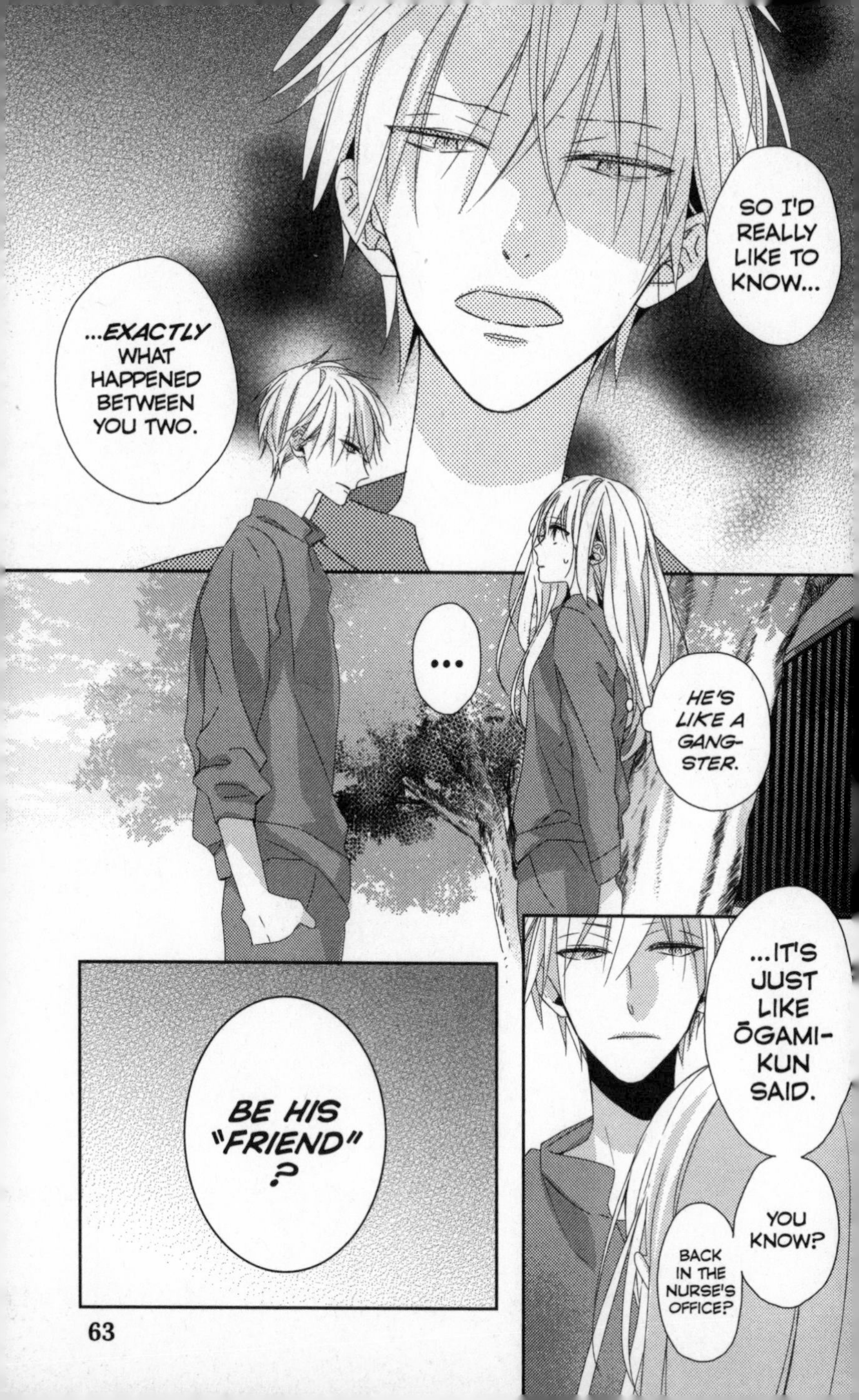
SO I'D REALLY LIKE TO KNOW...
...*EXACTLY* WHAT HAPPENED BETWEEN YOU TWO.
HE'S LIKE A GANG-STER.
...
...IT'S JUST LIKE ŌGAMI-KUN SAID.
YOU KNOW?
BACK IN THE NURSE'S OFFICE?
BE HIS "FRIEND"?

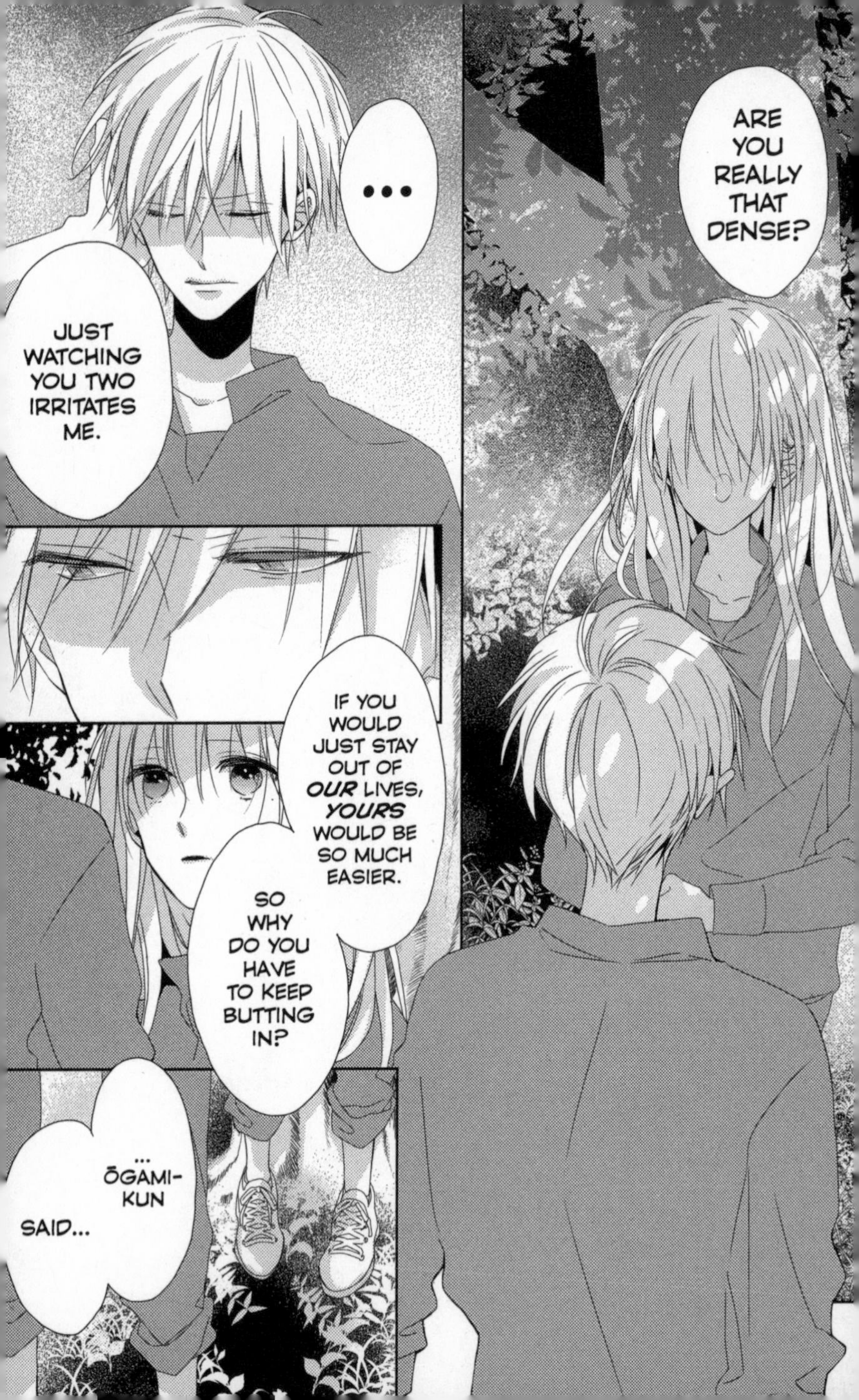
ARE YOU REALLY THAT DENSE?
...
JUST WATCHING YOU TWO IRRITATES ME.
IF YOU WOULD JUST STAY OUT OF OUR LIVES, YOURS WOULD BE SO MUCH EASIER.
SO WHY DO YOU HAVE TO KEEP BUTTING IN?
... ŌGAMI-KUN SAID...

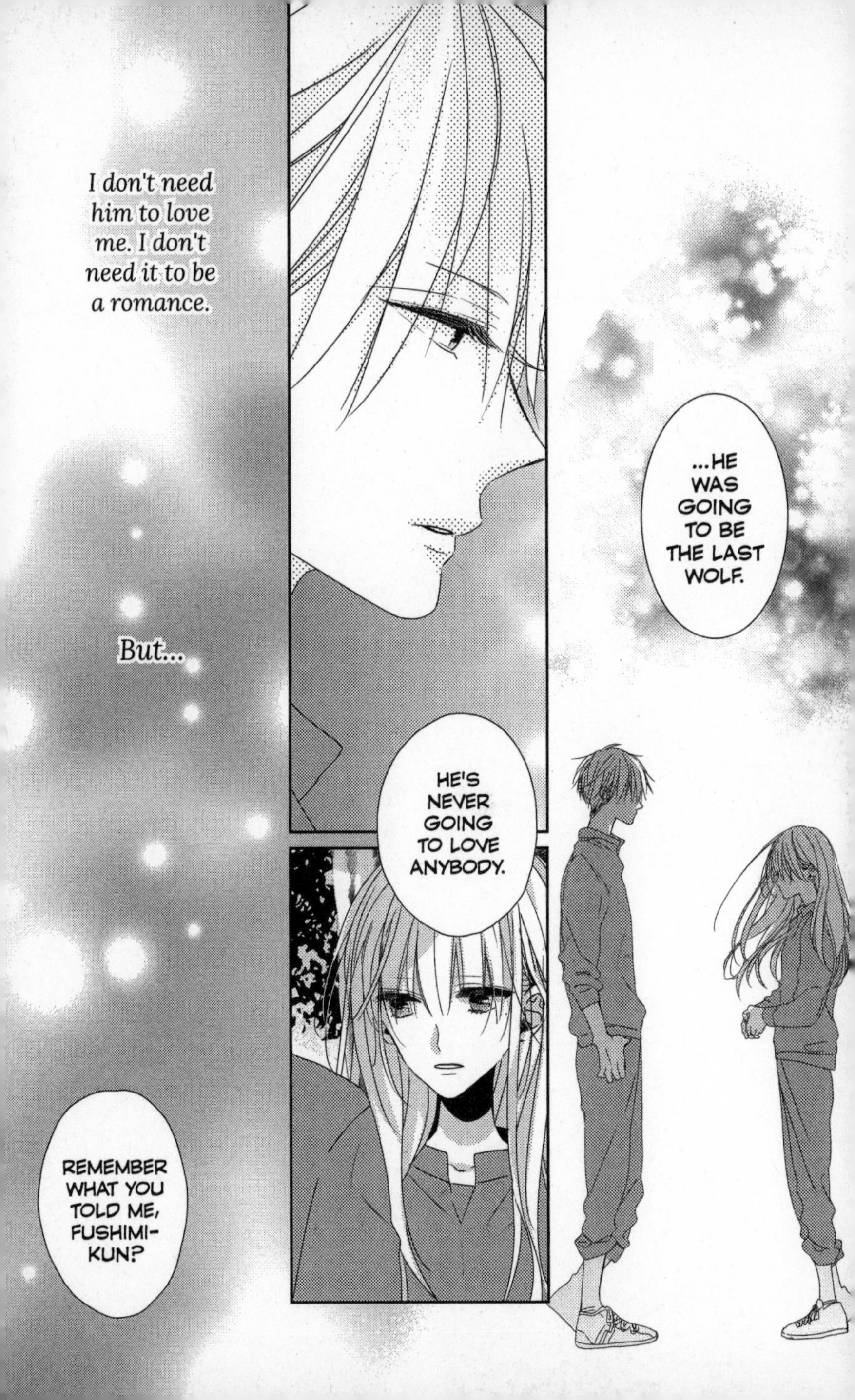

...HE WAS GOING TO BE THE LAST WOLF.
HE'S NEVER GOING TO LOVE ANYBODY.
I don't need him to love me. I don't need it to be a romance.
But...
REMEMBER WHAT YOU TOLD ME, FUSHIMI-KUN?

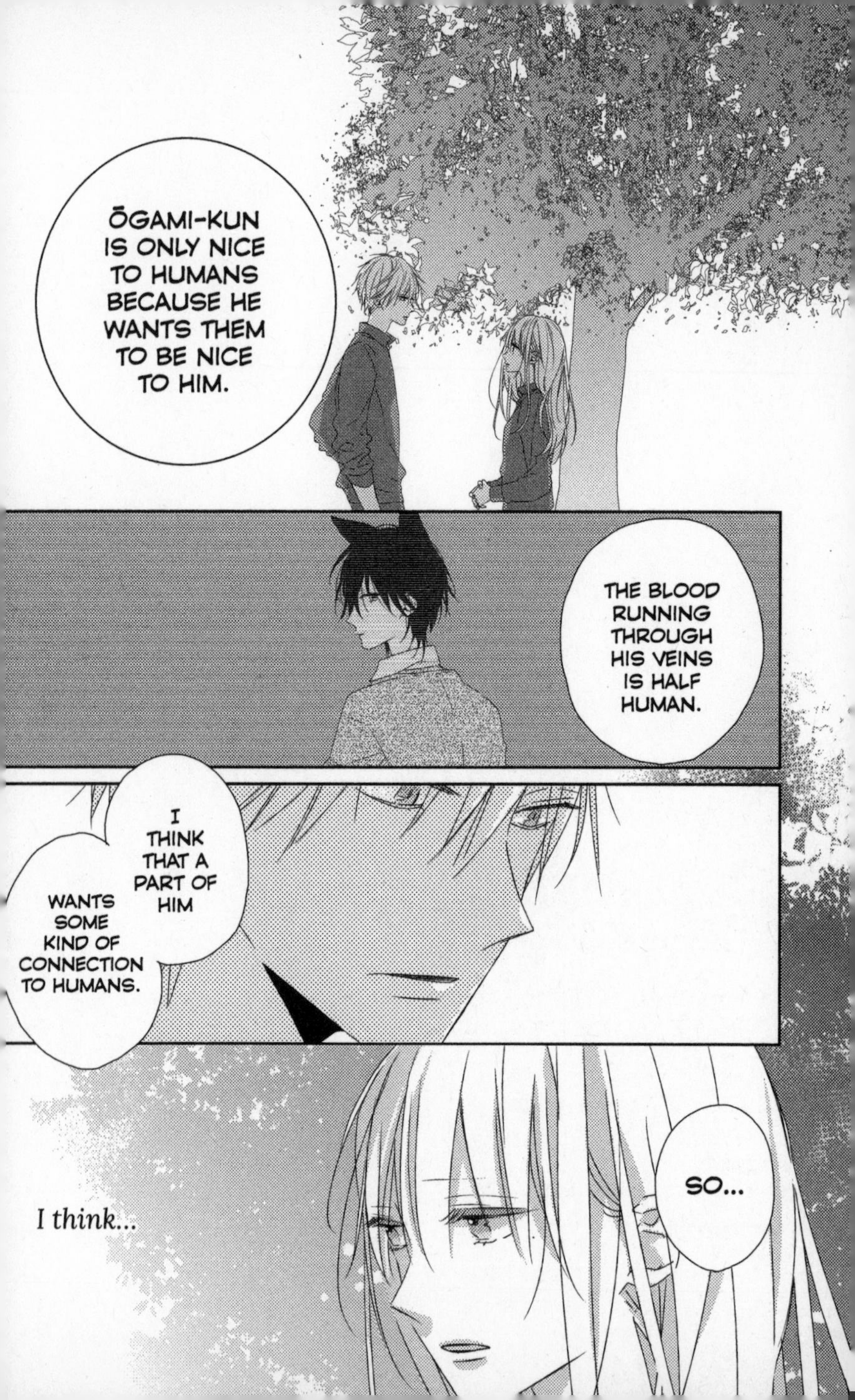
ŌGAMI-KUN IS ONLY NICE TO HUMANS BECAUSE HE WANTS THEM TO BE NICE TO HIM.
THE BLOOD RUNNING THROUGH HIS VEINS IS HALF HUMAN.
I THINK THAT A PART OF HIM
WANTS SOME KIND OF CONNECTION TO HUMANS.
SO...
I think...

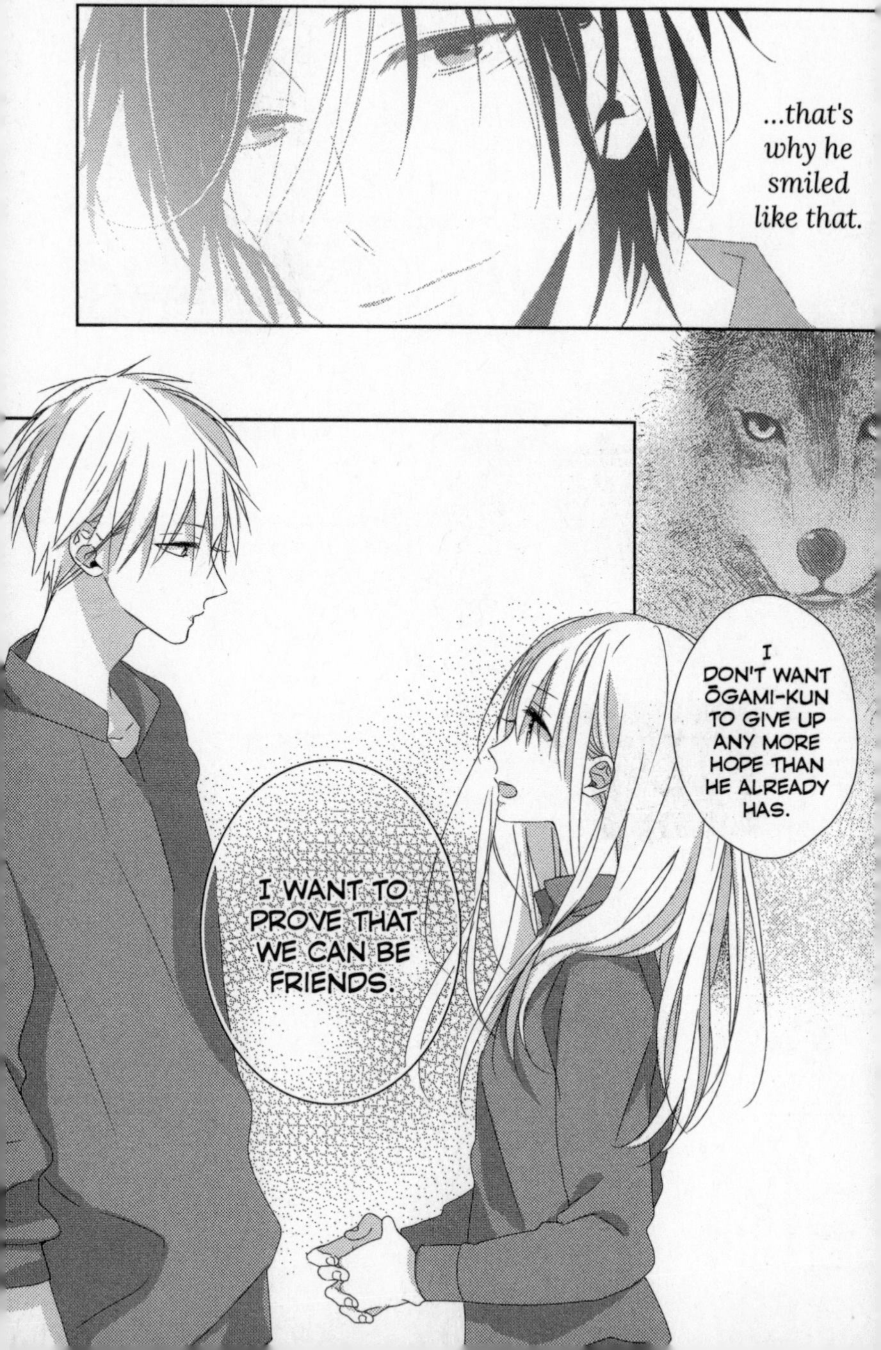
...that's why he smiled like that.
I DON'T WANT ŌGAMI-KUN TO GIVE UP ANY MORE HOPE THAN HE ALREADY HAS.
I WANT TO PROVE THAT WE CAN BE FRIENDS.

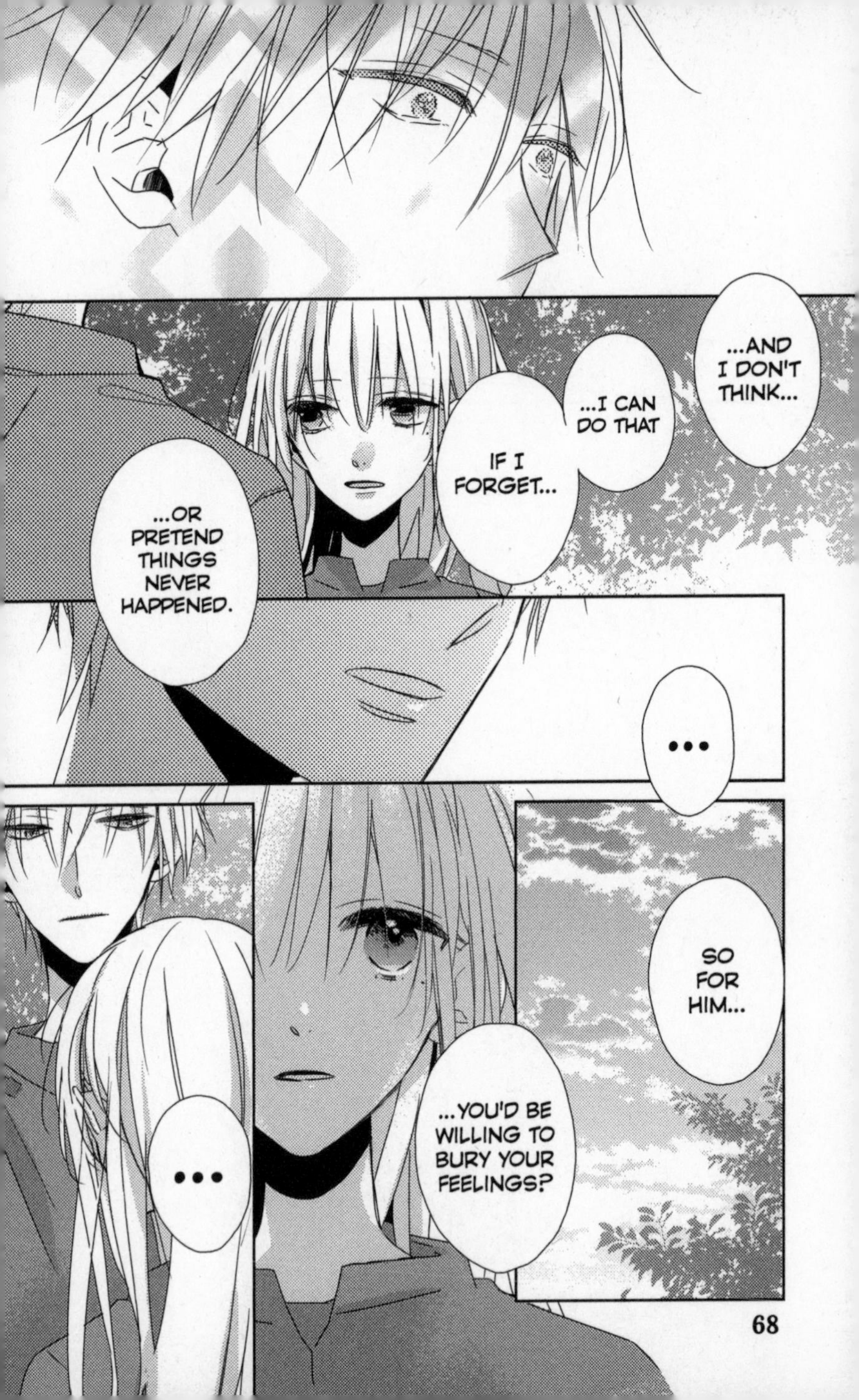
...AND I DON'T THINK...
...I CAN DO THAT
IF I FORGET...
...OR PRETEND THINGS NEVER HAPPENED.
...
SO FOR HIM...
...YOU'D BE WILLING TO BURY YOUR FEELINGS?
...

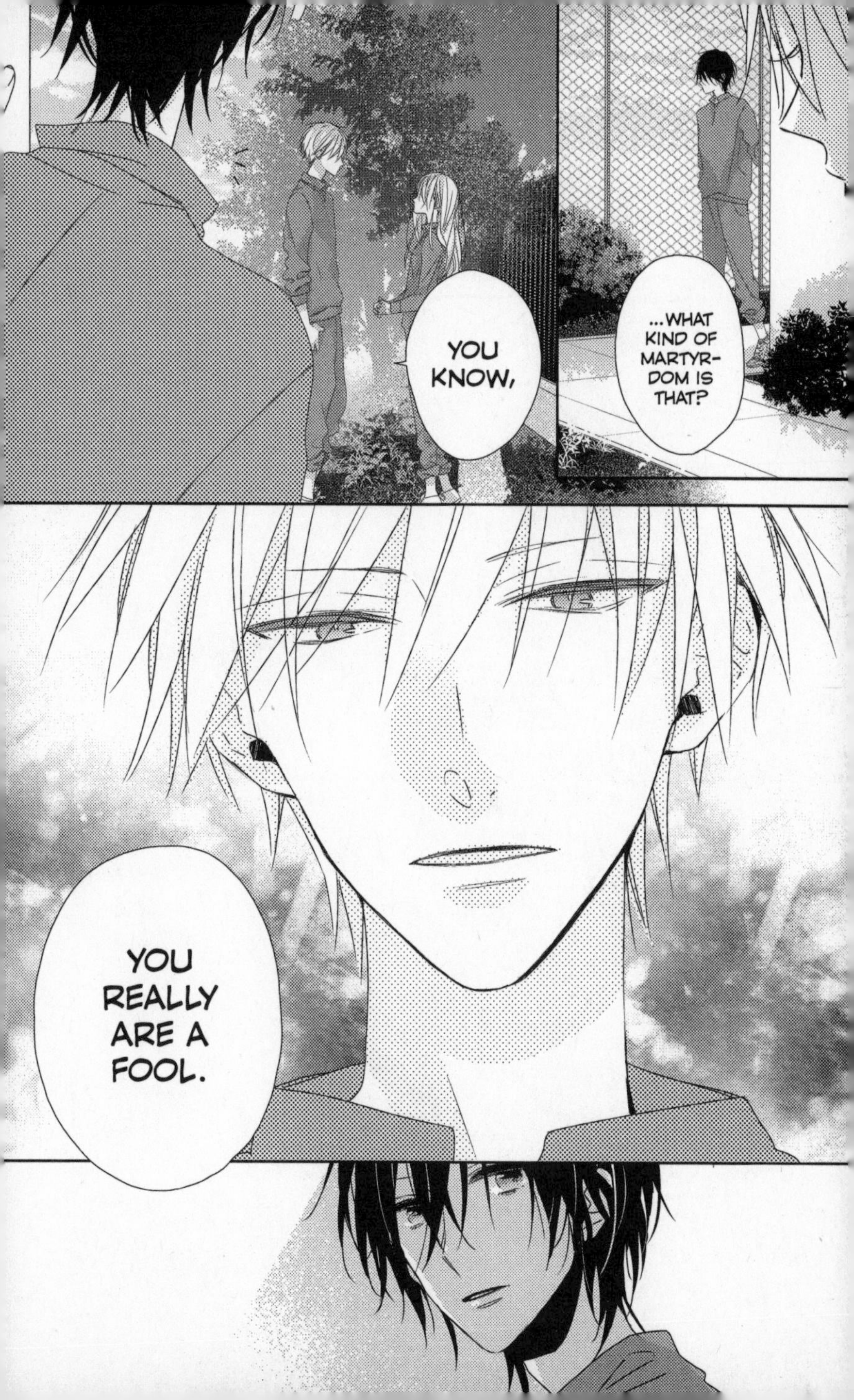
...WHAT KIND OF MARTYR-DOM IS THAT?
YOU KNOW,
YOU REALLY ARE A FOOL.

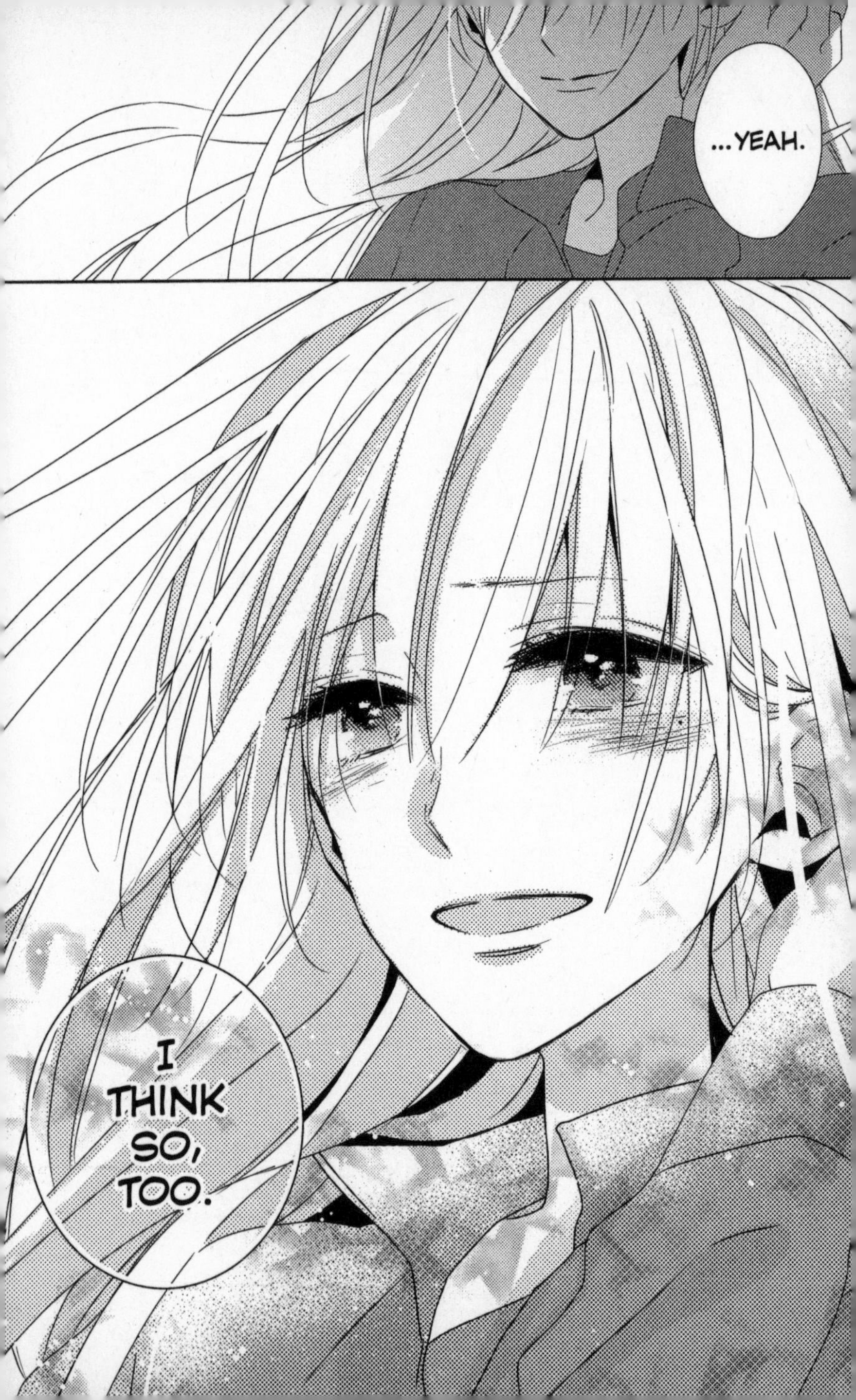
...YEAH.
I THINK SO, TOO.

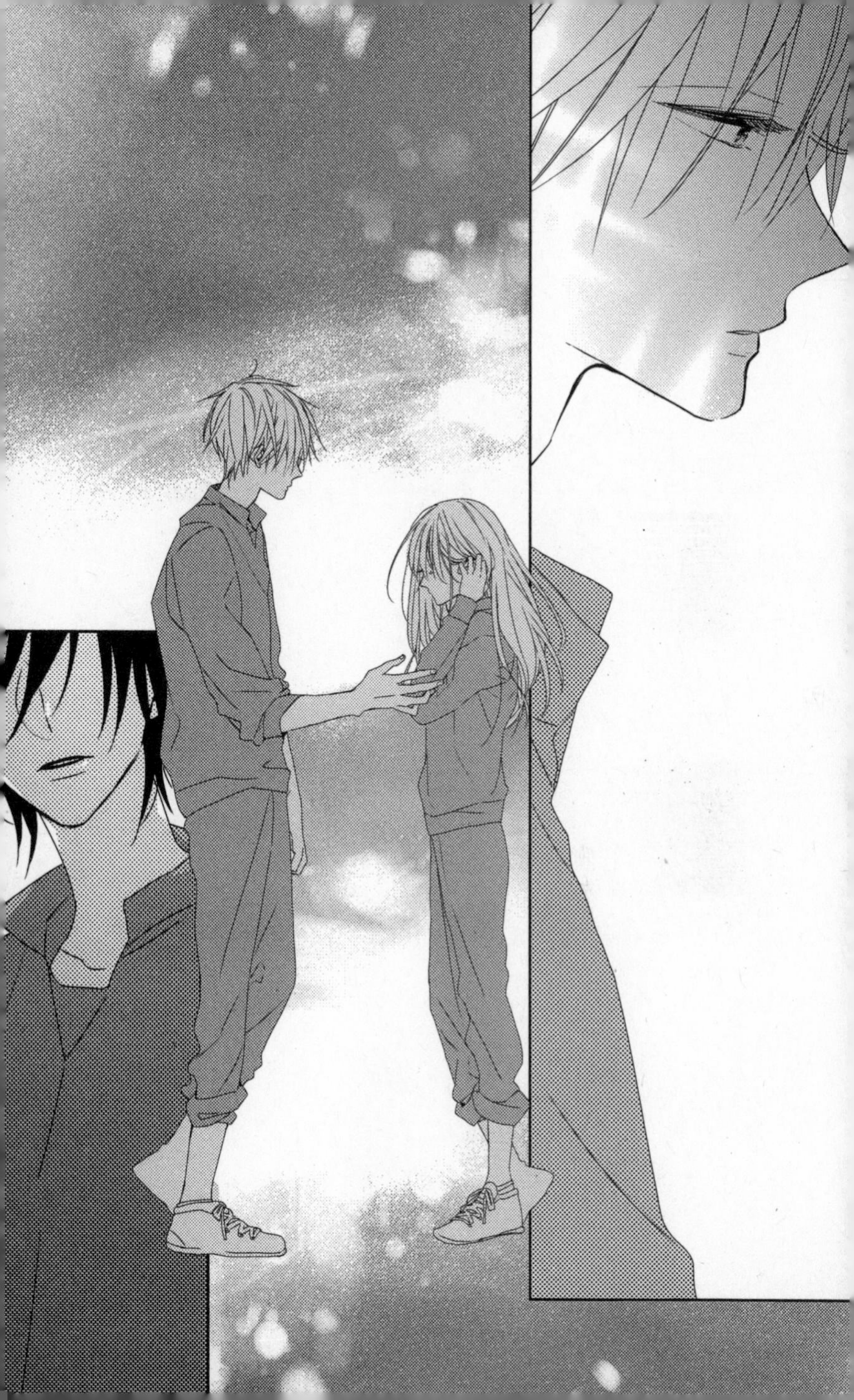

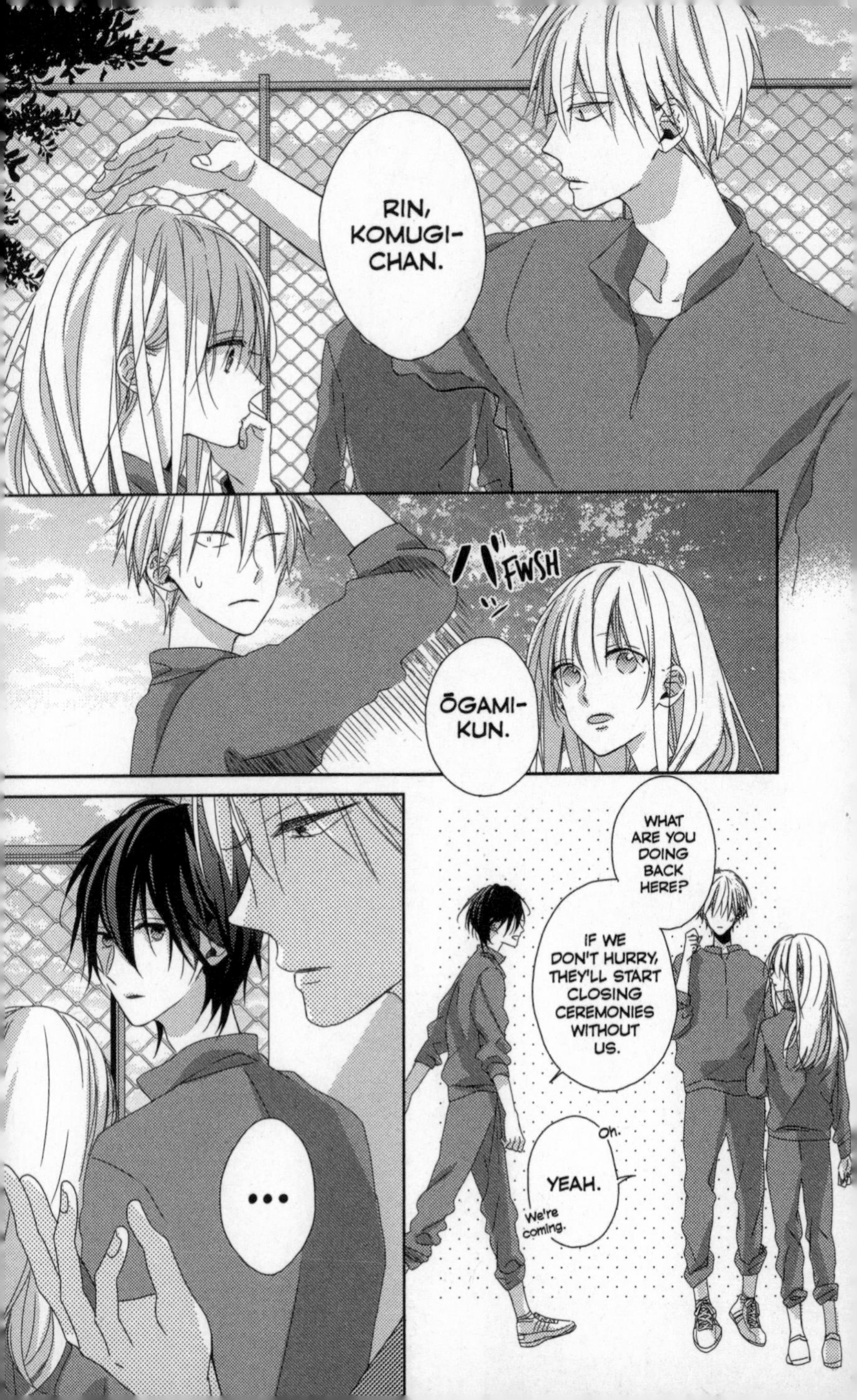
RIN, KOMUGI-CHAN.
バ FWSH
ŌGAMI-KUN.
WHAT ARE YOU DOING BACK HERE?
IF WE DON'T HURRY, THEY'LL START CLOSING CEREMONIES WITHOUT US.
Oh.
YEAH.
We're coming.
...

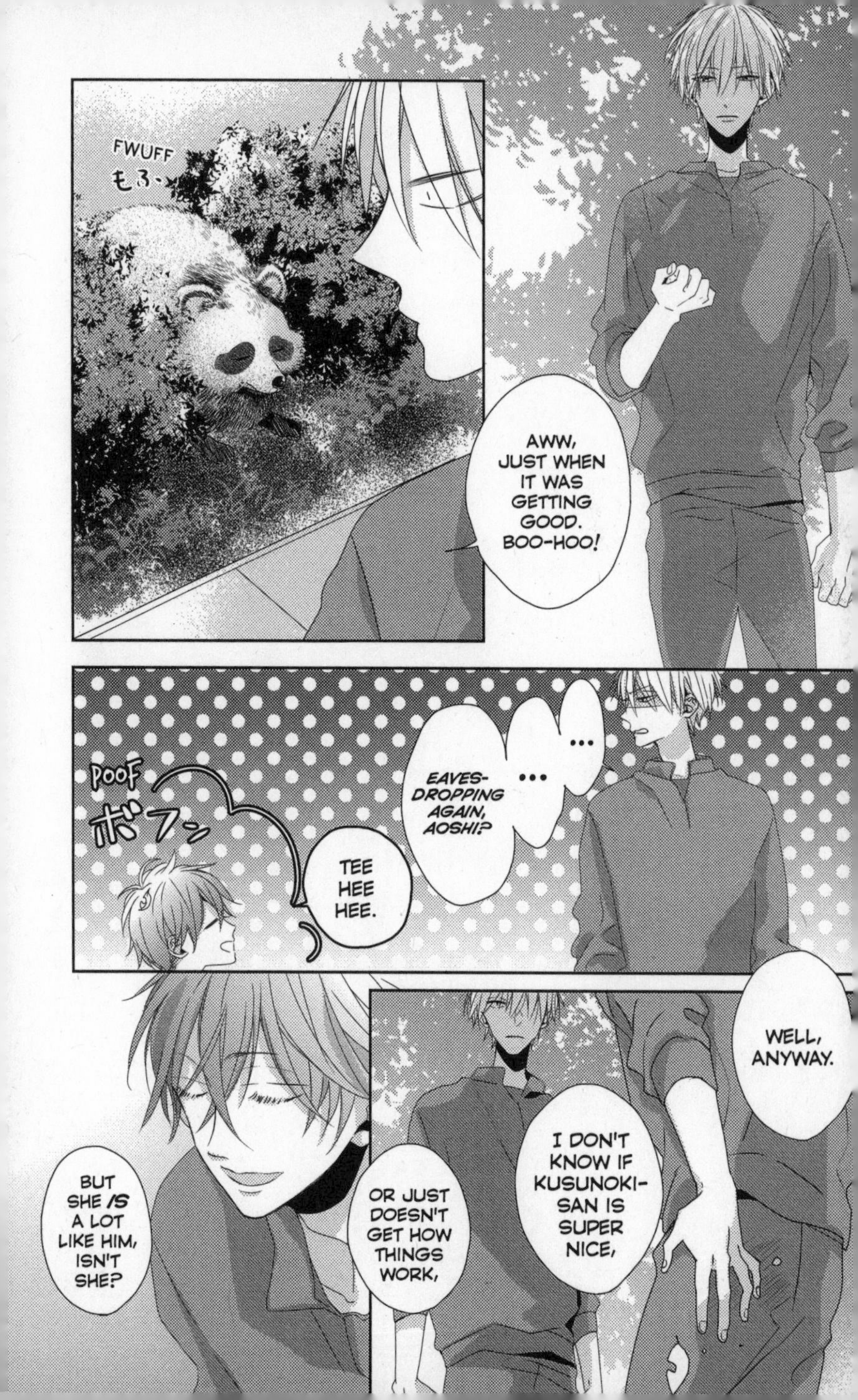
AWW, JUST WHEN IT WAS GETTING GOOD. BOO-HOO!
FWUFF
もふ
...
...
EAVES-DROPPING AGAIN, AOSHI?
TEE HEE HEE.
POOF
ボフン
WELL, ANYWAY.
I DON'T KNOW IF KUSUNOKI-SAN IS SUPER NICE,
OR JUST DOESN'T GET HOW THINGS WORK,
BUT SHE IS A LOT LIKE HIM, ISN'T SHE?

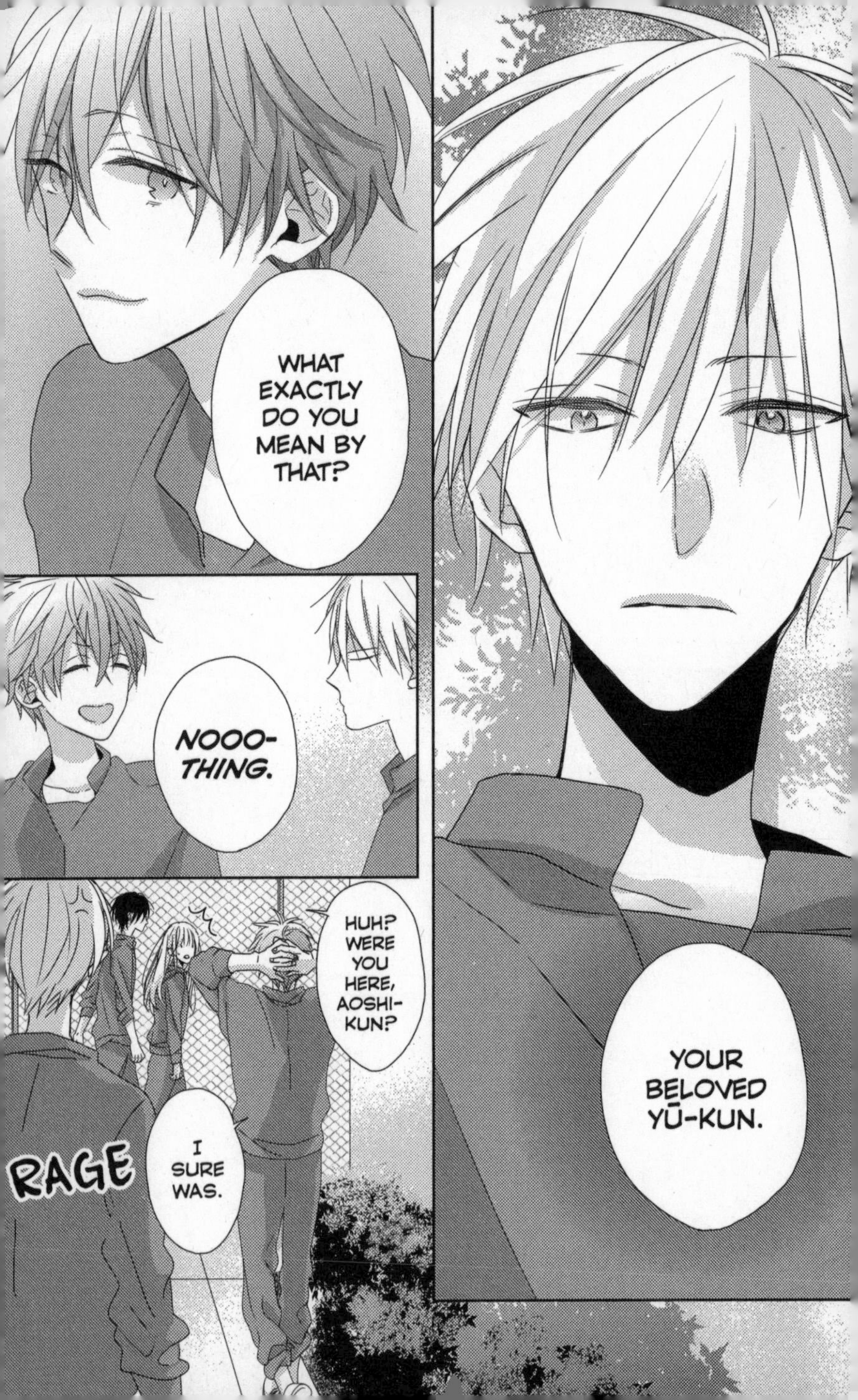
YOUR BELOVED YŪ-KUN.
WHAT EXACTLY DO YOU MEAN BY THAT?
NOOO-THING.
HUH? WERE YOU HERE, AOSHI-KUN?
I SURE WAS.
RAGE

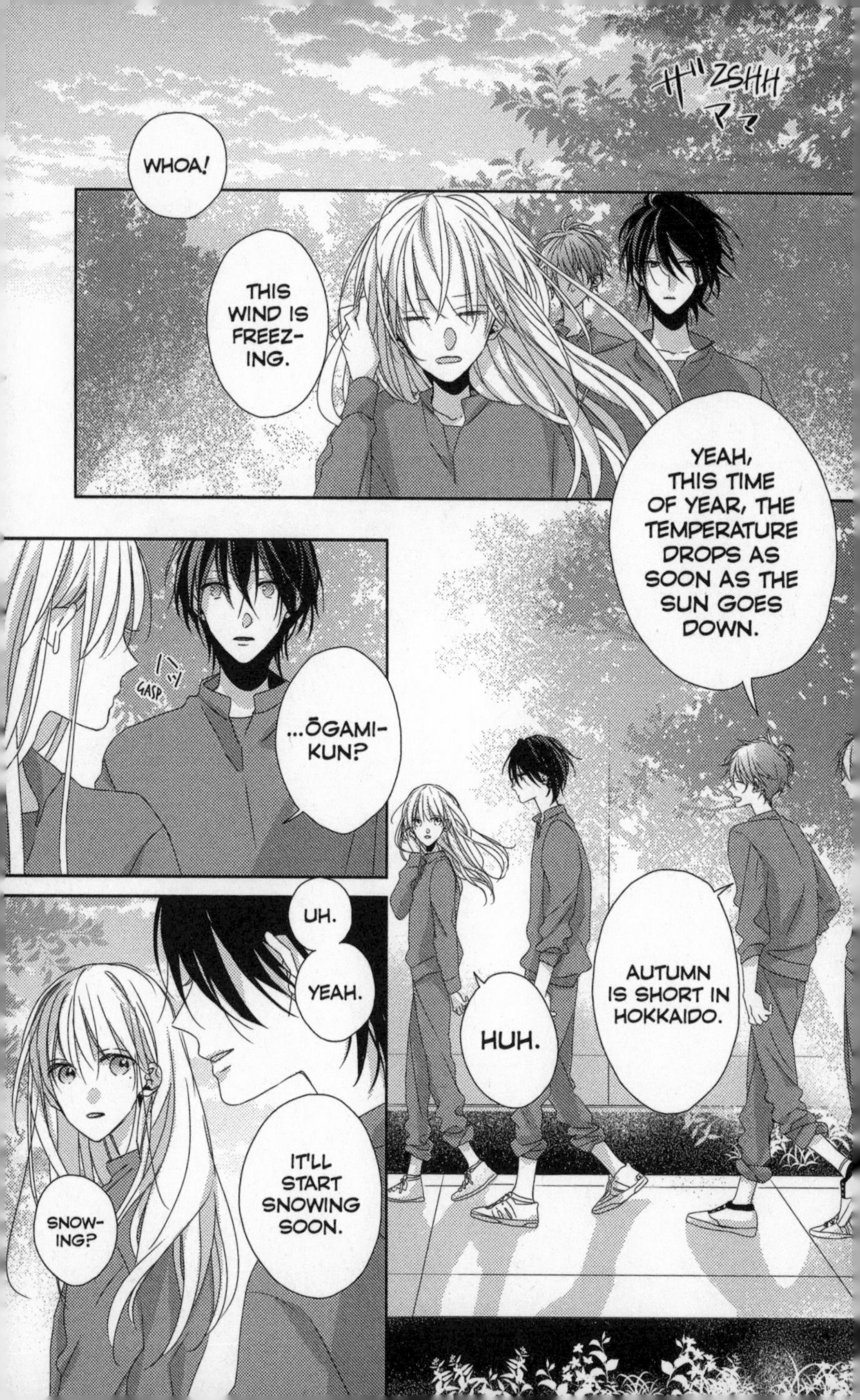
ZSHH
WHOA!
THIS WIND IS FREEZ-ING.
YEAH, THIS TIME OF YEAR, THE TEMPERATURE DROPS AS SOON AS THE SUN GOES DOWN.
AUTUMN IS SHORT IN HOKKAIDO.
HUH.
GASP
...ŌGAMI-KUN?
UH.
YEAH.
IT'LL START SNOWING SOON.
SNOW-ING?

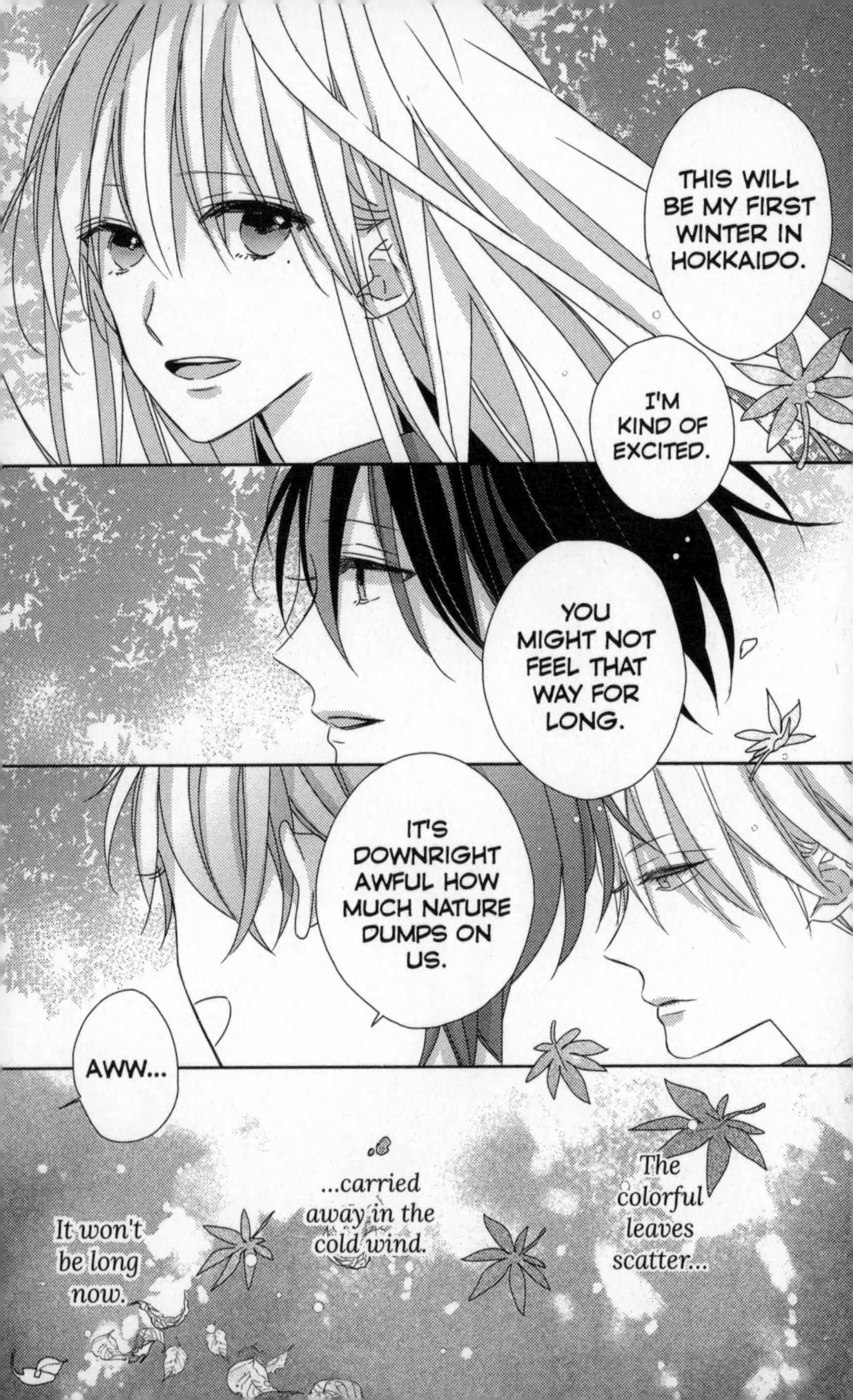
THIS WILL BE MY FIRST WINTER IN HOKKAIDO.
I'M KIND OF EXCITED.
YOU MIGHT NOT FEEL THAT WAY FOR LONG.
IT'S DOWNRIGHT AWFUL HOW MUCH NATURE DUMPS ON US.
AWW...
The colorful leaves scatter...
...carried away in the cold wind.
It won't be long now.

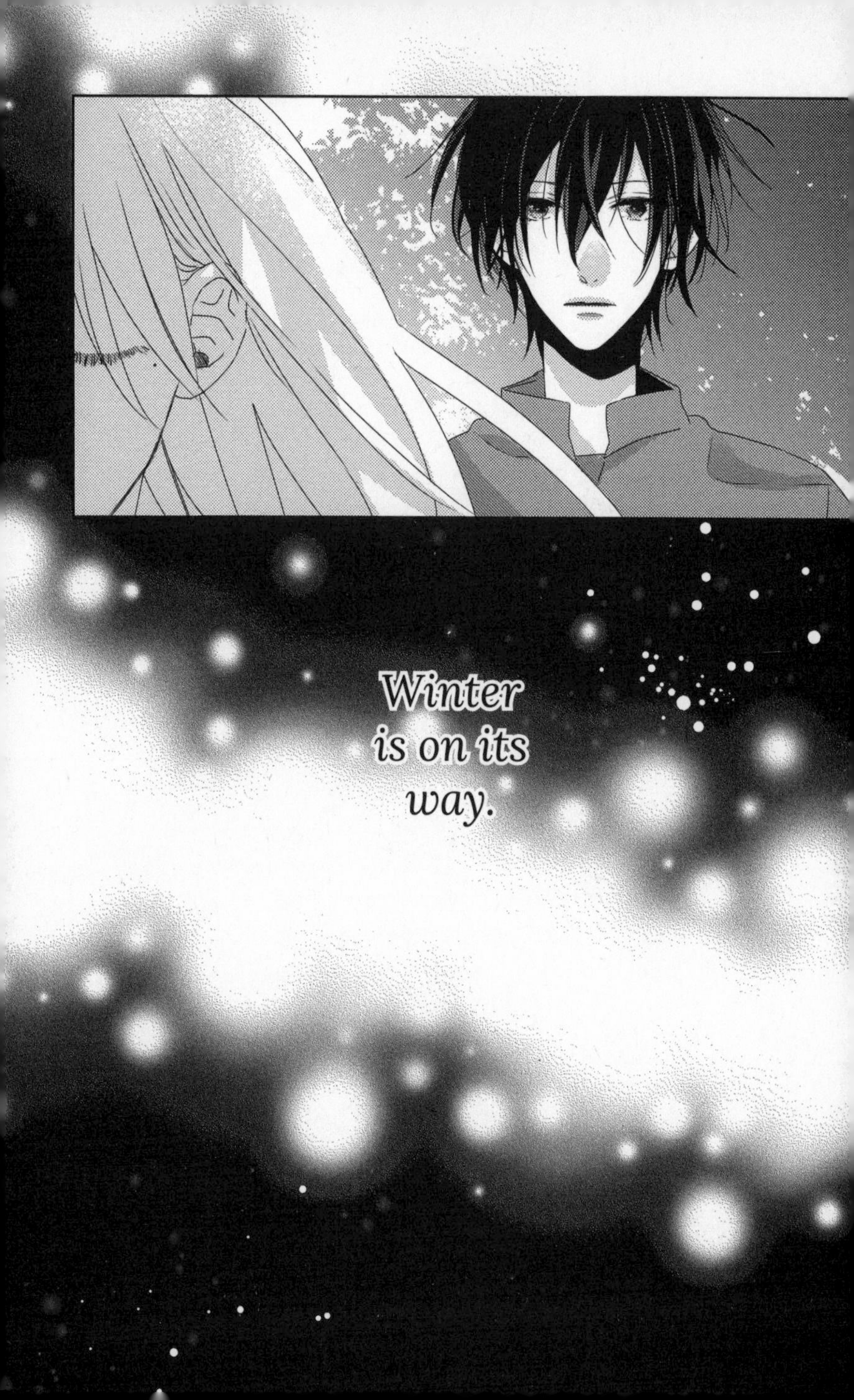
Winter is on its way.

GLANCE
チラ.

That Wolf-Boy is Mine!

Chapter 7

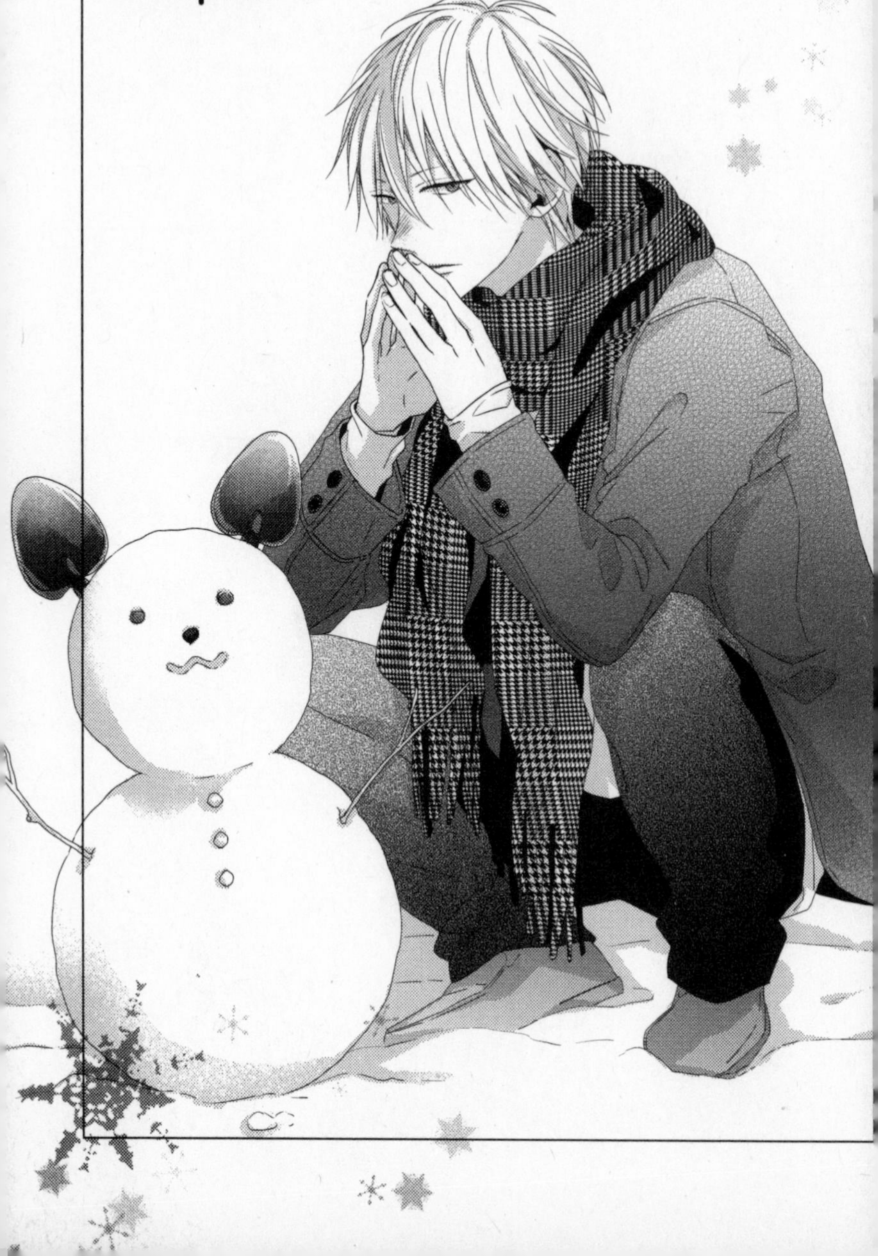

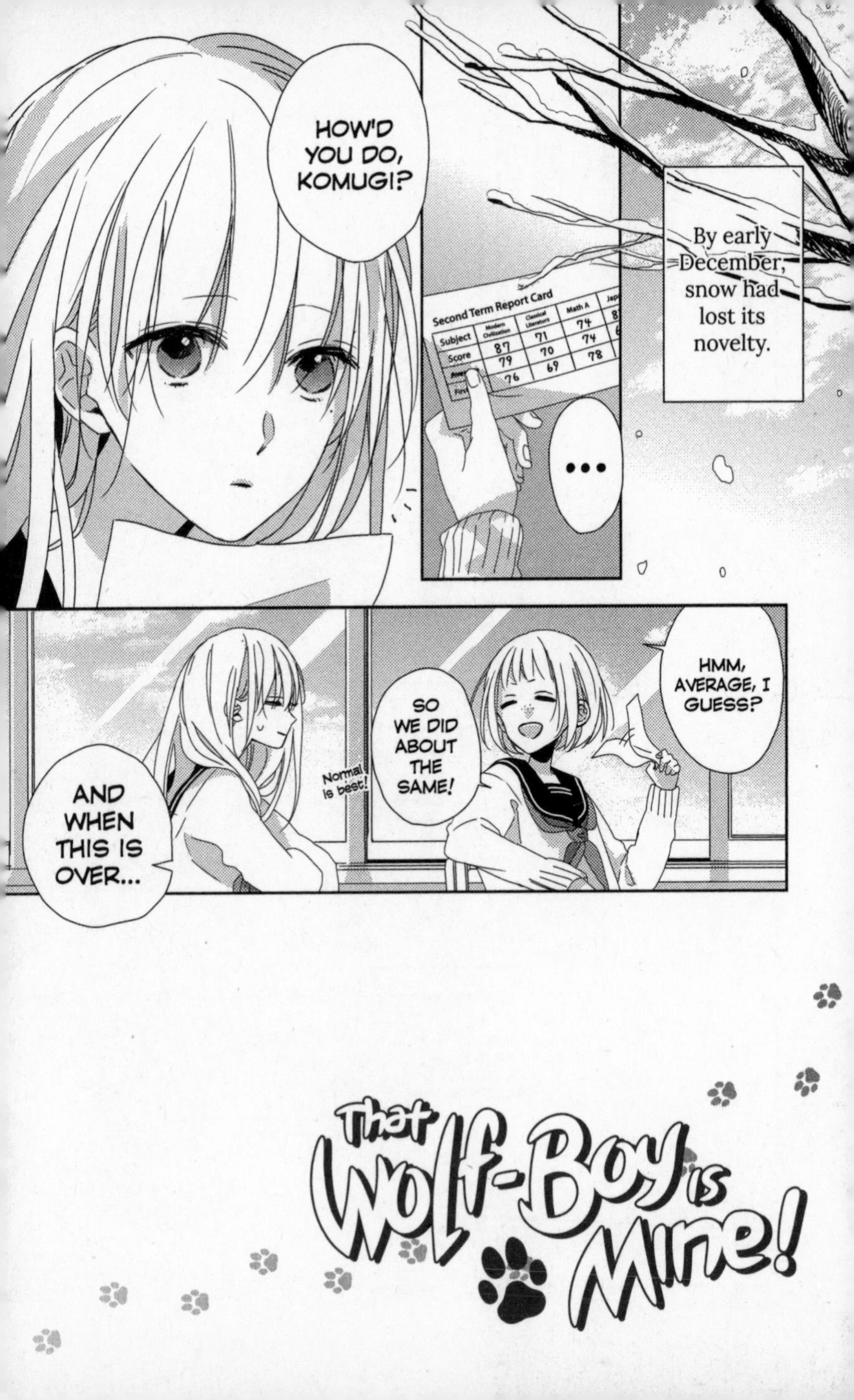
By early December, snow had lost its novelty.
Second Term Report Card
Subject
Score
Modern Civilization
Classical Literature
Math A
87 71 74
79 70 74
76 69 78
...
HOW'D YOU DO, KOMUGI?
HMM, AVERAGE, I GUESS?
SO WE DID ABOUT THE SAME!
Normal is best!
AND WHEN THIS IS OVER...
That Wolf-Boy is Mine!

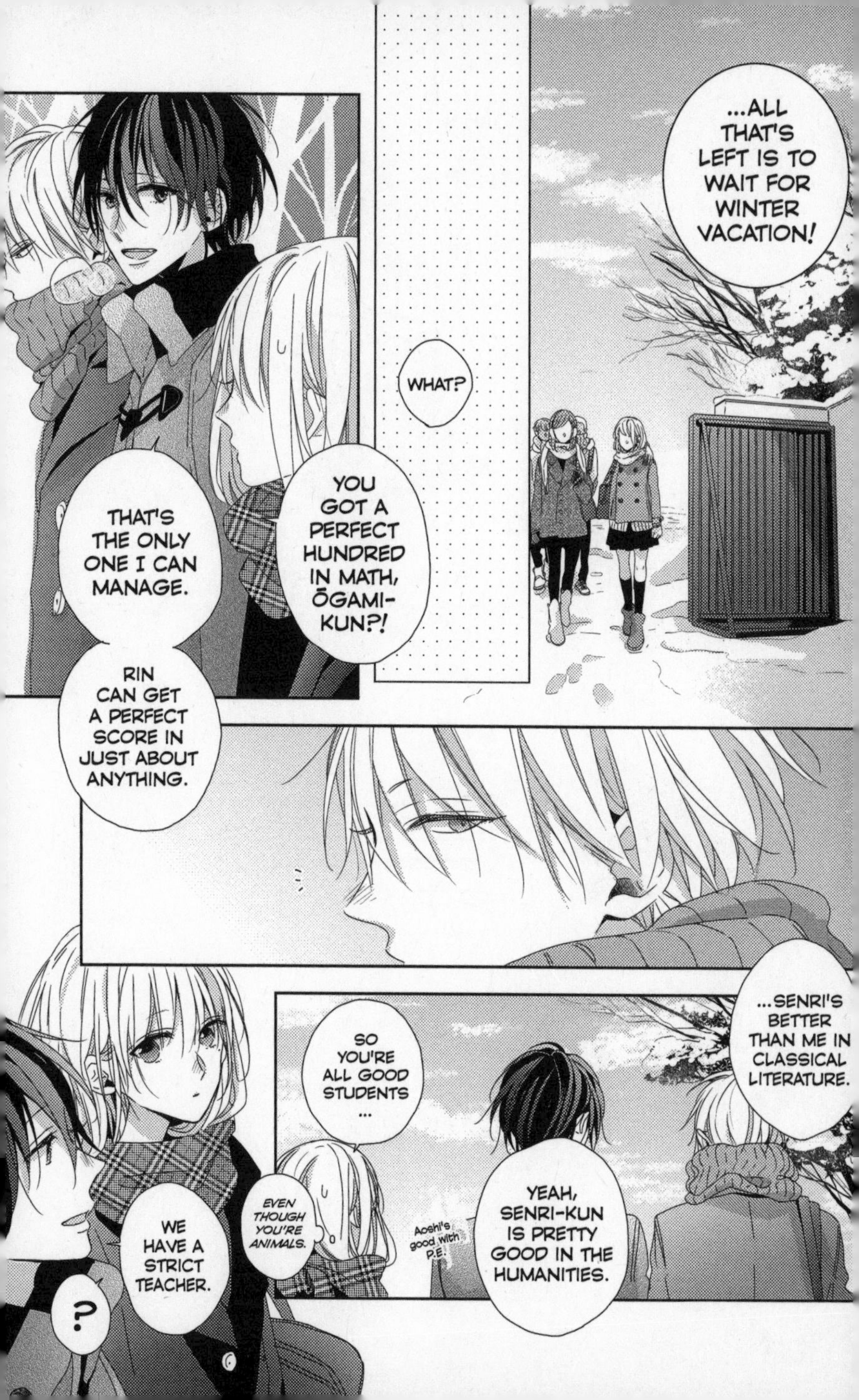
...ALL THAT'S LEFT IS TO WAIT FOR WINTER VACATION!
WHAT?
YOU GOT A PERFECT HUNDRED IN MATH, ŌGAMI-KUN?!
THAT'S THE ONLY ONE I CAN MANAGE.
RIN CAN GET A PERFECT SCORE IN JUST ABOUT ANYTHING.
...SENRI'S BETTER THAN ME IN CLASSICAL LITERATURE.
YEAH, SENRI-KUN IS PRETTY GOOD IN THE HUMANITIES.
Aoshi's good with P.E.
SO YOU'RE ALL GOOD STUDENTS...
EVEN THOUGH YOU'RE ANIMALS.
WE HAVE A STRICT TEACHER.
?

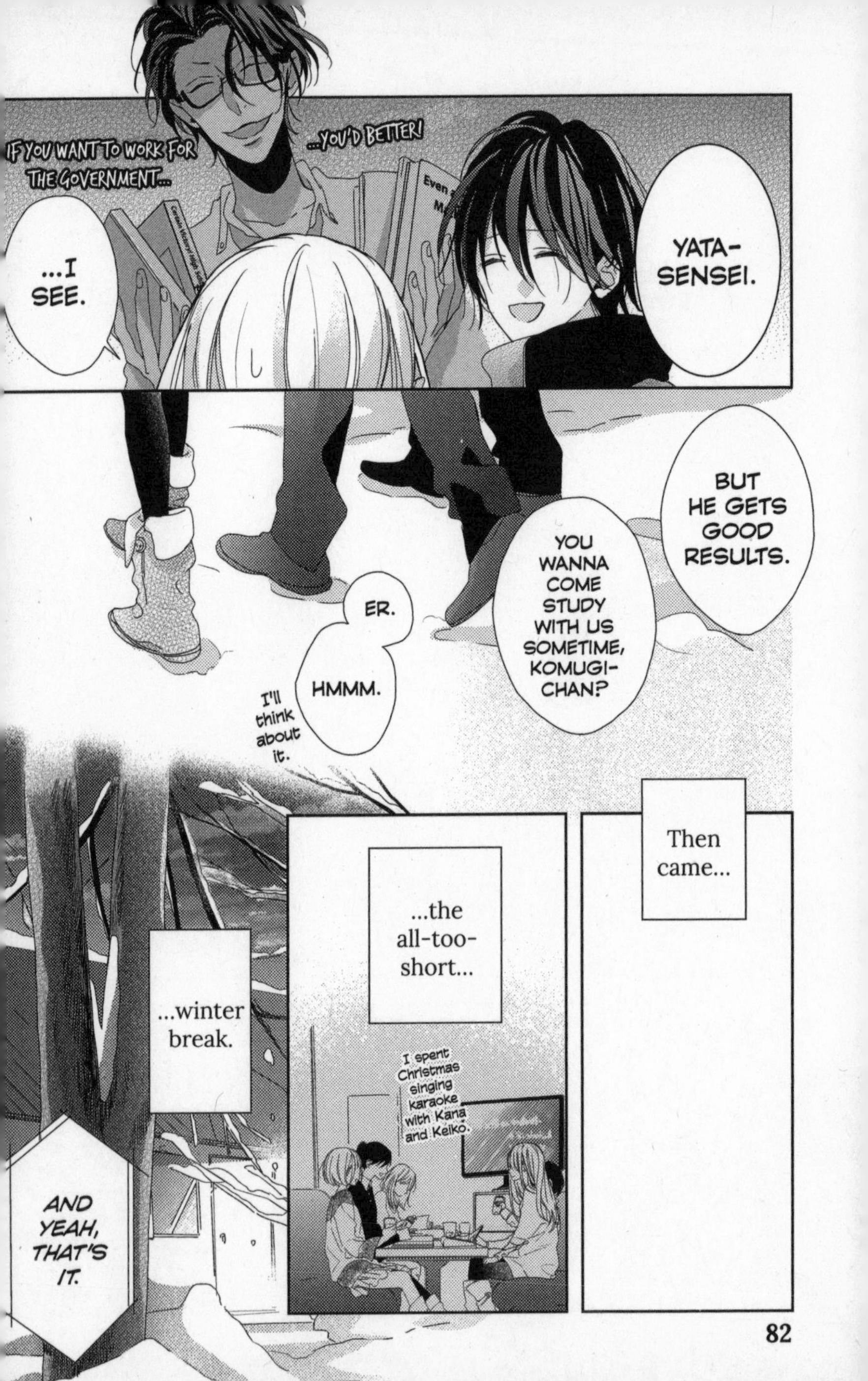
YATA-SENSEI.
IF YOU WANT TO WORK FOR THE GOVERNMENT...
...YOU'D BETTER!
...I SEE.
BUT HE GETS GOOD RESULTS.
YOU WANNA COME STUDY WITH US SOMETIME, KOMUGI-CHAN?
ER.
HMMM.
I'll think about it.
Then came...
...the all-too-short...
I spent Christmas singing karaoke with Kana and Keiko.
...winter break.
AND YEAH, THAT'S IT.

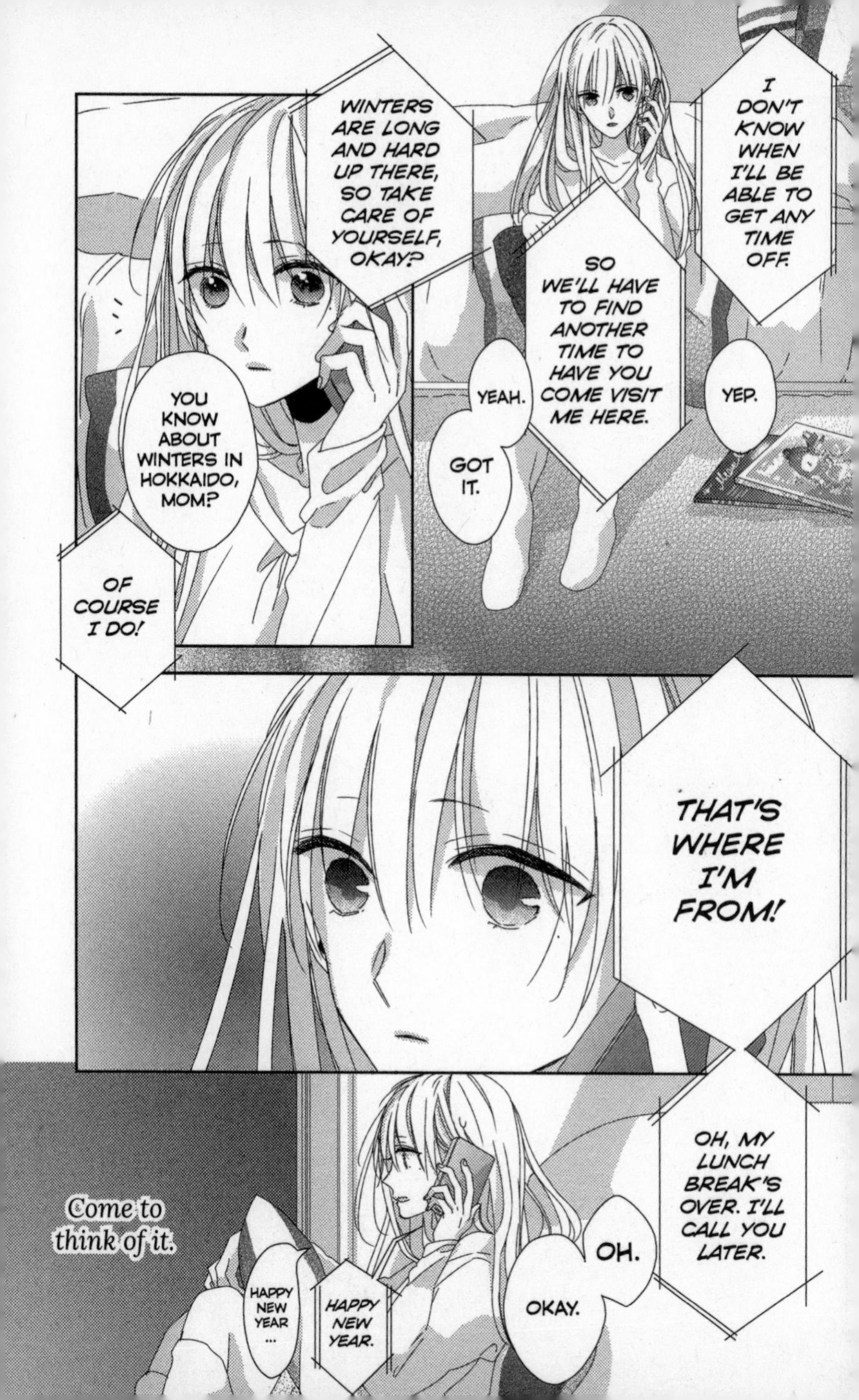

I DON'T KNOW WHEN I'LL BE ABLE TO GET ANY TIME OFF.
YEP.
SO WE'LL HAVE TO FIND ANOTHER TIME TO HAVE YOU COME VISIT ME HERE.
YEAH.
GOT IT.
WINTERS ARE LONG AND HARD UP THERE, SO TAKE CARE OF YOURSELF, OKAY?
YOU KNOW ABOUT WINTERS IN HOKKAIDO, MOM?
OF COURSE I DO!
THAT'S WHERE I'M FROM!
OH, MY LUNCH BREAK'S OVER. I'LL CALL YOU LATER.
OH.
OKAY.
HAPPY NEW YEAR.
HAPPY NEW YEAR...
Come to think of it.

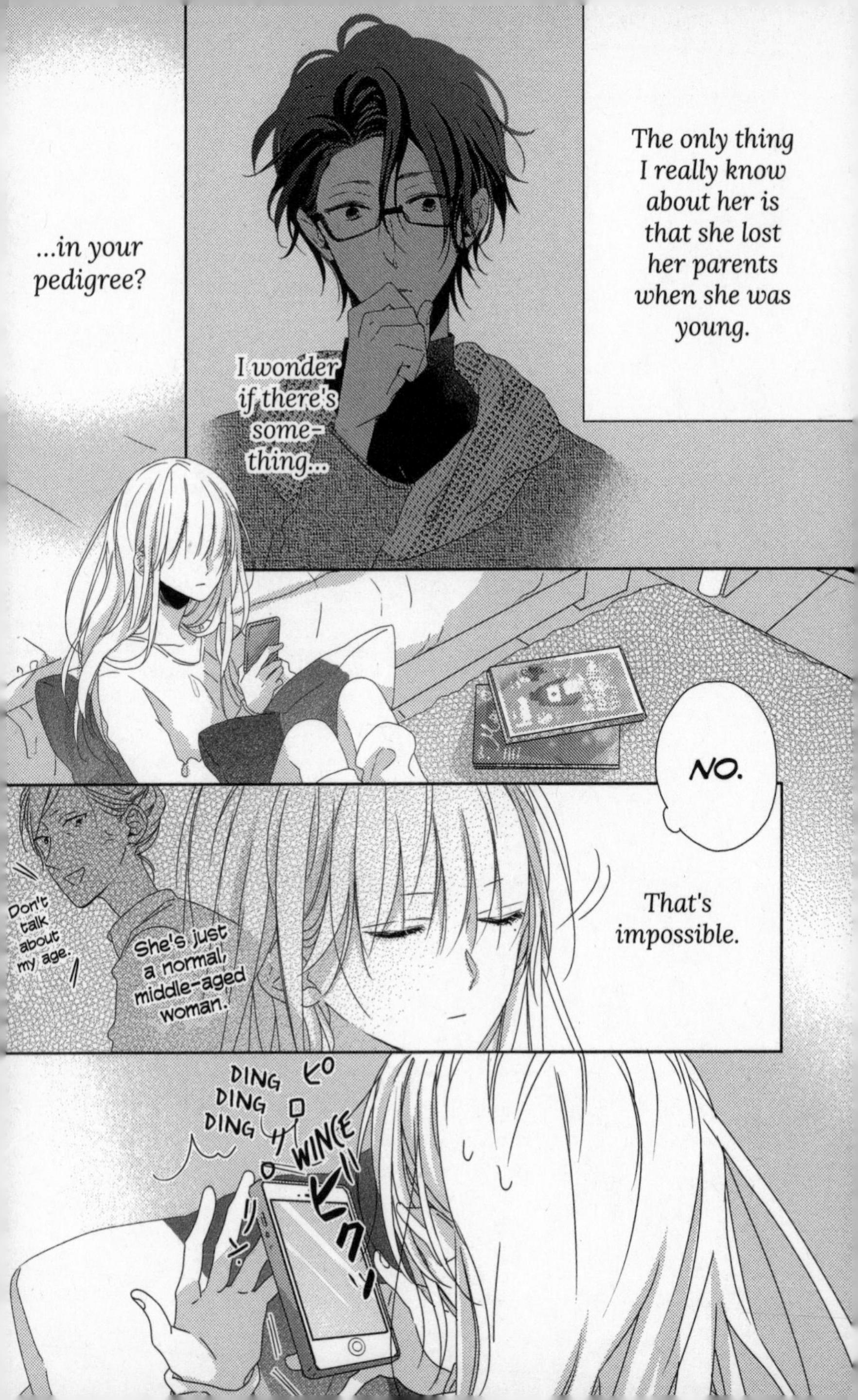
The only thing I really know about her is that she lost her parents when she was young.
I wonder if there's some-thing...
...in your pedigree?
NO.
That's impossible.
She's just a normal, middle-aged woman.
Don't talk about my age.
DING DING DING
WINCE

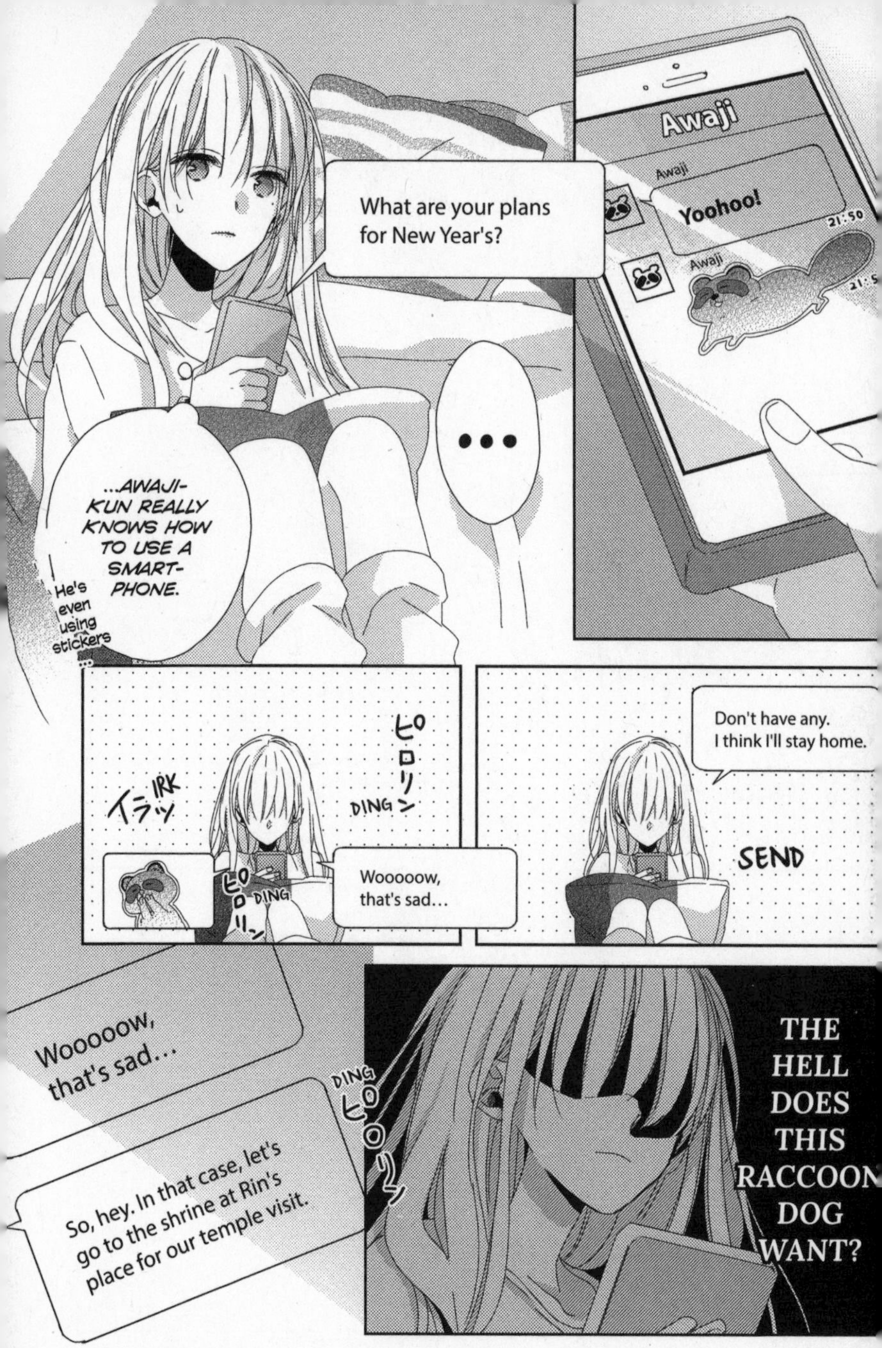
Awaji
Awaji
Yoohoo!
21:50
Awaji
What are your plans for New Year's?
...
...AWAJI-KUN REALLY KNOWS HOW TO USE A SMARTPHONE.
He's even using stickers...
Don't have any. I think I'll stay home.
SEND
ピロリン DING
イラッ IRK
Woooow, that's sad...
ピロリン DING
THE HELL DOES THIS RACCOON DOG WANT?
ピロリン DING
Woooow, that's sad...
So, hey. In that case, let's go to the shrine at Rin's place for our temple visit.

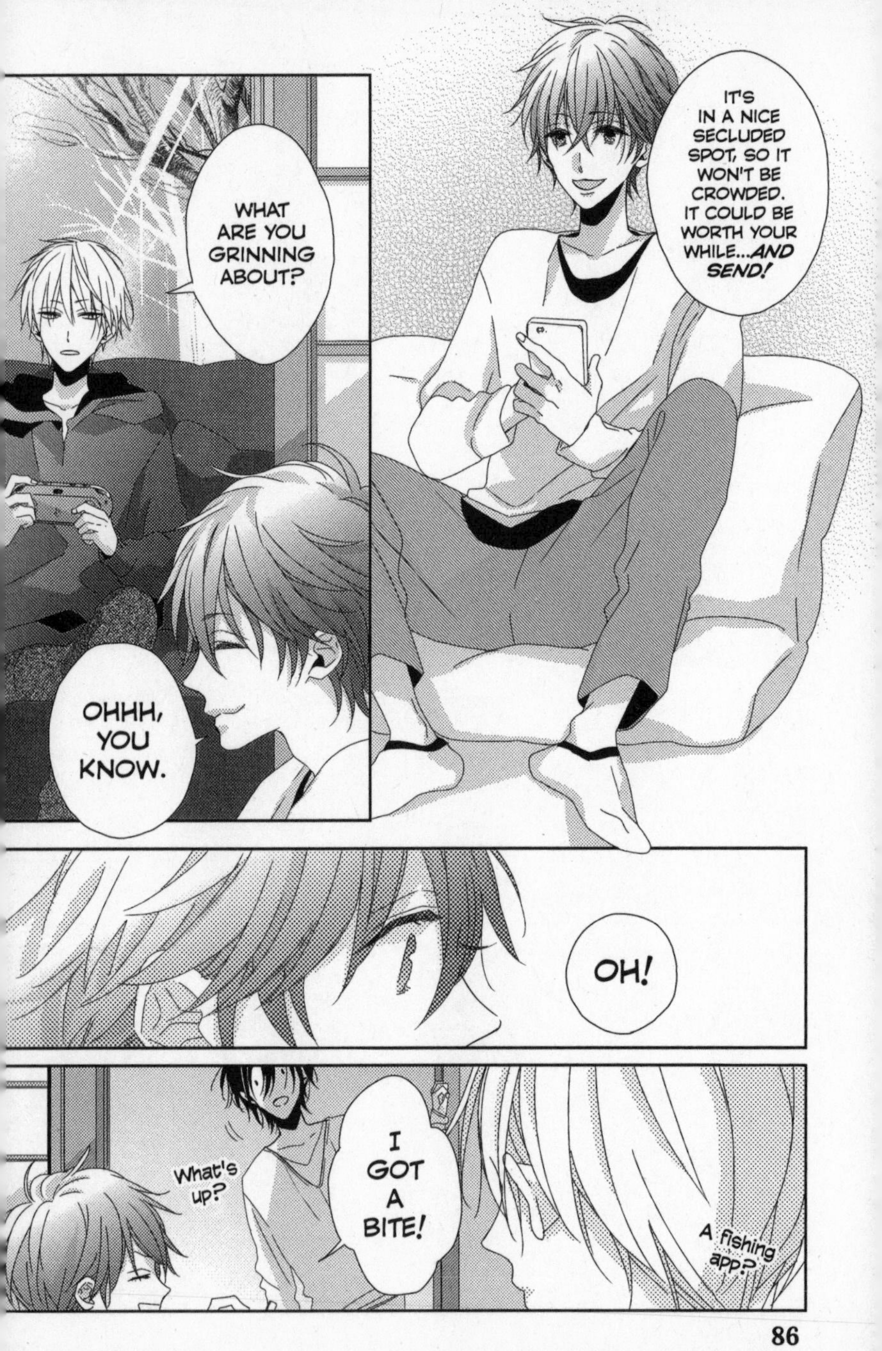
IT'S IN A NICE SECLUDED SPOT, SO IT WON'T BE CROWDED. IT COULD BE WORTH YOUR WHILE...*AND SEND!*
WHAT ARE YOU GRINNING ABOUT?
OHHH, YOU KNOW.
OH!
A fishing app?
I GOT A BITE!
What's up?

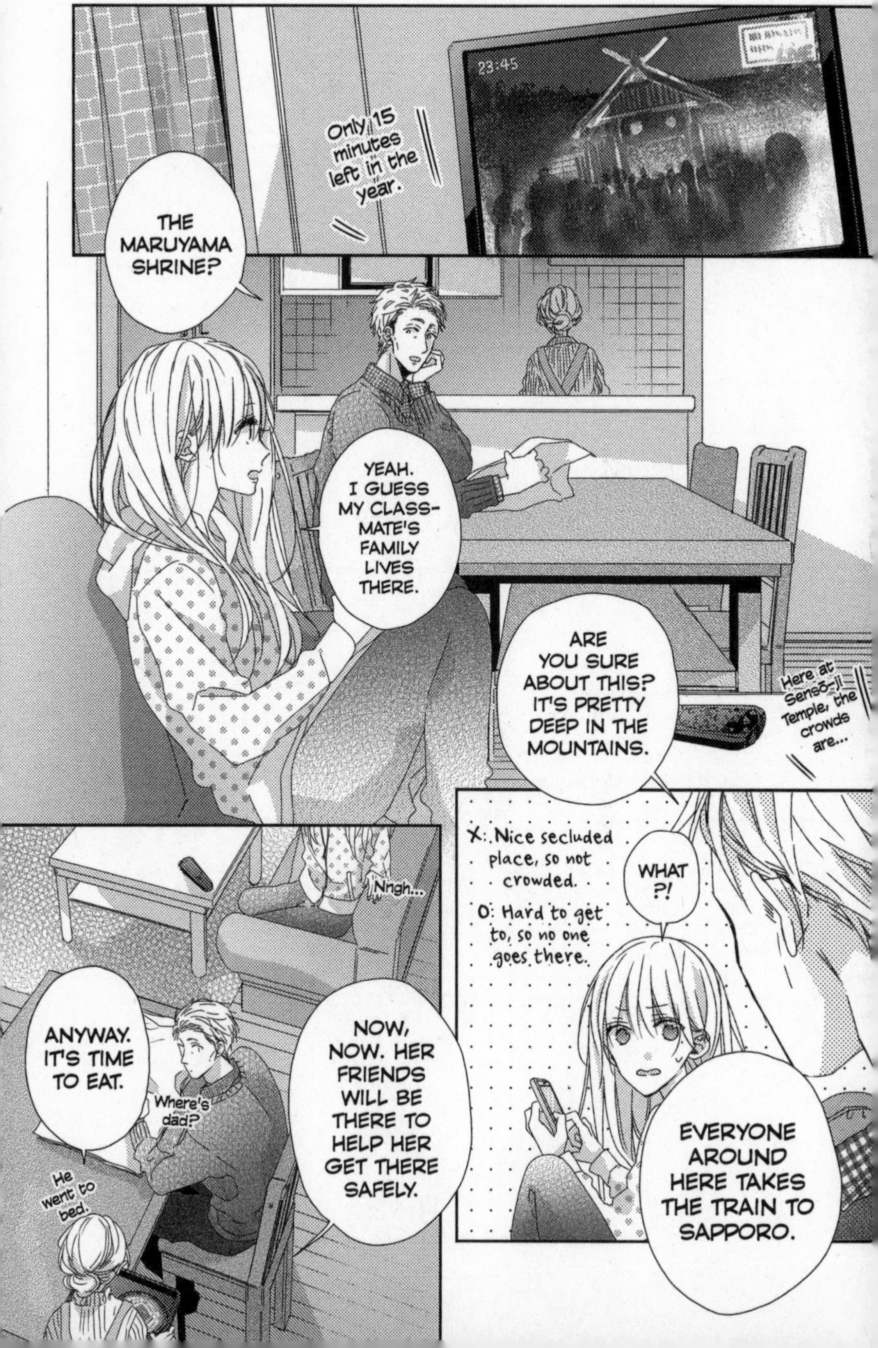
23:45
Only 15 minutes left in the year.
THE MARUYAMA SHRINE?
YEAH. I GUESS MY CLASS-MATE'S FAMILY LIVES THERE.
ARE YOU SURE ABOUT THIS? IT'S PRETTY DEEP IN THE MOUNTAINS.
Here at Sensō-ji Temple, the crowds are...
WHAT?!
X: Nice secluded place, so not crowded.
O: Hard to get to, so no one goes there.
EVERYONE AROUND HERE TAKES THE TRAIN TO SAPPORO.
Nngh...
NOW, NOW. HER FRIENDS WILL BE THERE TO HELP HER GET THERE SAFELY.
ANYWAY. IT'S TIME TO EAT.
Where's dad?
He went to bed.

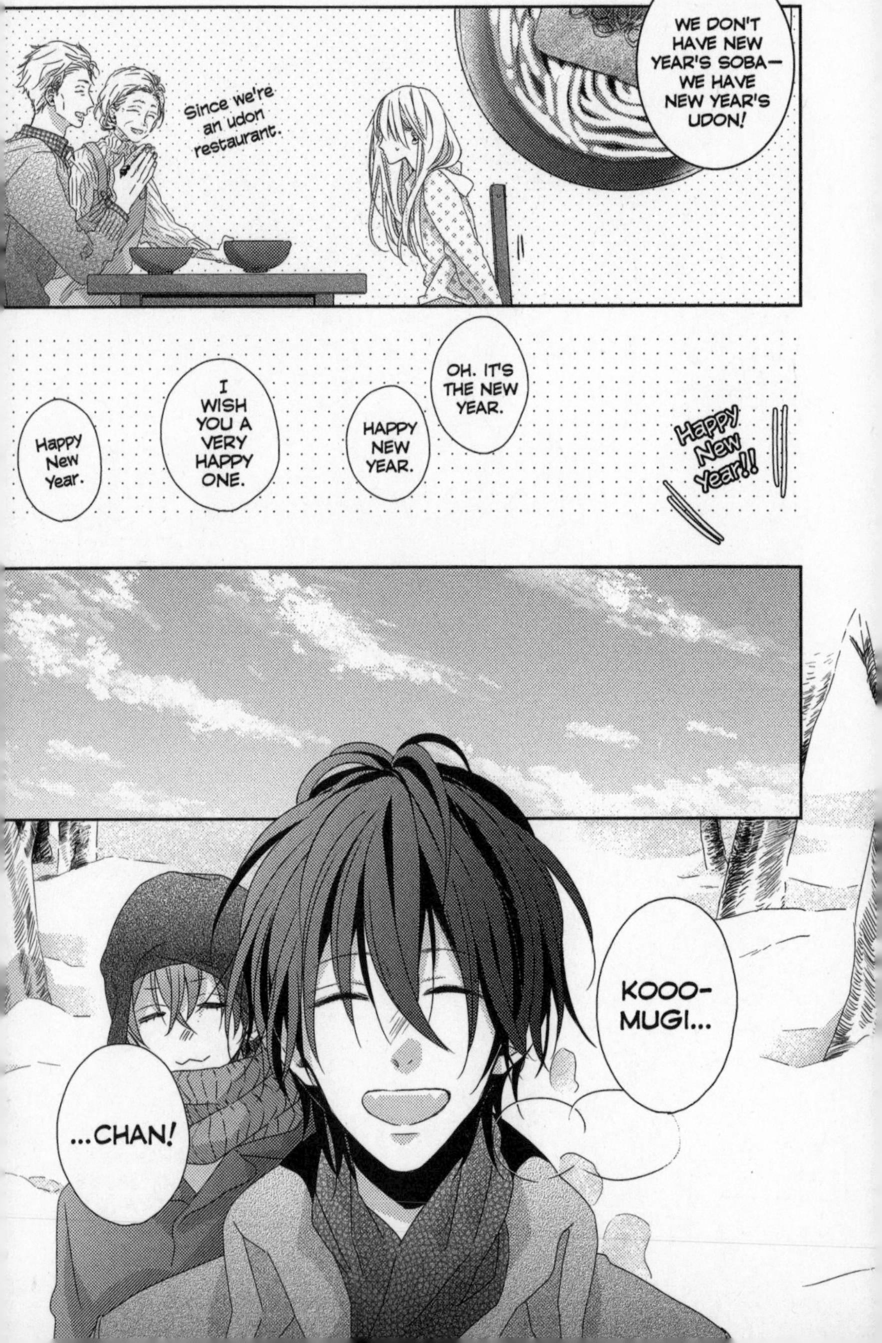
WE DON'T HAVE NEW YEAR'S SOBA—WE HAVE NEW YEAR'S UDON!
Since we're an udon restaurant.
Happy New Year!!
OH. IT'S THE NEW YEAR.
HAPPY NEW YEAR.
I WISH YOU A VERY HAPPY ONE.
Happy New Year.
KOOO-MUGI...
...CHAN!

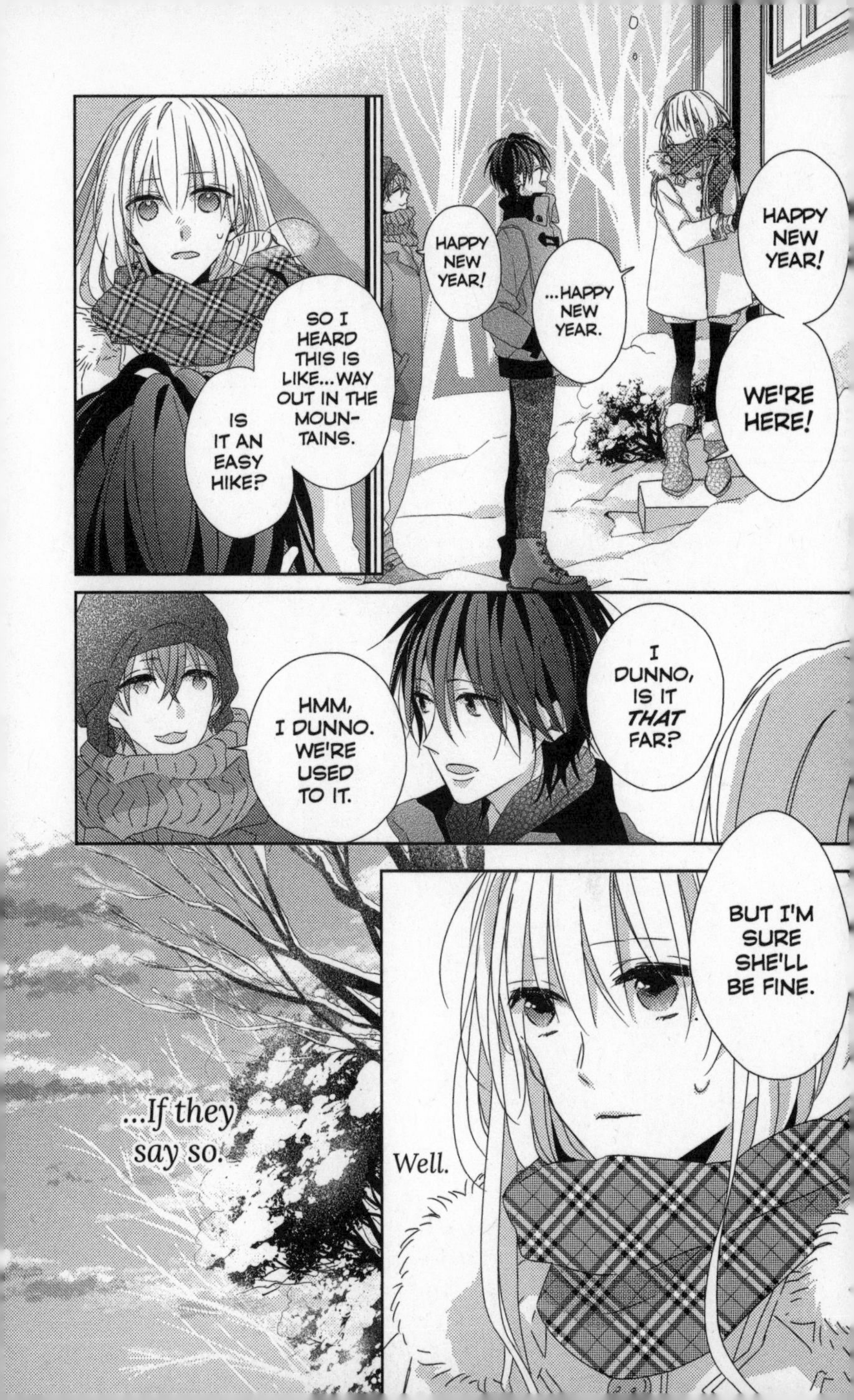
HAPPY NEW YEAR!
WE'RE HERE!
...HAPPY NEW YEAR.
HAPPY NEW YEAR!
SO I HEARD THIS IS LIKE...WAY OUT IN THE MOUN-TAINS.
IS IT AN EASY HIKE?
I DUNNO, IS IT *THAT* FAR?
HMM, I DUNNO. WE'RE USED TO IT.
BUT I'M SURE SHE'LL BE FINE.
Well.
...If they say so.

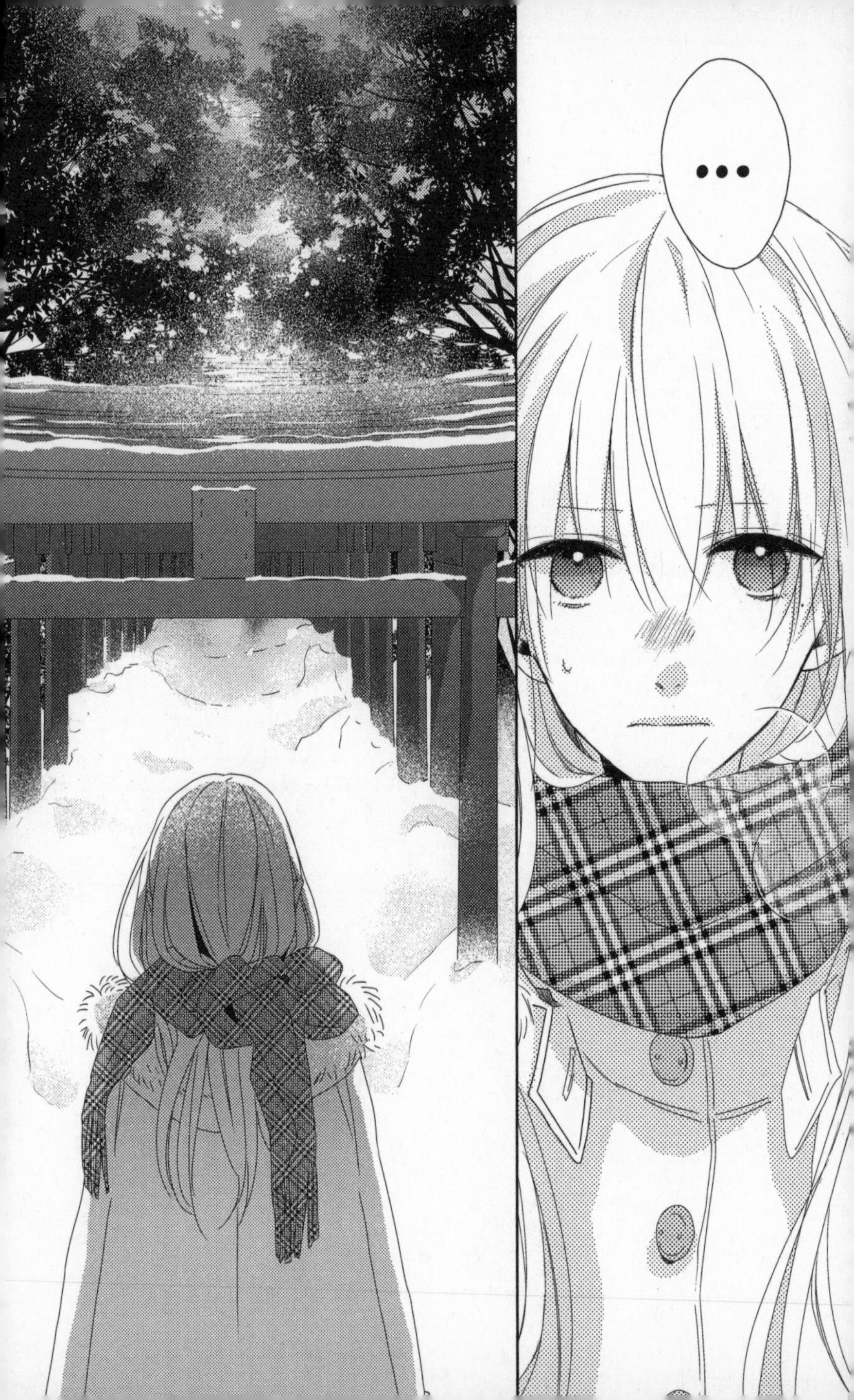
...

We are here.

I've been had...

↑ Shrine

IT'S OKAY. IT'S A BIT OF A CLIMB, BUT IT'S ALL IN A STRAIGHT LINE.

...YEAH.

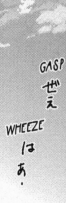

GASP ぜぇ

WHEEZE はぁ.

Yeah!

Let's just stay positive!

I WISH I'D BUNDLED UP MORE...

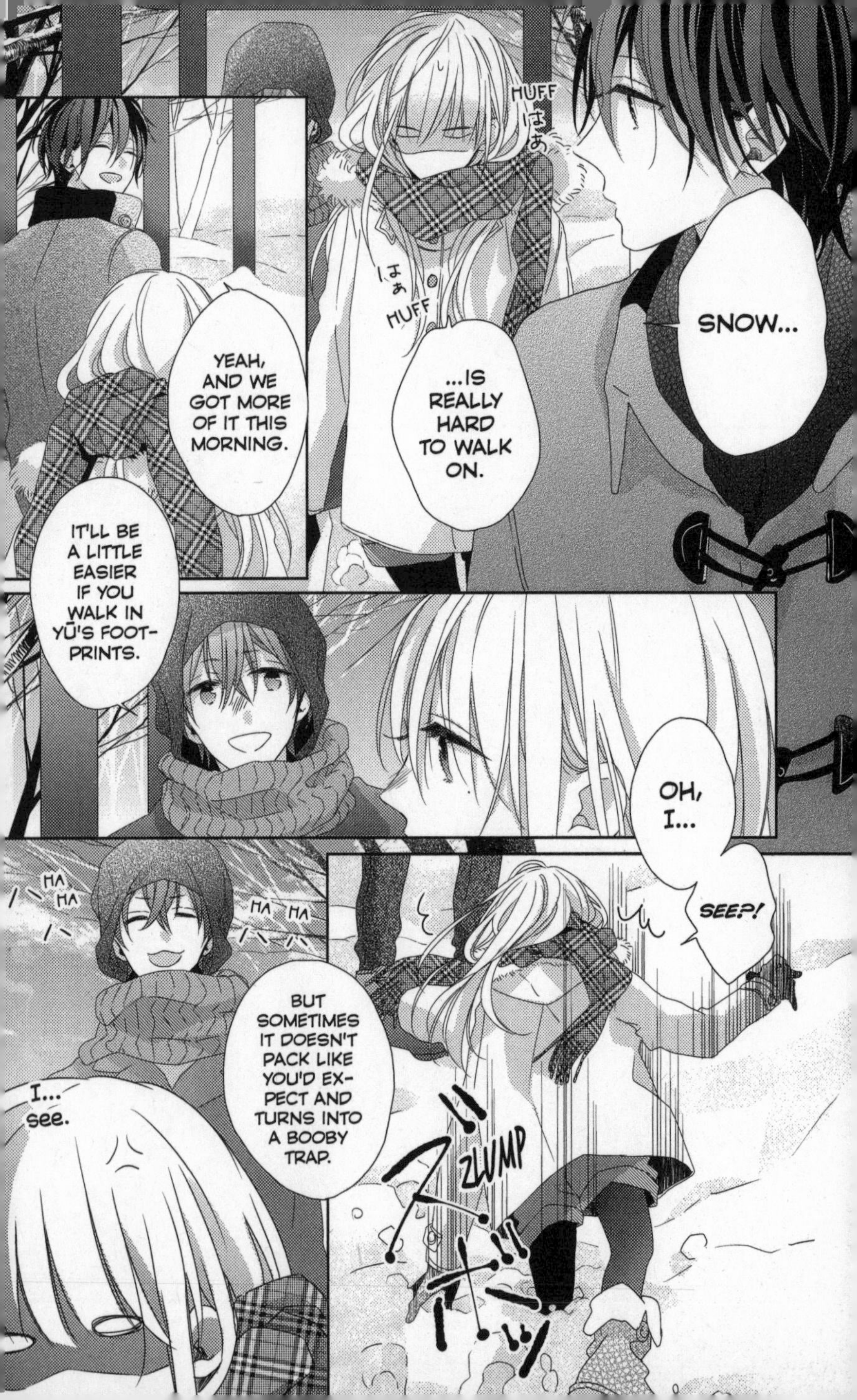
SNOW...
HUFF
はぁ
...IS REALLY HARD TO WALK ON.
はぁ
HUFF
YEAH, AND WE GOT MORE OF IT THIS MORNING.
IT'LL BE A LITTLE EASIER IF YOU WALK IN YŪ'S FOOT-PRINTS.
OH, I...
SEE?!
ZUMP
HA HA
HA HA
BUT SOMETIMES IT DOESN'T PACK LIKE YOU'D EX-PECT AND TURNS INTO A BOOBY TRAP.
I... see.

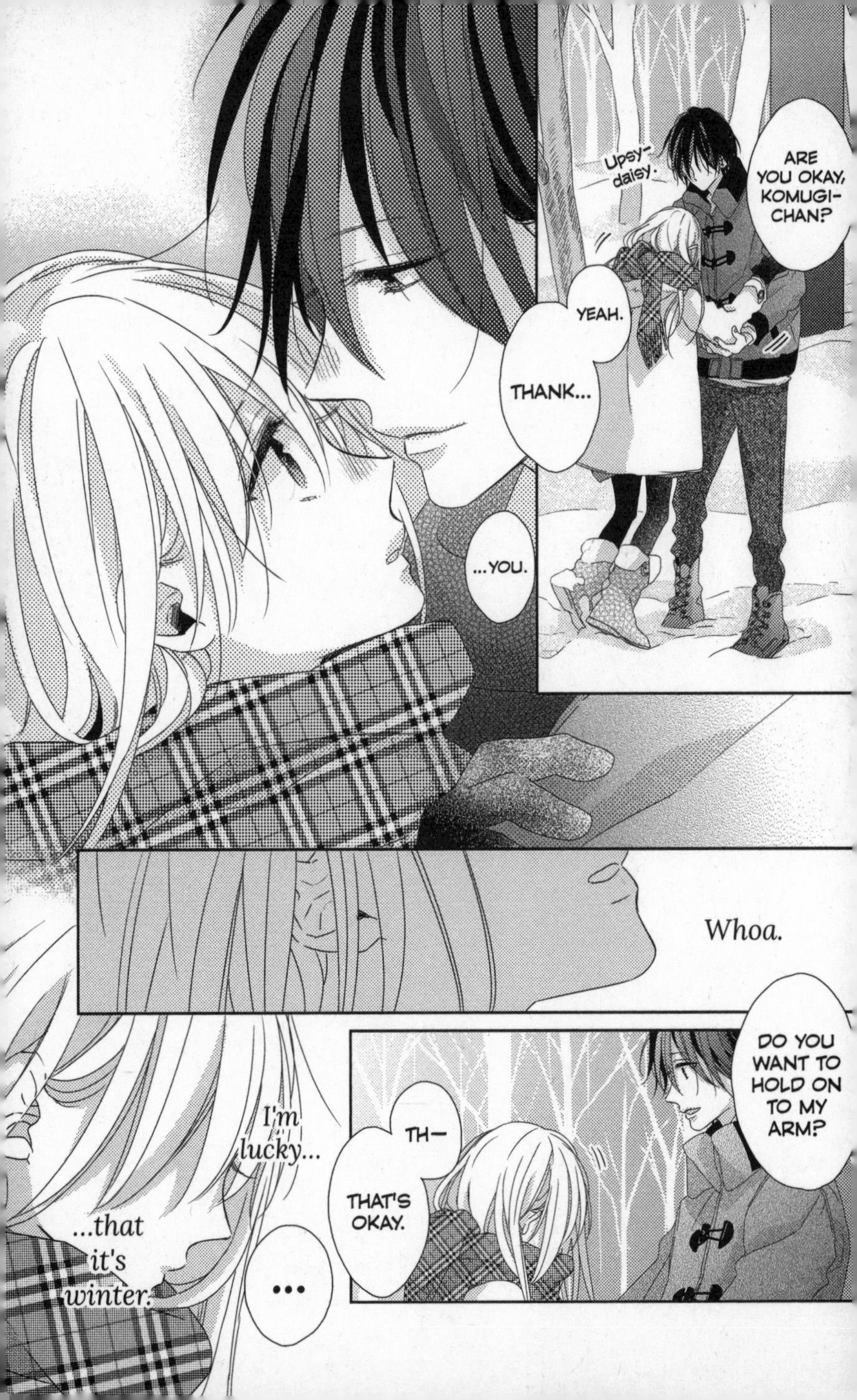
ARE YOU OKAY, KOMUGI-CHAN?
Upsy-daisy.
YEAH.
THANK...
...YOU.
Whoa.
DO YOU WANT TO HOLD ON TO MY ARM?
TH—
THAT'S OKAY.
...
I'm lucky...
...that it's winter.

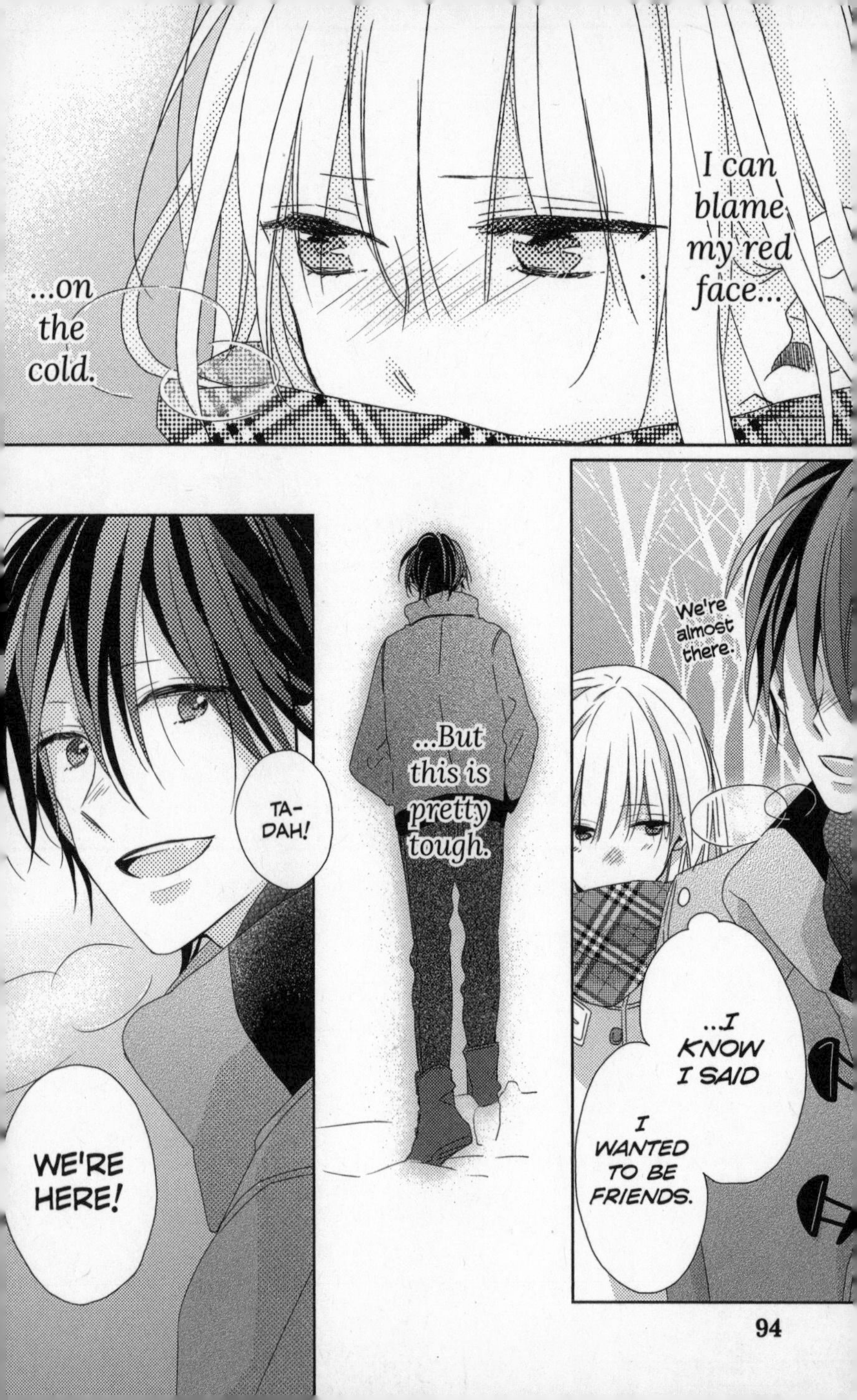
I can blame my red face...
...on the cold.
We're almost there.
...I KNOW I SAID
I WANTED TO BE FRIENDS.
...But this is pretty tough.
TA-DAH!
WE'RE HERE!

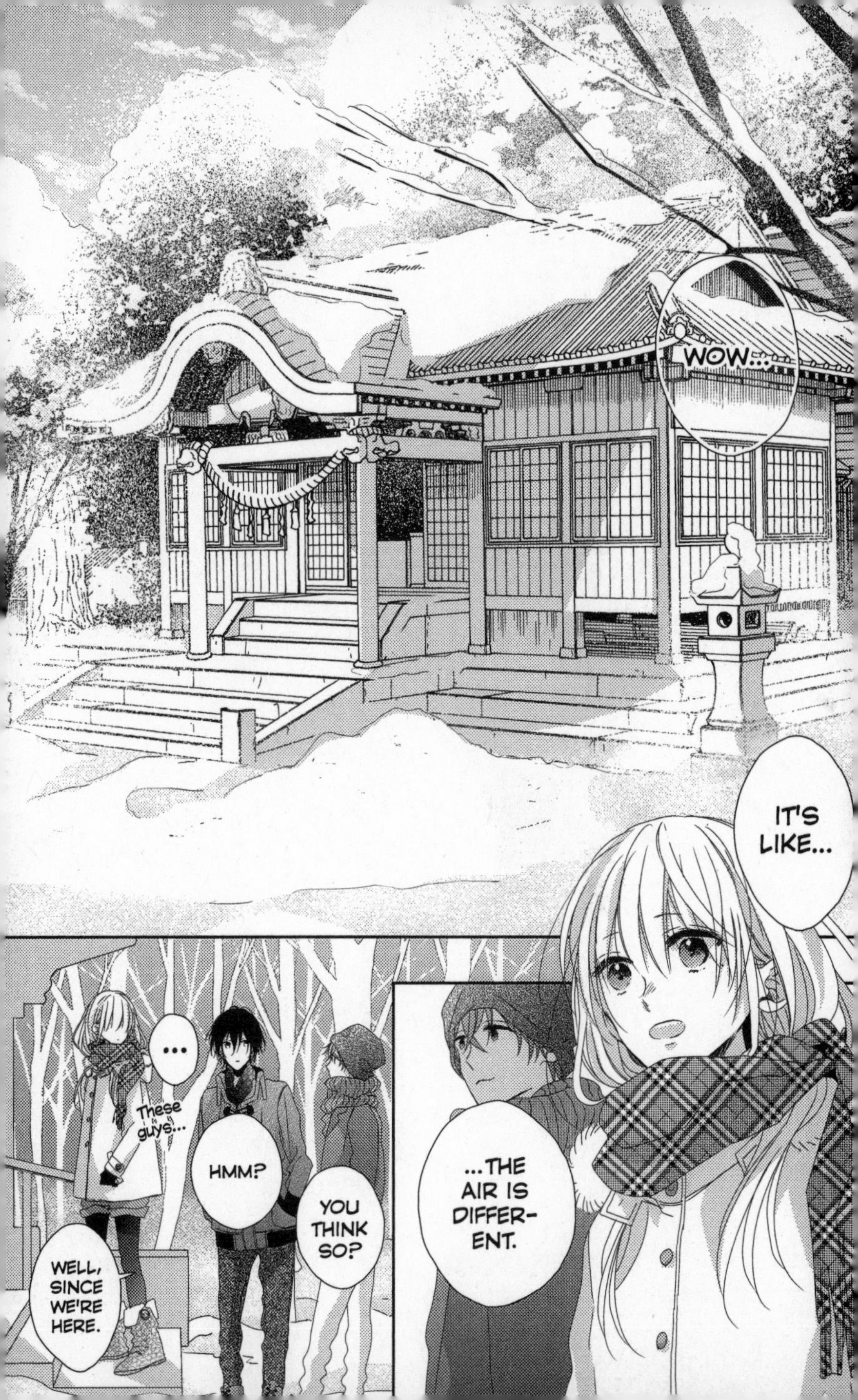
WOW...
IT'S LIKE...
...THE AIR IS DIFFER-ENT.
...
These guys...
HMM?
YOU THINK SO?
WELL, SINCE WE'RE HERE.

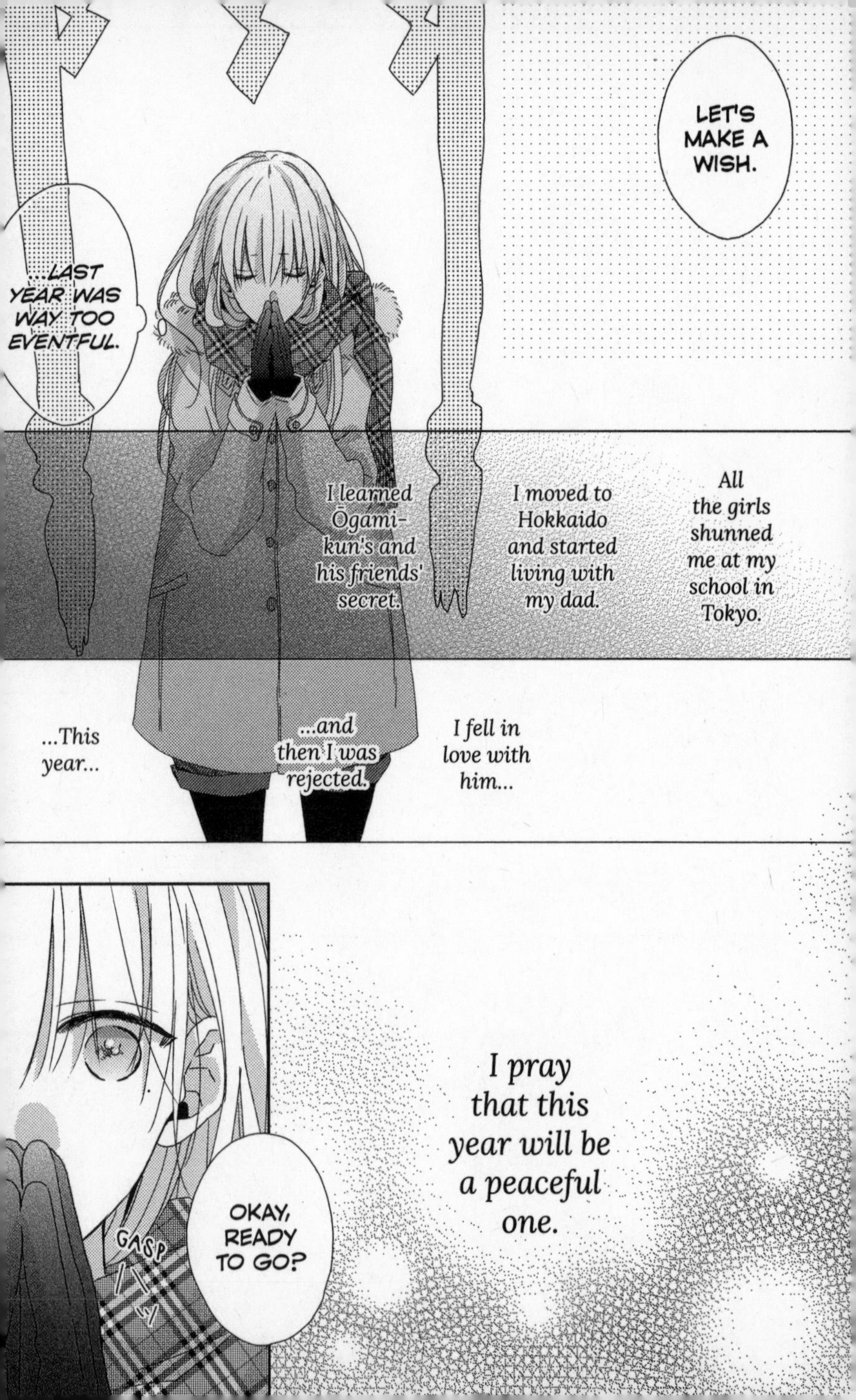
LET'S MAKE A WISH.
...LAST YEAR WAS WAY TOO EVENTFUL.
All the girls shunned me at my school in Tokyo.
I moved to Hokkaido and started living with my dad.
I learned Ōgami-kun's and his friends' secret.
I fell in love with him...
...and then I was rejected.
...This year...
I pray that this year will be a peaceful one.
OKAY, READY TO GO?
GASP

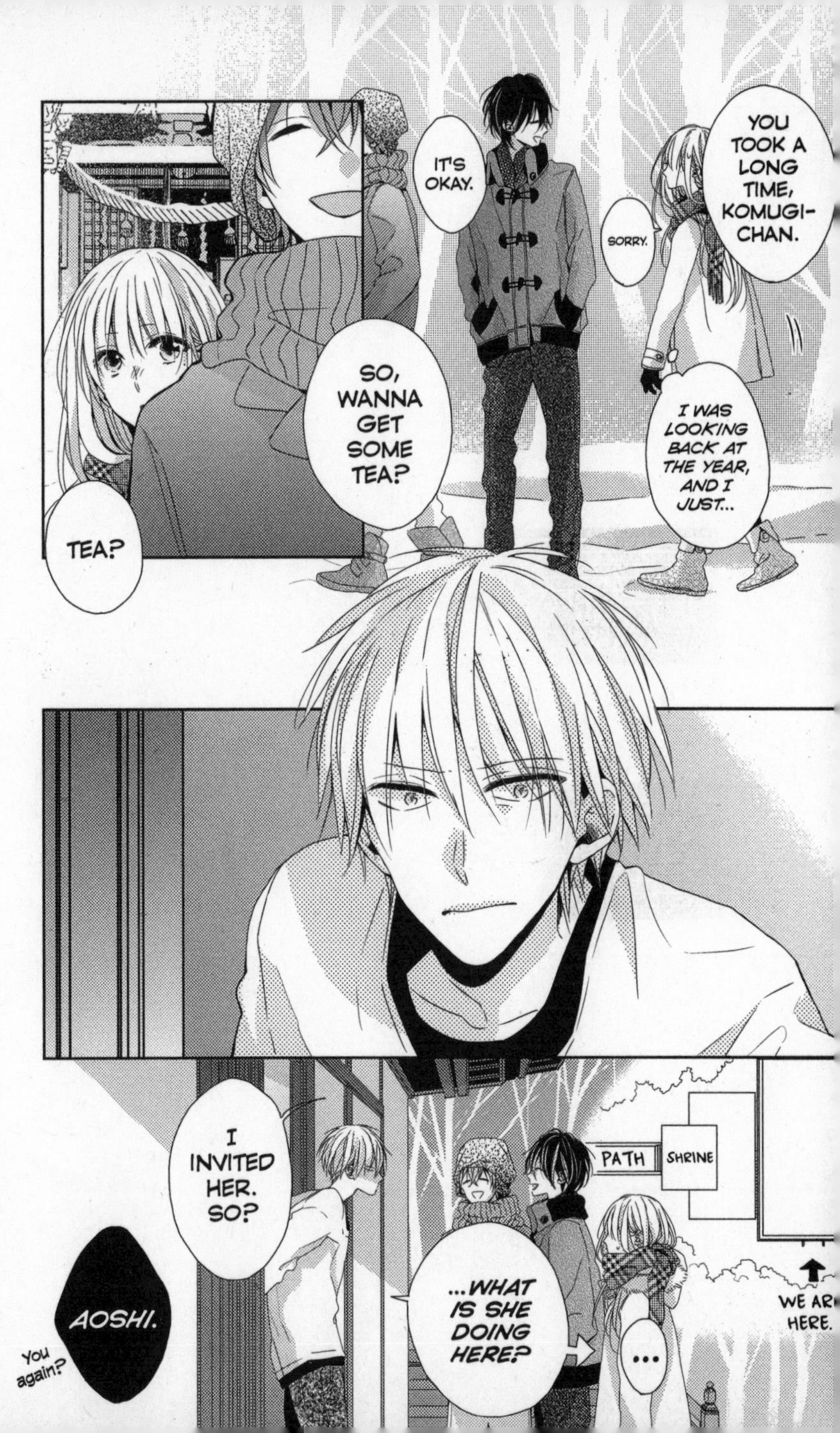
YOU TOOK A LONG TIME, KOMUGI-CHAN.
SORRY.
I WAS LOOKING BACK AT THE YEAR, AND I JUST...
IT'S OKAY.
SO, WANNA GET SOME TEA?
TEA?
SHRINE
PATH
WE AR HERE.
...
...WHAT IS SHE DOING HERE?
I INVITED HER. SO?
AOSHI.
You again?

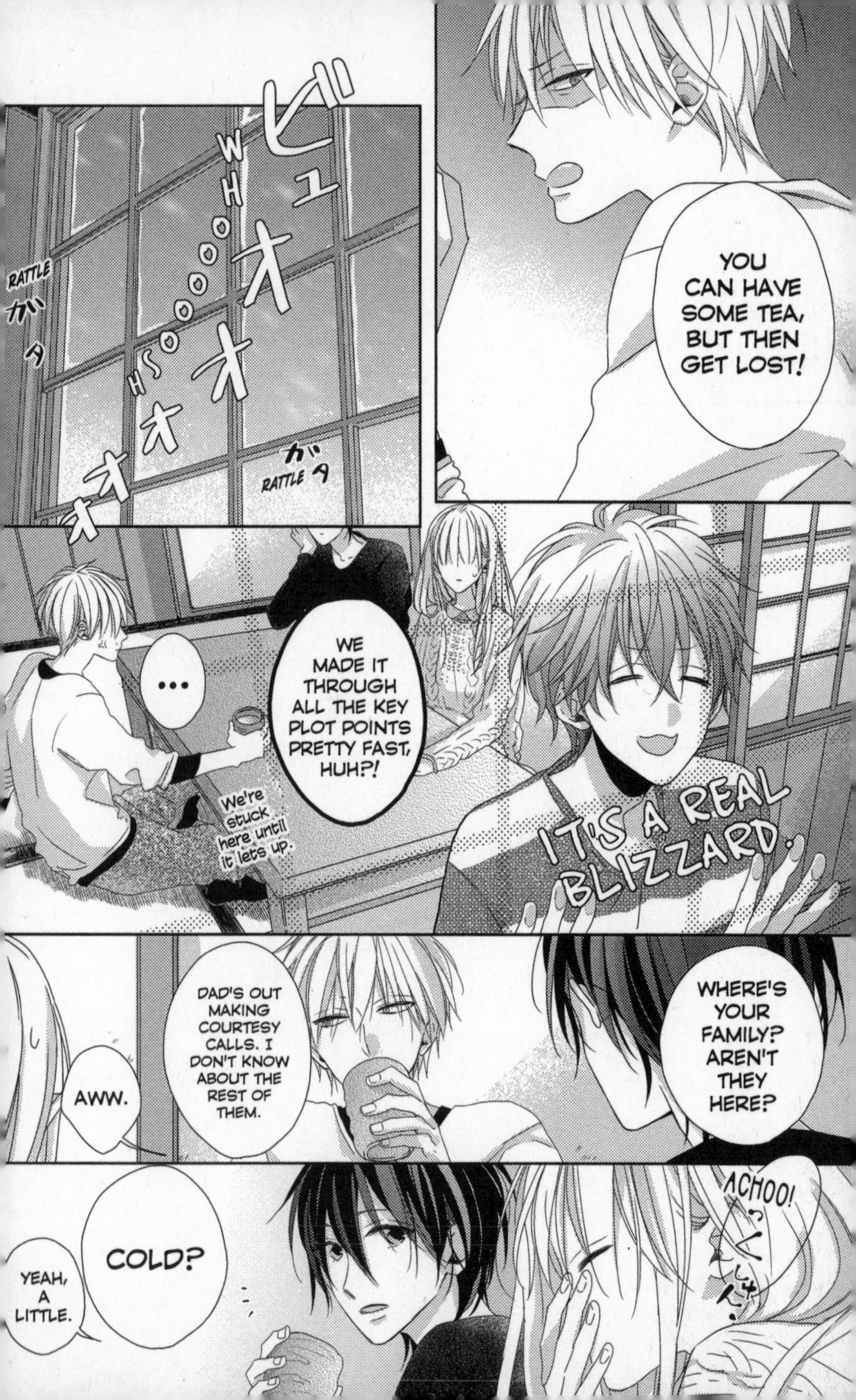
YOU CAN HAVE SOME TEA, BUT THEN GET LOST!
ビュオオオオ
WHOOOOSH
RATTLE ガタ
RATTLE ガタ
IT'S A REAL BLIZZARD.
WE MADE IT THROUGH ALL THE KEY PLOT POINTS PRETTY FAST, HUH?!
We're stuck here until it lets up.
...
WHERE'S YOUR FAMILY? AREN'T THEY HERE?
DAD'S OUT MAKING COURTESY CALLS. I DON'T KNOW ABOUT THE REST OF THEM.
AWW.
ACHOO!
くしゅん
COLD?
YEAH, A LITTLE.

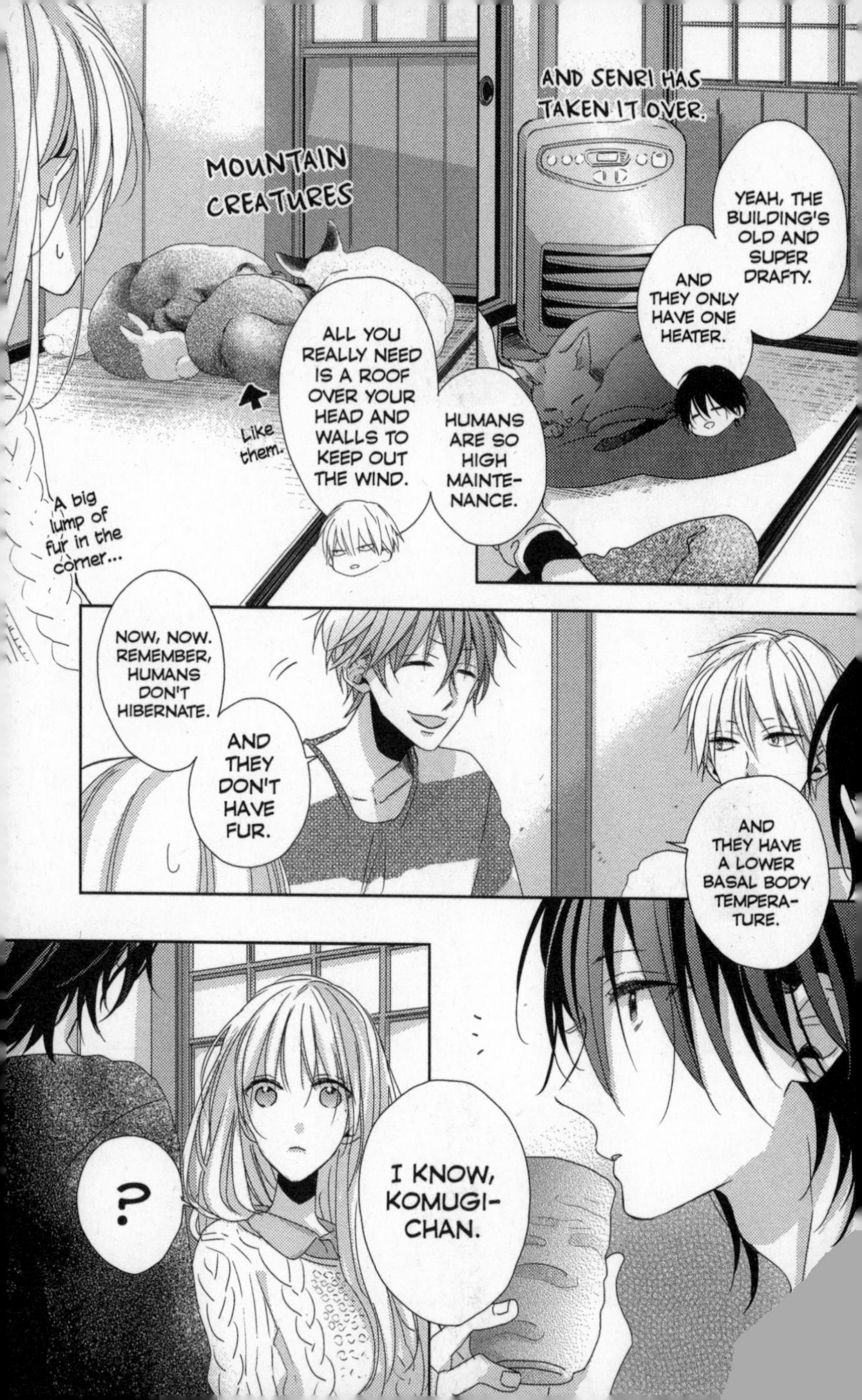
AND SENRI HAS TAKEN IT OVER.
YEAH, THE BUILDING'S OLD AND SUPER DRAFTY.
AND THEY ONLY HAVE ONE HEATER.
MOUNTAIN CREATURES
HUMANS ARE SO HIGH MAINTE-NANCE.
ALL YOU REALLY NEED IS A ROOF OVER YOUR HEAD AND WALLS TO KEEP OUT THE WIND.
Like them.
A big lump of fur in the corner...
AND THEY HAVE A LOWER BASAL BODY TEMPERA-TURE.
NOW, NOW. REMEMBER, HUMANS DON'T HIBERNATE.
AND THEY DON'T HAVE FUR.
I KNOW, KOMUGI-CHAN.
?

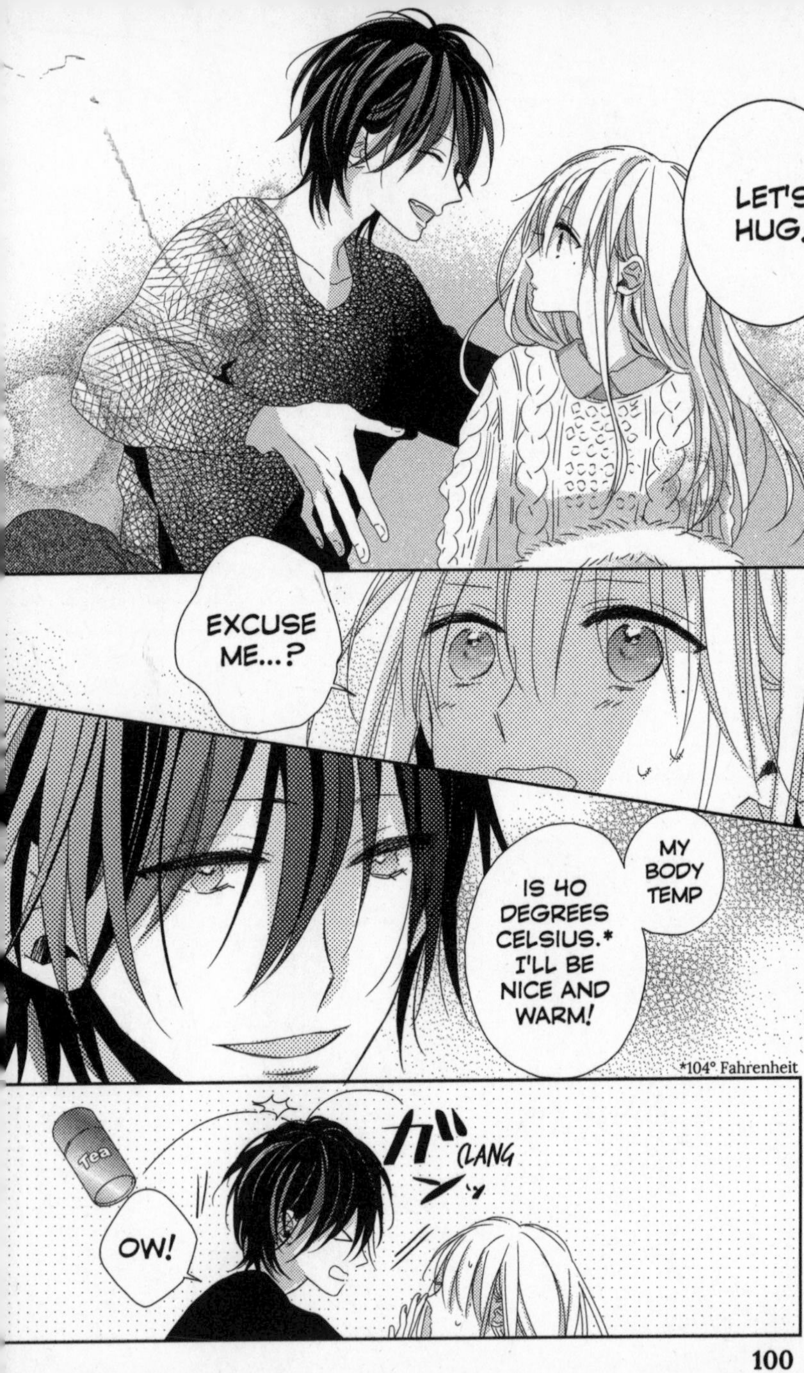
LET'S HUG!
EXCUSE ME...?
MY BODY TEMP IS 40 DEGREES CELSIUS.* I'LL BE NICE AND WARM!
ガッ
CLANG
Tea
OW!

*104° Fahrenheit

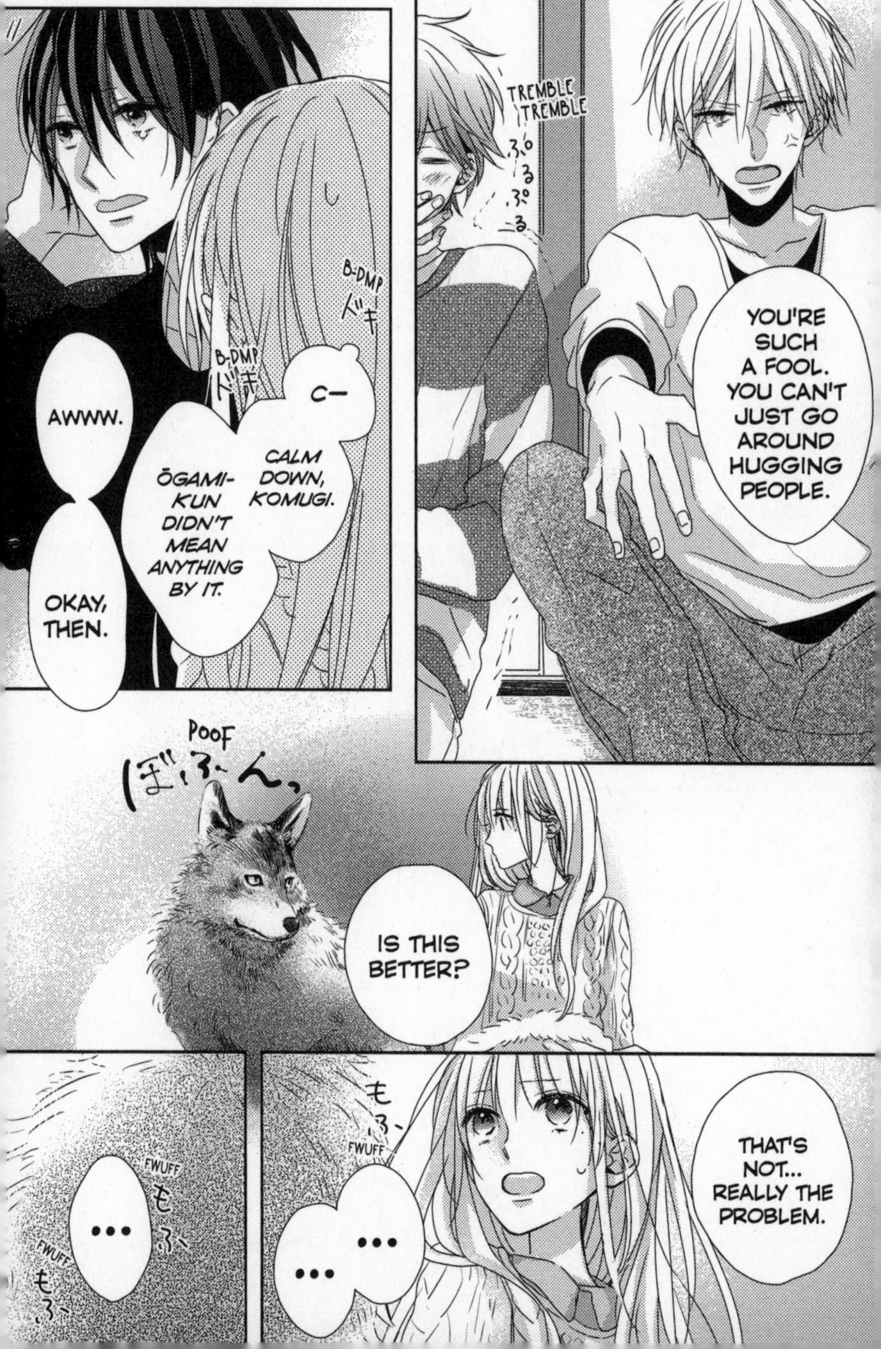
TREMBLE TREMBLE
ぷるぷる
YOU'RE SUCH A FOOL. YOU CAN'T JUST GO AROUND HUGGING PEOPLE.
B-DMP
ドキ
B-DMP
ドキ
C—
CALM DOWN, KOMUGI.
ŌGAMI-KUN DIDN'T MEAN ANYTHING BY IT.
AWWW.
OKAY, THEN.
POOF
ぼふん
IS THIS BETTER?
THAT'S NOT... REALLY THE PROBLEM.
FWUFF
もふ
...
...
FWUFF
もふ
FWUFF
もふ
...

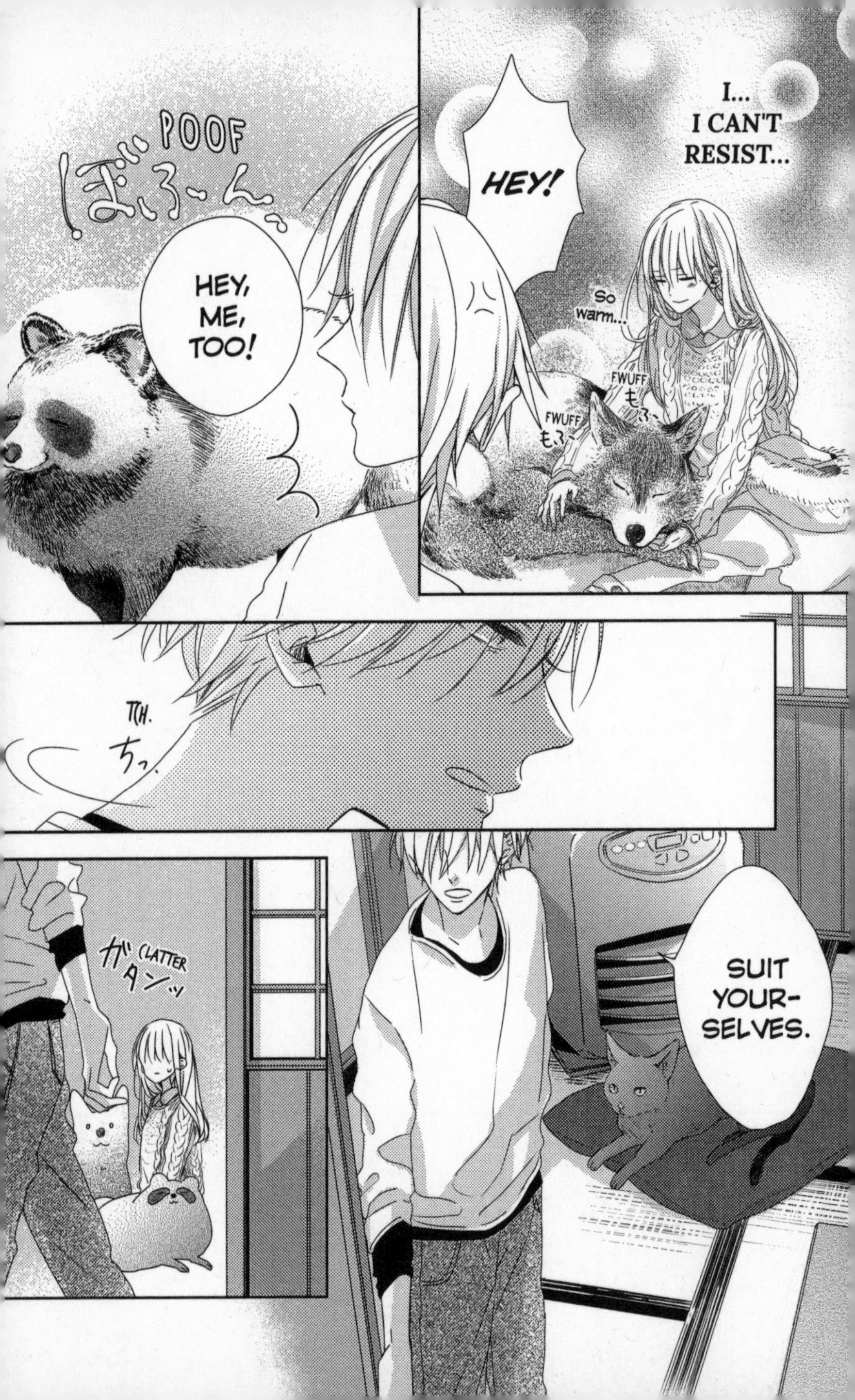
I...
I CAN'T
RESIST...
HEY!
So
warm...
FWUFF
もふ
FWUFF
もふ
POOF
ぼふ~ん
HEY,
ME,
TOO!
TCH.
ちっ
SUIT
YOUR-
SELVES.
ガタンッ
CLATTER

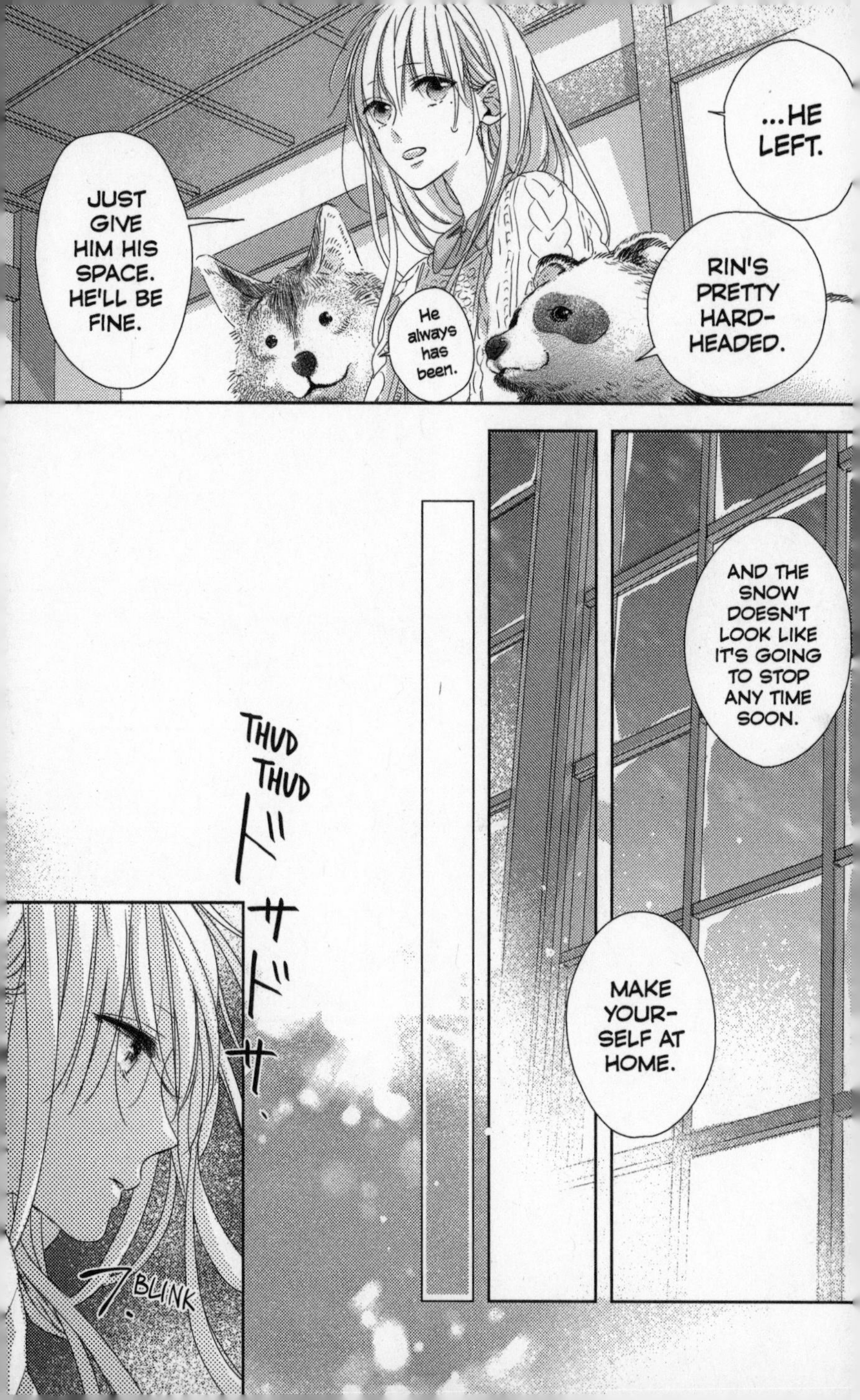
...HE LEFT.
RIN'S PRETTY HARD-HEADED.
He always has been.
JUST GIVE HIM HIS SPACE. HE'LL BE FINE.
AND THE SNOW DOESN'T LOOK LIKE IT'S GOING TO STOP ANY TIME SOON.
MAKE YOUR-SELF AT HOME.
THUD THUD
ドサドサ
BLINK

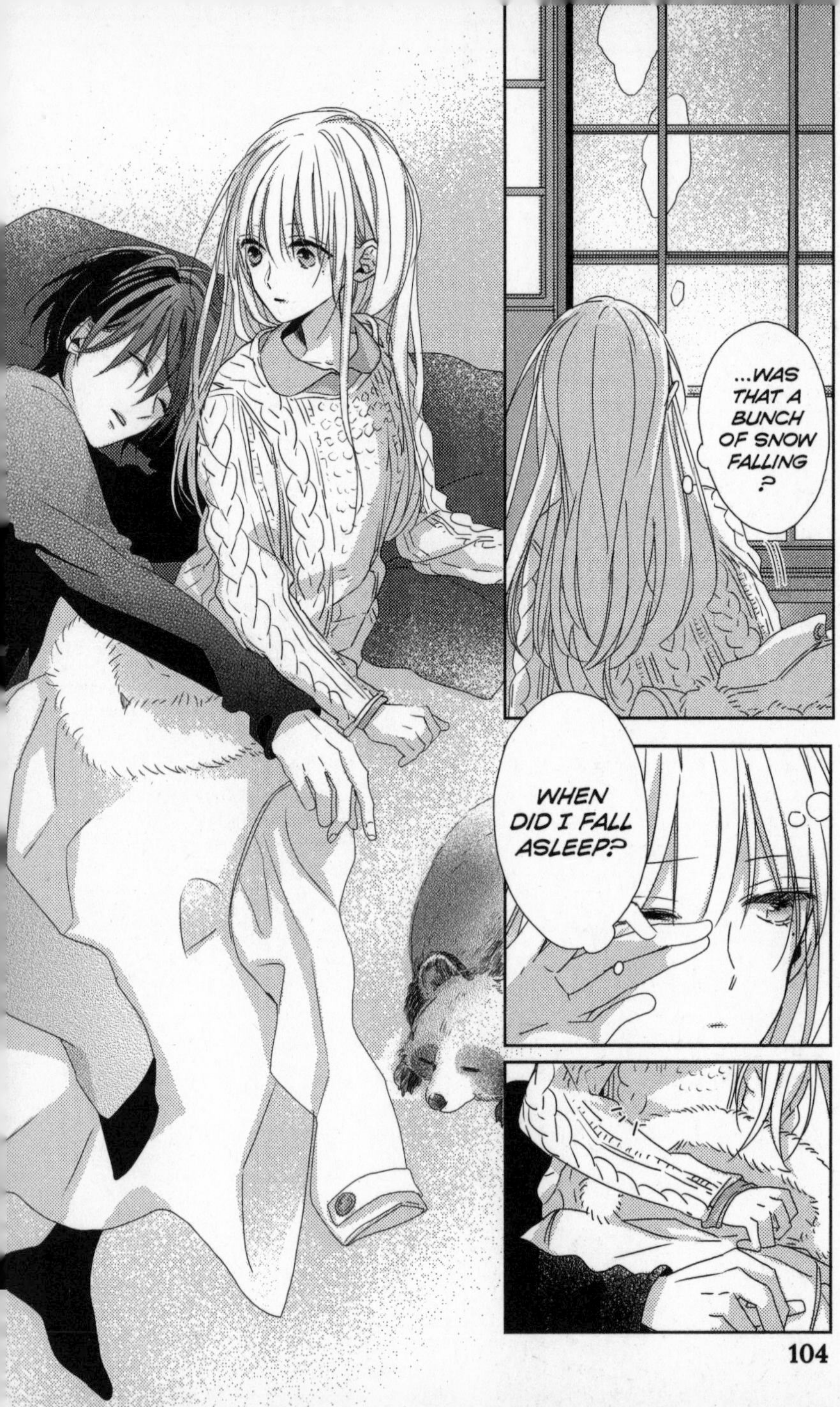
...WAS THAT A BUNCH OF SNOW FALLING ?
WHEN DID I FALL ASLEEP?

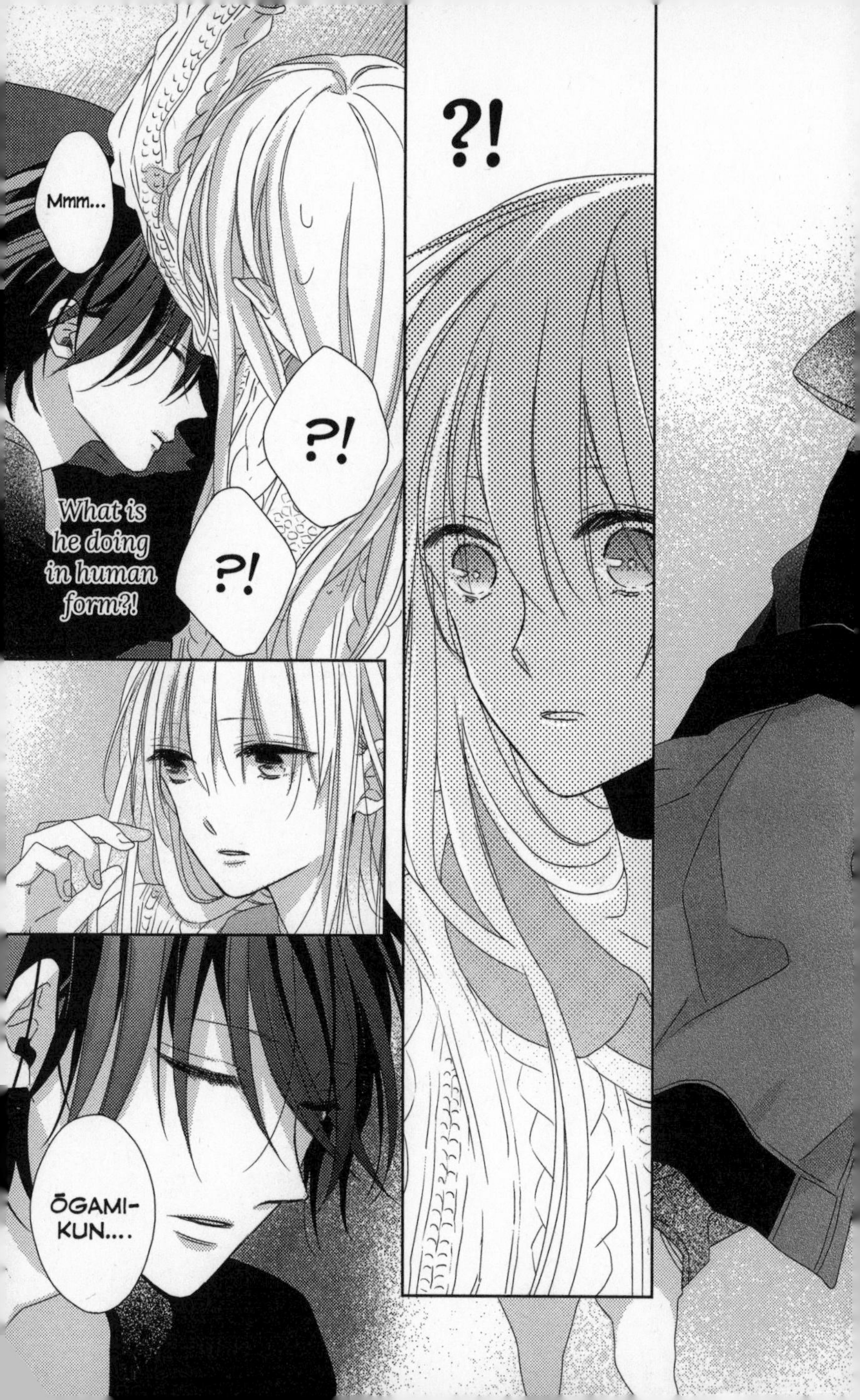
?!
Mmm...
?!
?!
What is he doing in human form?!
ŌGAMI-KUN....

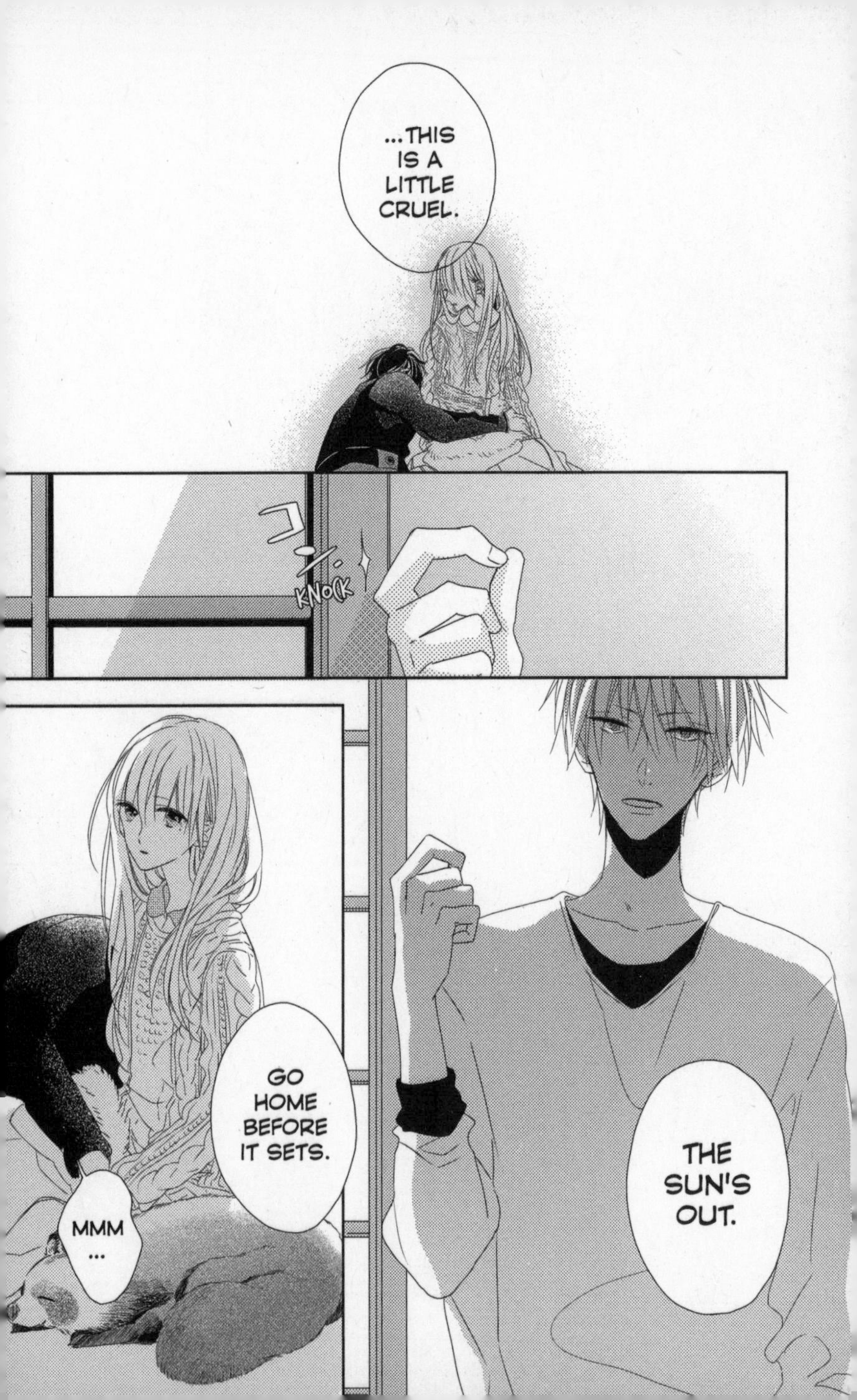
...THIS IS A LITTLE CRUEL.
KNOCK
THE SUN'S OUT.
GO HOME BEFORE IT SETS.
MMM ...

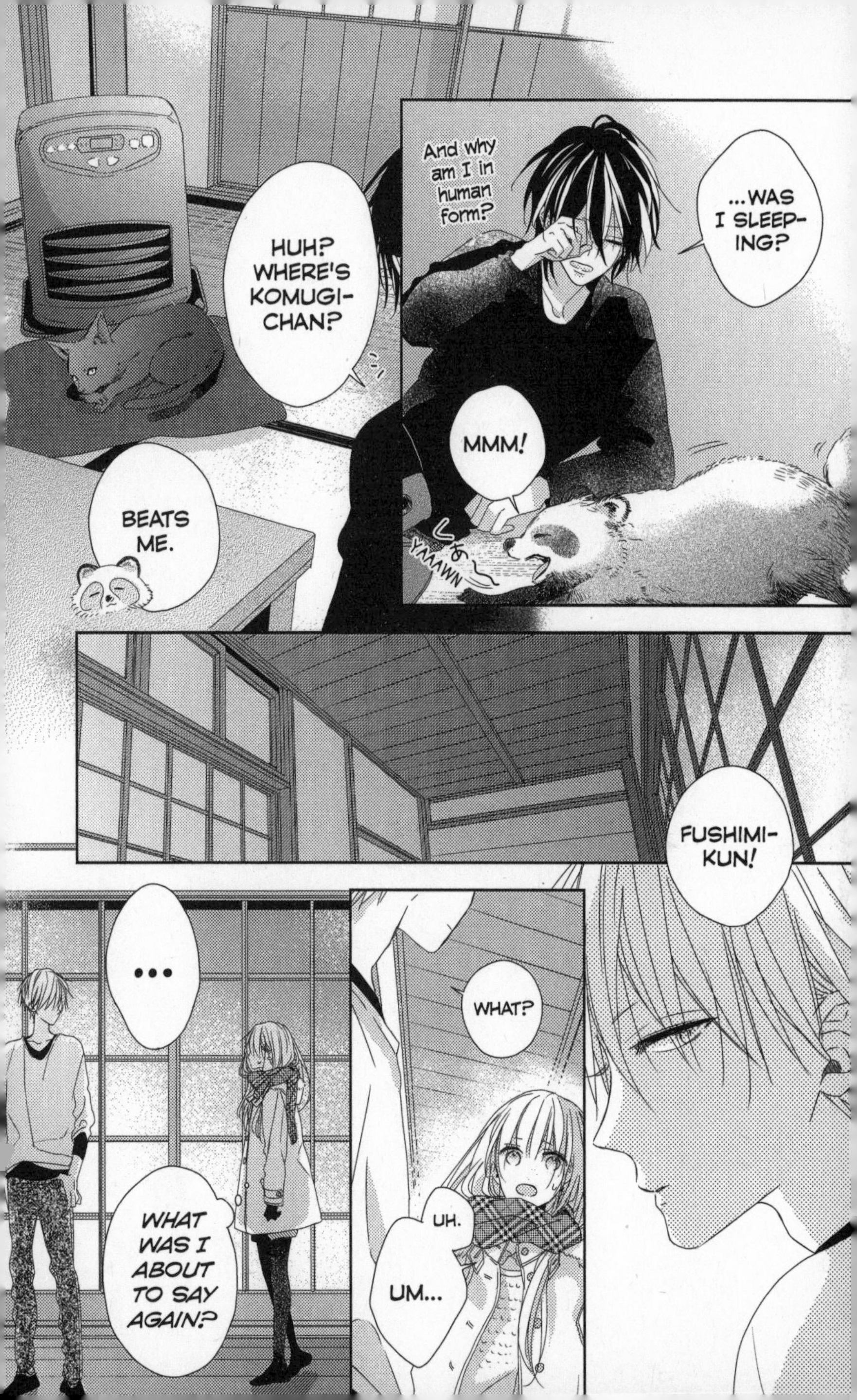
...WAS I SLEEPING?
And why am I in human form?
MMM!
YAAAWN
HUH? WHERE'S KOMUGI-CHAN?
BEATS ME.
FUSHIMI-KUN!
WHAT?
UH.
UM...
...
WHAT WAS I ABOUT TO SAY AGAIN?

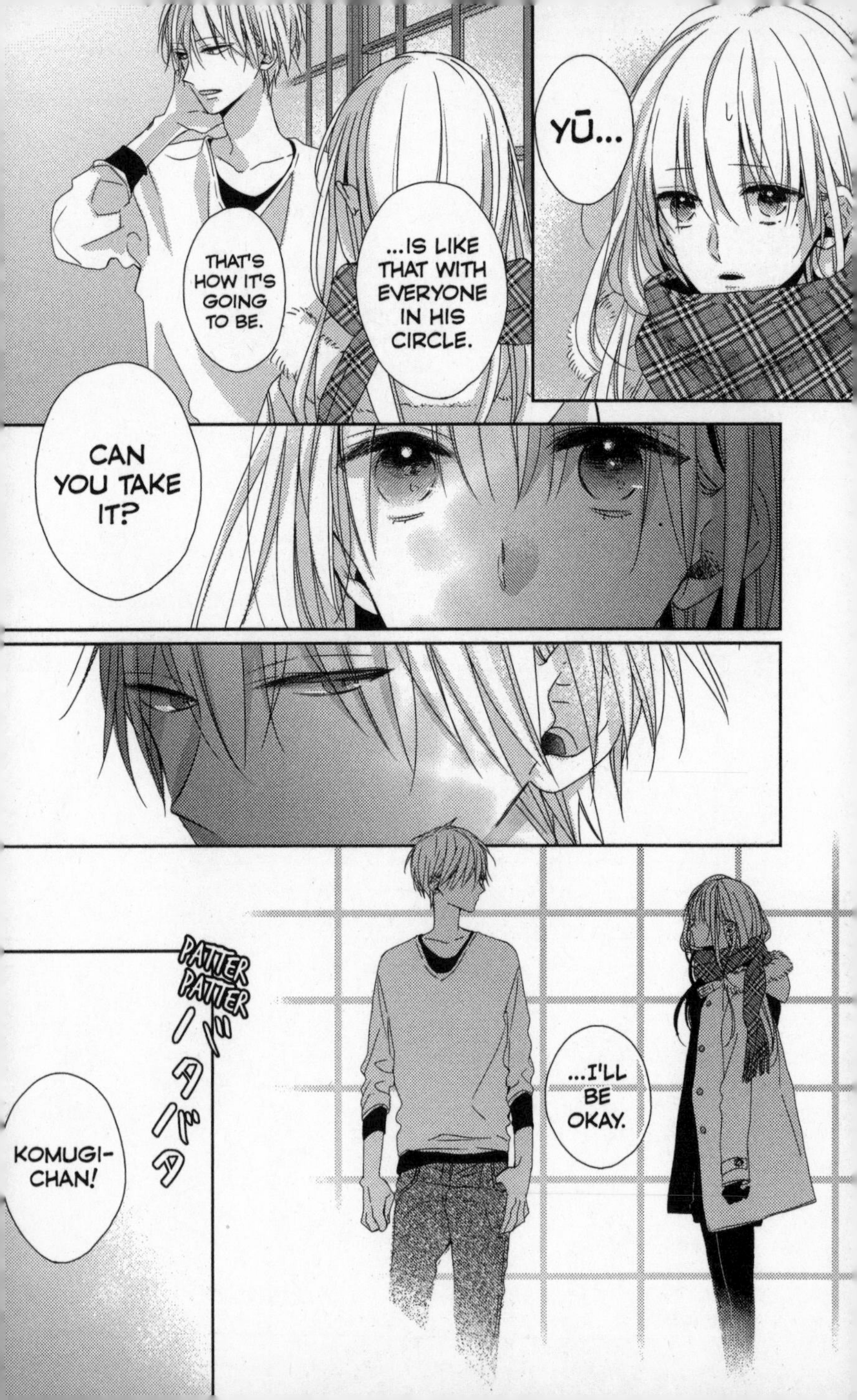
YŪ...
...IS LIKE THAT WITH EVERYONE IN HIS CIRCLE.
THAT'S HOW IT'S GOING TO BE.
CAN YOU TAKE IT?
...I'LL BE OKAY.
PATTER PATTER
パタパタ
KOMUGI-CHAN!

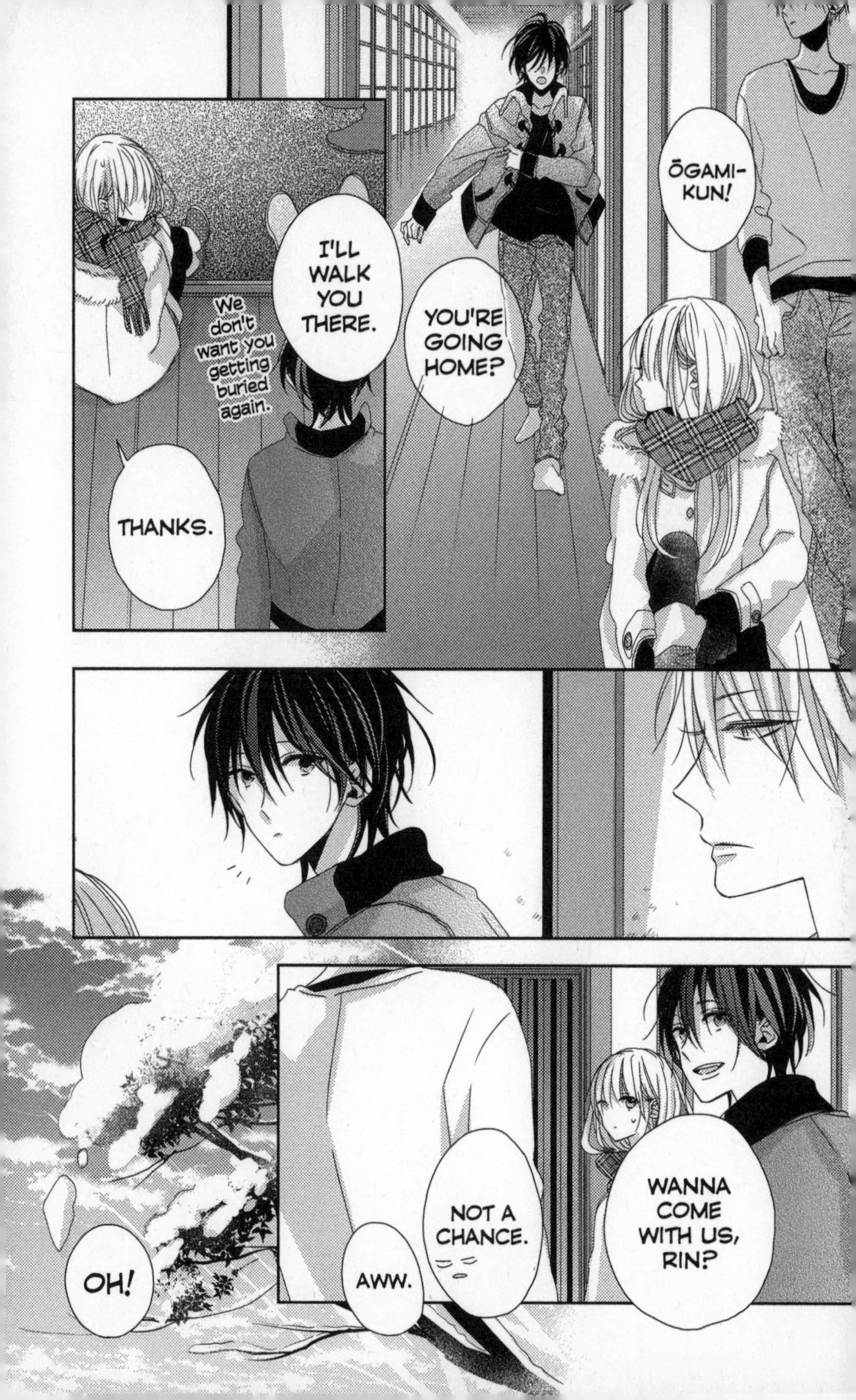
ŌGAMI-KUN!
YOU'RE GOING HOME?
I'LL WALK YOU THERE.
We don't want you getting buried again.
THANKS.
WANNA COME WITH US, RIN?
NOT A CHANCE.
AWW.
OH!

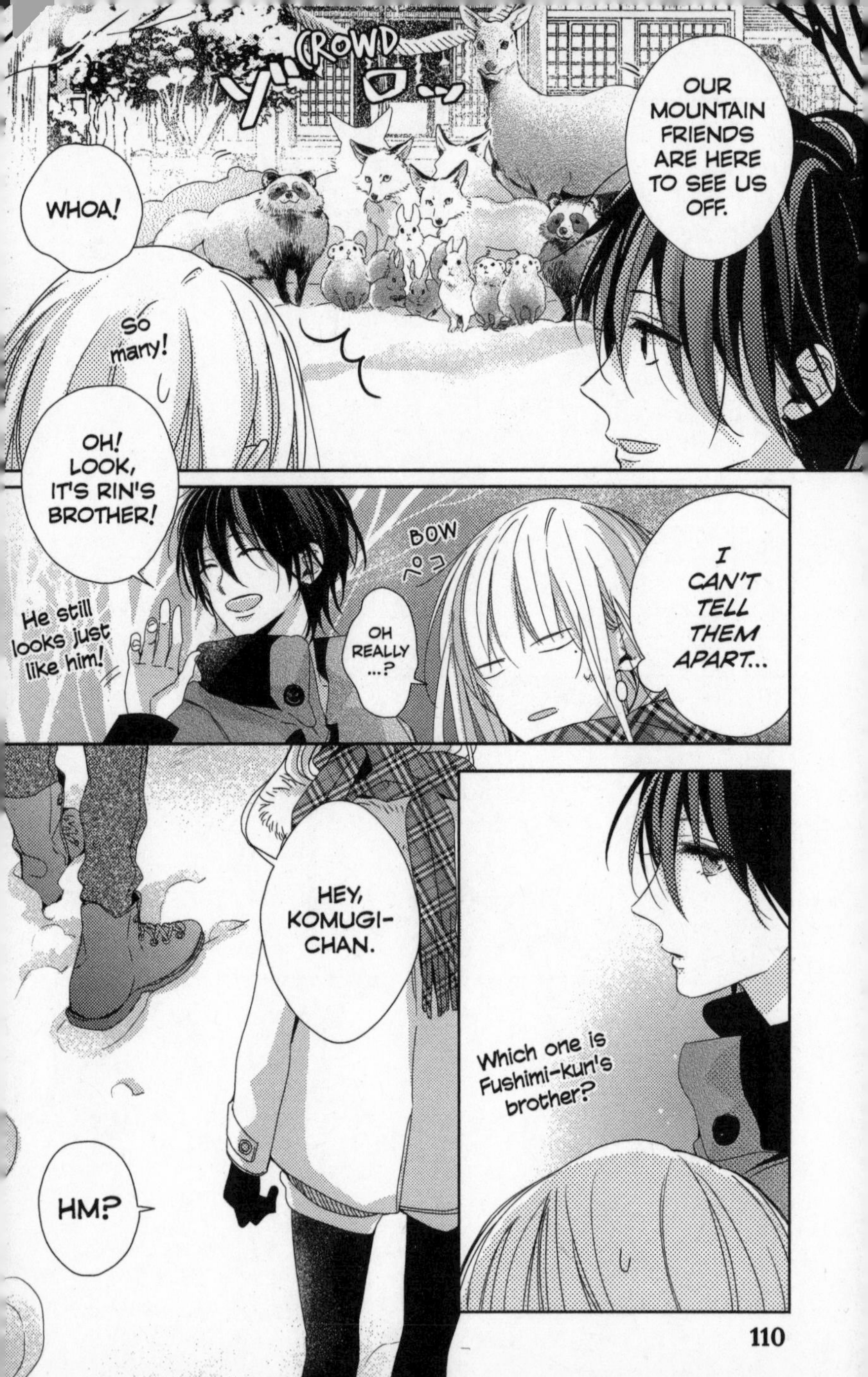
OUR MOUNTAIN FRIENDS ARE HERE TO SEE US OFF.
CROWD
WHOA!
So many!
I CAN'T TELL THEM APART...
BOW
OH REALLY ...?
OH! LOOK, IT'S RIN'S BROTHER!
He still looks just like him!
Which one is Fushimi-kun's brother?
HEY, KOMUGI-CHAN.
HM?

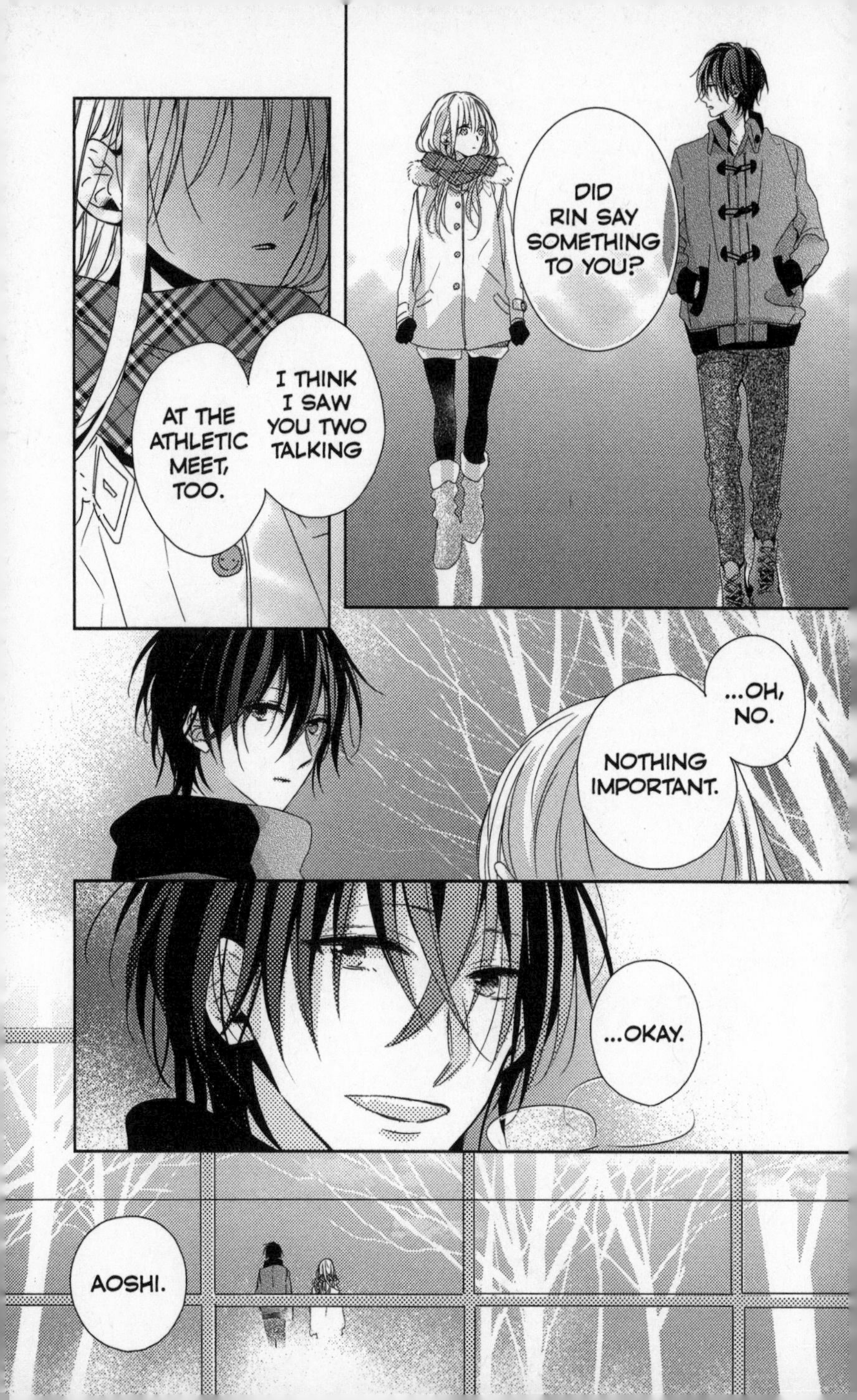
DID RIN SAY SOMETHING TO YOU?
I THINK I SAW YOU TWO TALKING
AT THE ATHLETIC MEET, TOO.
...OH, NO.
NOTHING IMPORTANT.
...OKAY.
AOSHI.

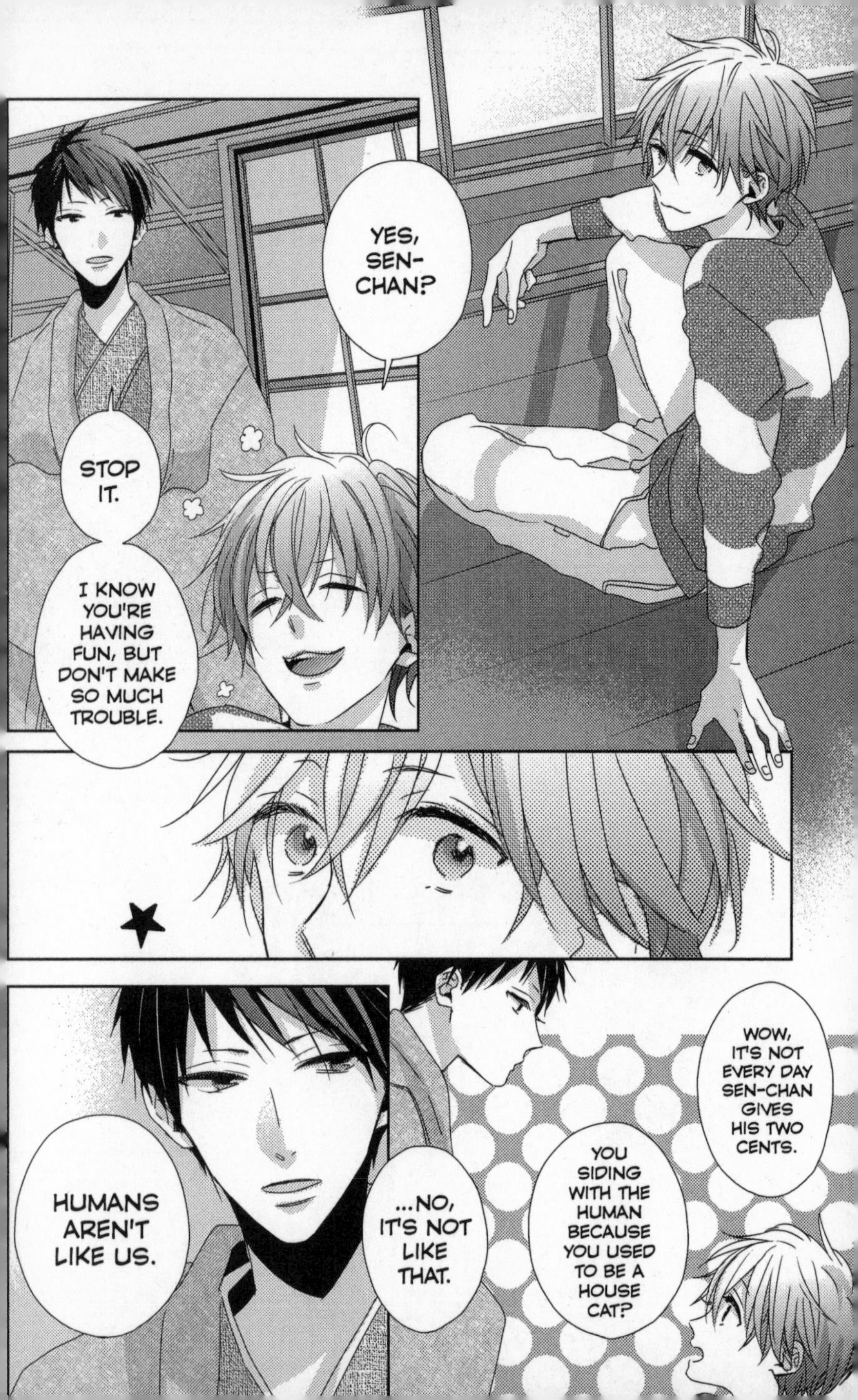
YES, SEN-CHAN?
STOP IT.
I KNOW YOU'RE HAVING FUN, BUT DON'T MAKE SO MUCH TROUBLE.
WOW, IT'S NOT EVERY DAY SEN-CHAN GIVES HIS TWO CENTS.
YOU SIDING WITH THE HUMAN BECAUSE YOU USED TO BE A HOUSE CAT?
...NO, IT'S NOT LIKE THAT.
HUMANS AREN'T LIKE US.

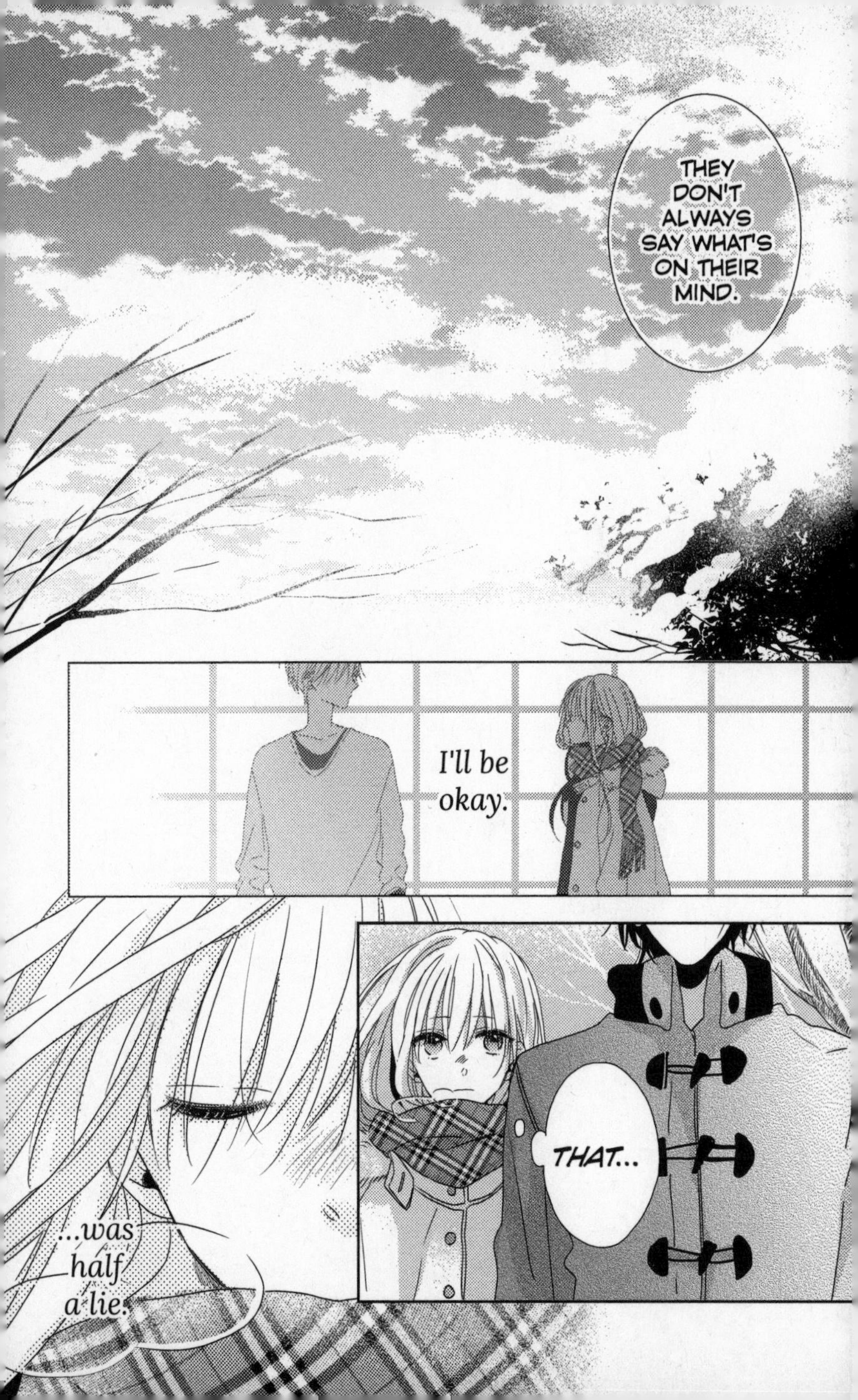
THEY DON'T ALWAYS SAY WHAT'S ON THEIR MIND.
I'll be okay.
THAT...
...was half a lie.

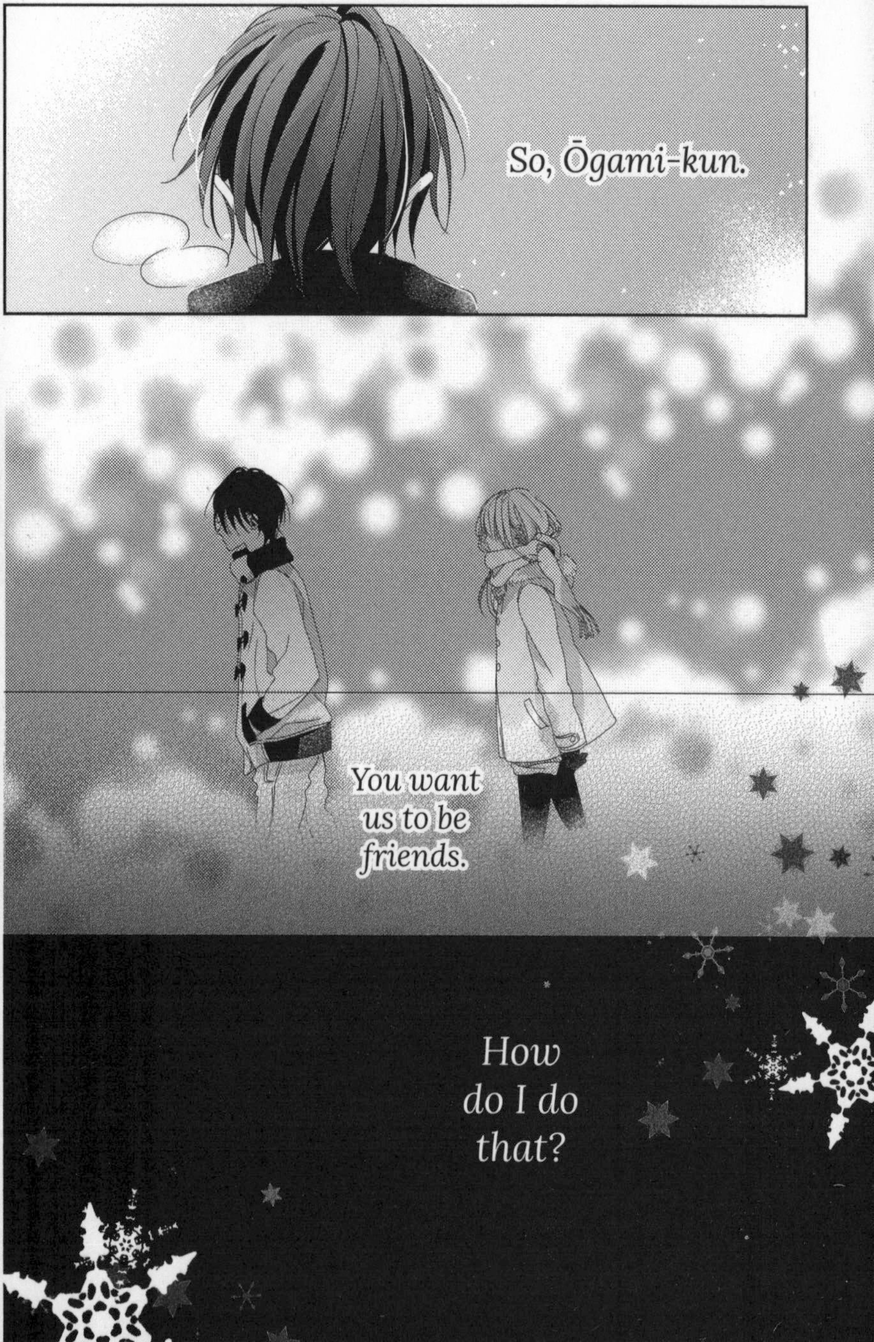
So, Ōgami-kun.
You want us to be friends.
How do I do that?

That Wolf-Boy is Mine!

That Wolf-Boy is Mine!

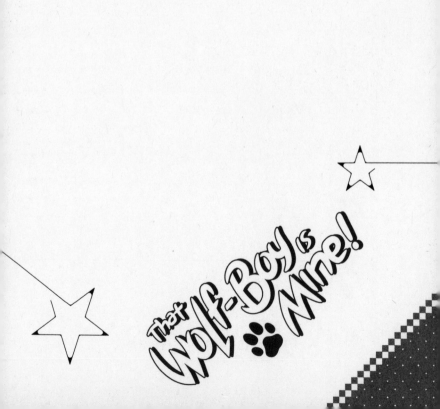

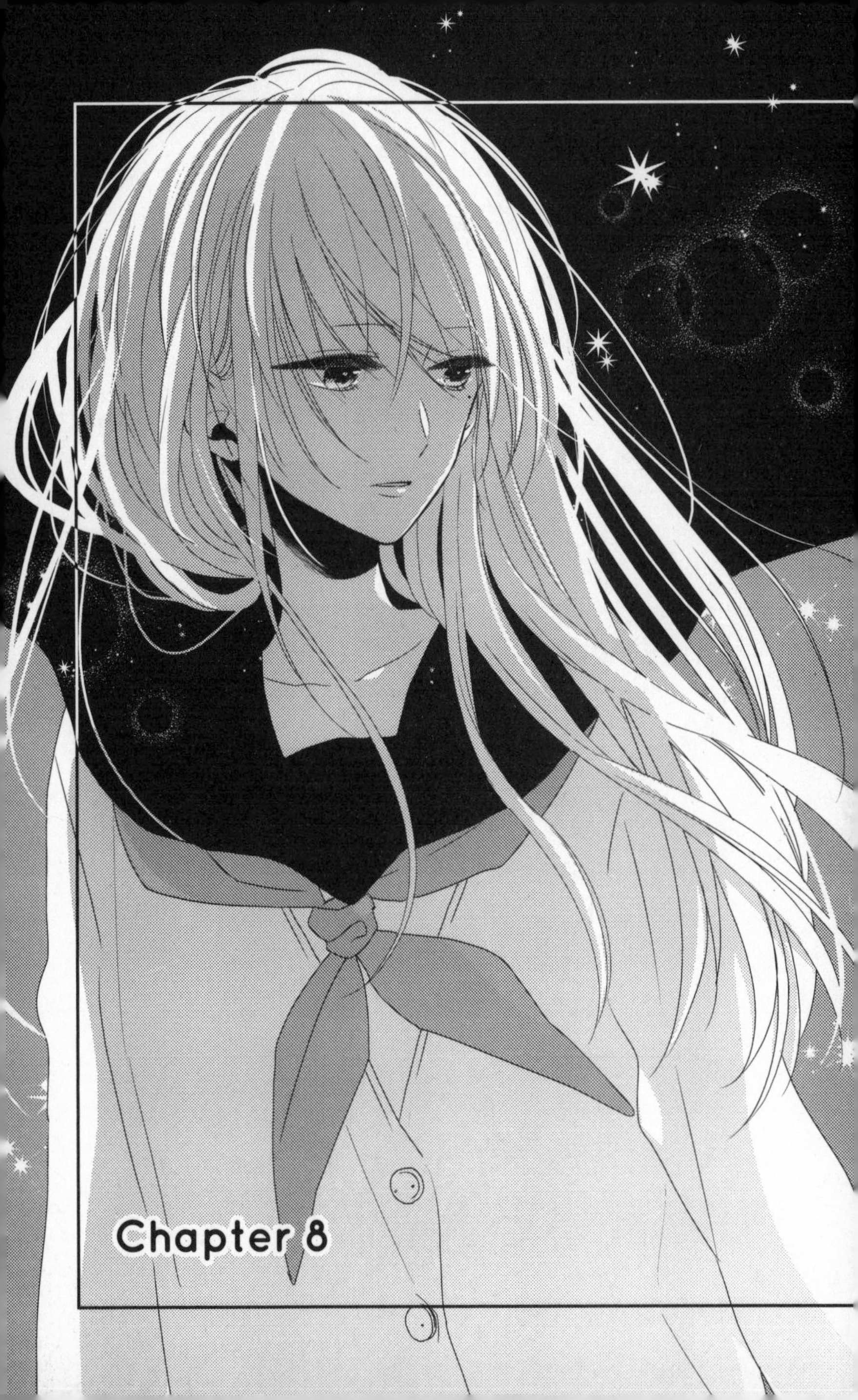
Chapter 8

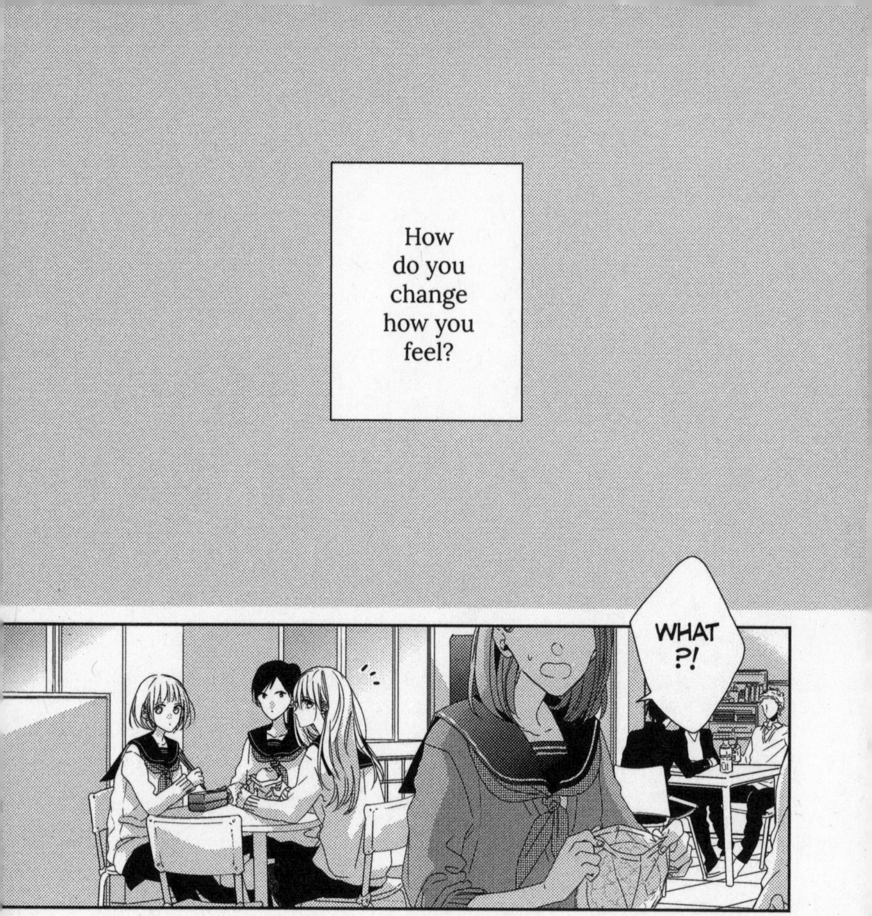
How do you change how you feel?
WHAT?!

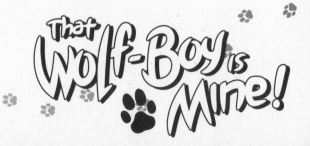

That Wolf-Boy is Mine!

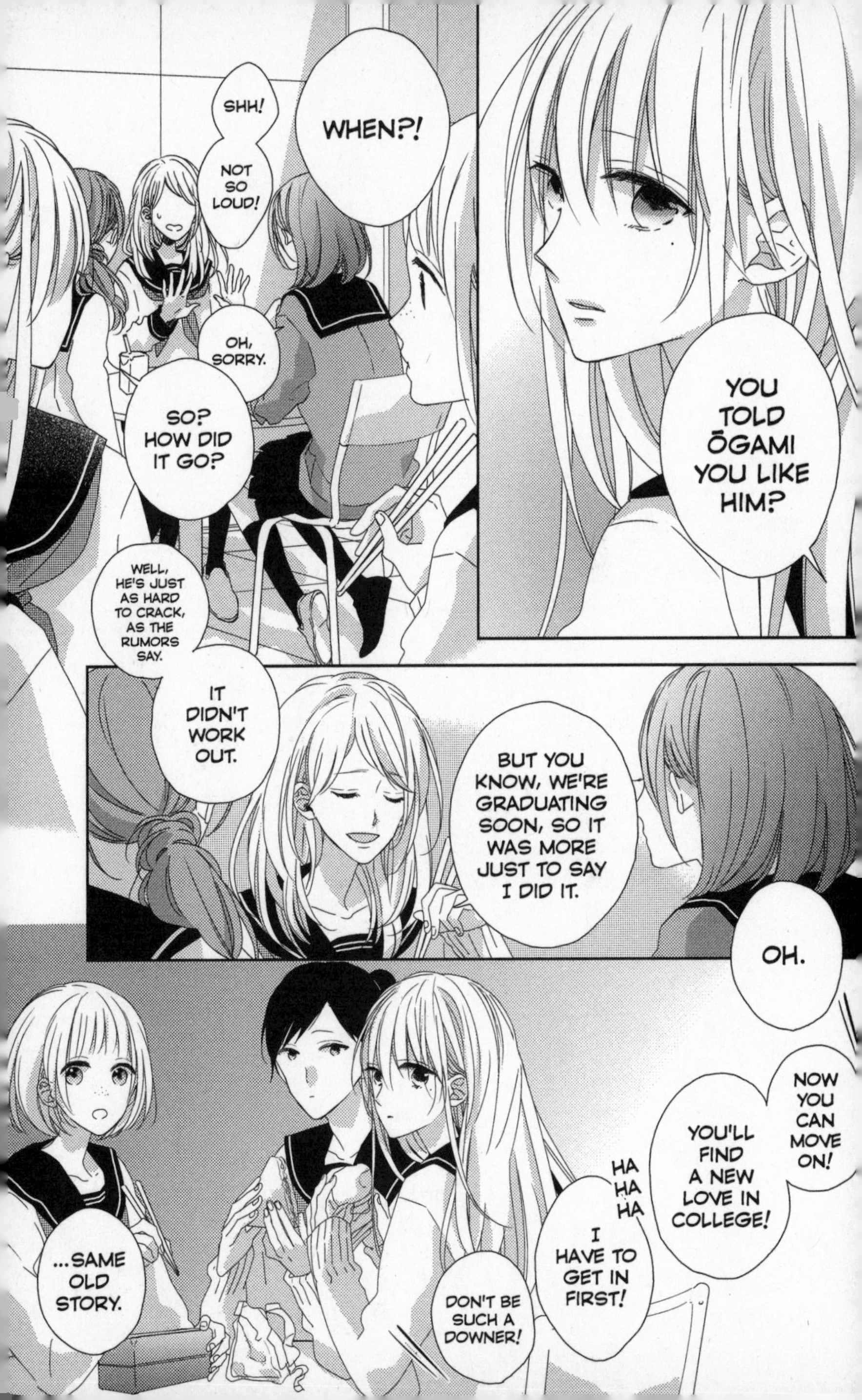
YOU TOLD ŌGAMI YOU LIKE HIM?
WHEN?!
SHH!
NOT SO LOUD!
OH, SORRY.
SO? HOW DID IT GO?
WELL, HE'S JUST AS HARD TO CRACK, AS THE RUMORS SAY.
IT DIDN'T WORK OUT.
BUT YOU KNOW, WE'RE GRADUATING SOON, SO IT WAS MORE JUST TO SAY I DID IT.
OH.
NOW YOU CAN MOVE ON!
YOU'LL FIND A NEW LOVE IN COLLEGE!
HA HA HA
I HAVE TO GET IN FIRST!
DON'T BE SUCH A DOWNER!
...SAME OLD STORY.

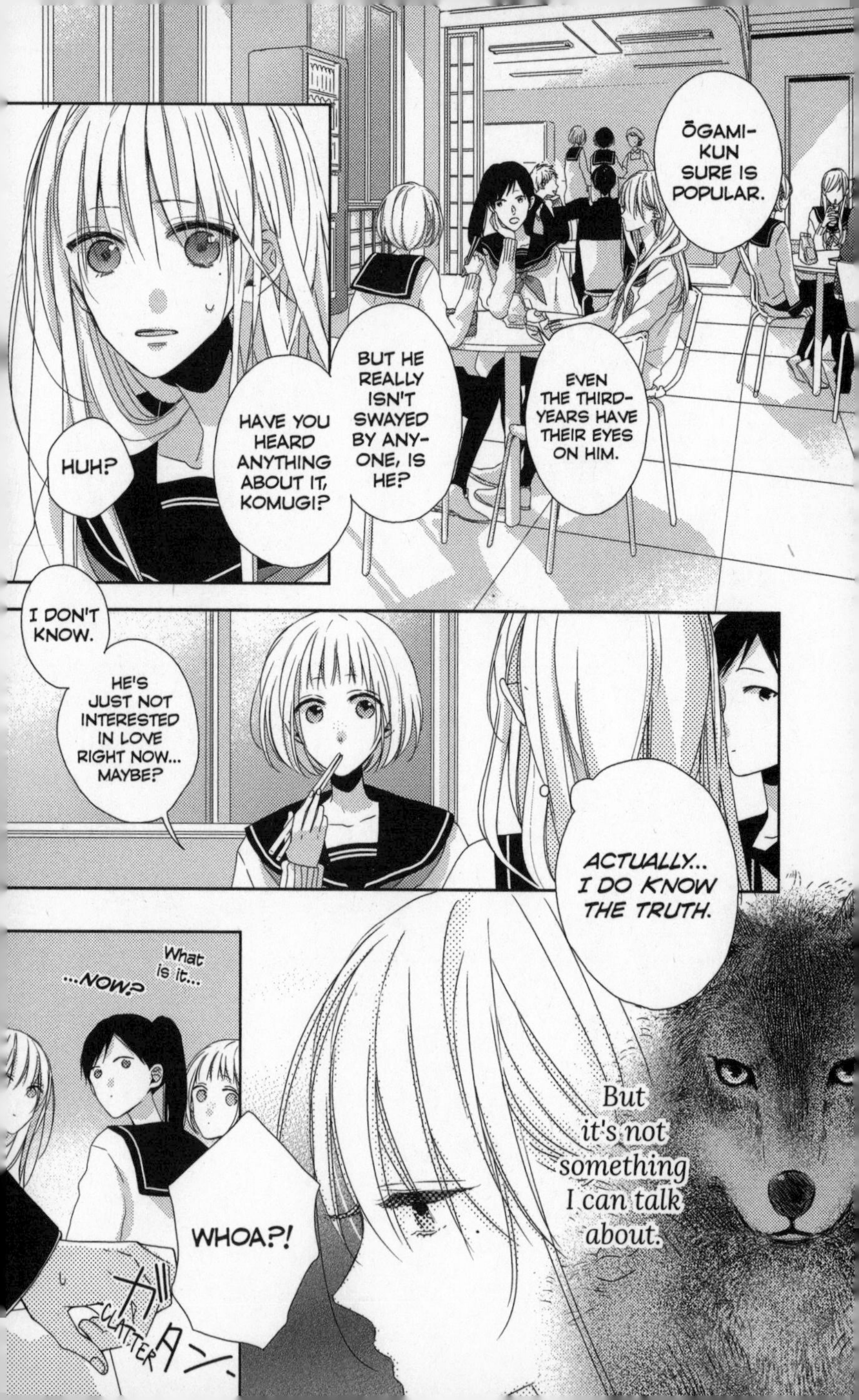
ŌGAMI-KUN SURE IS POPULAR.
EVEN THE THIRD-YEARS HAVE THEIR EYES ON HIM.
BUT HE REALLY ISN'T SWAYED BY ANY-ONE, IS HE?
HAVE YOU HEARD ANYTHING ABOUT IT, KOMUGI?
HUH?
I DON'T KNOW.
HE'S JUST NOT INTERESTED IN LOVE RIGHT NOW... MAYBE?
ACTUALLY... I DO KNOW THE TRUTH.
But it's not something I can talk about.
What is it...
...NOW?
WHOA?!
CLATTER

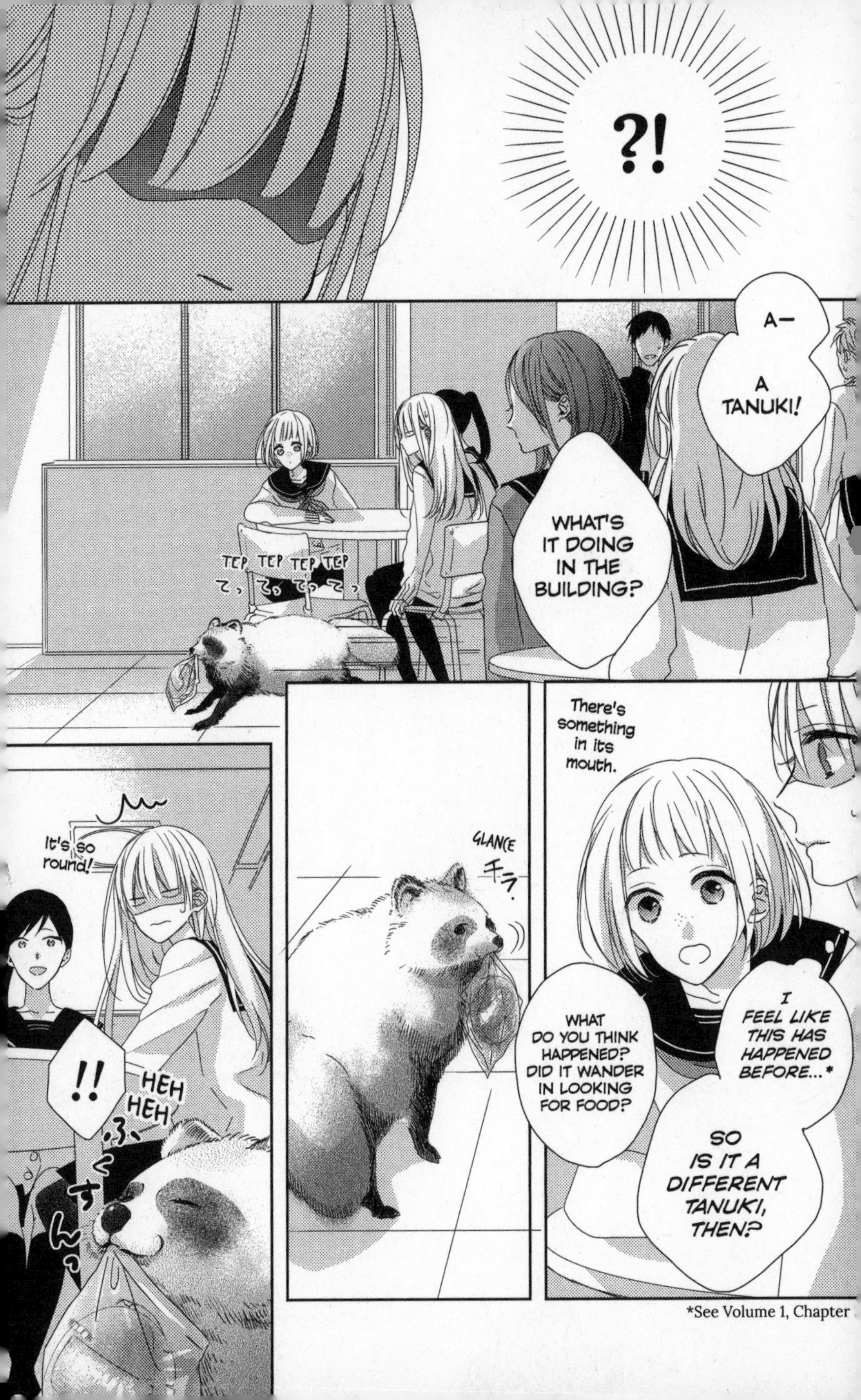
?!
A—
A TANUKI!
WHAT'S IT DOING IN THE BUILDING?
TEP TEP TEP TEP
て、て、て、て、
There's something in its mouth.
I FEEL LIKE THIS HAS HAPPENED BEFORE...*
WHAT DO YOU THINK HAPPENED? DID IT WANDER IN LOOKING FOR FOOD?
SO IS IT A DIFFERENT TANUKI, THEN?
GLANCE
チラ
It's so round!
!!
HEH HEH
ふくすん

*See Volume 1, Chapter

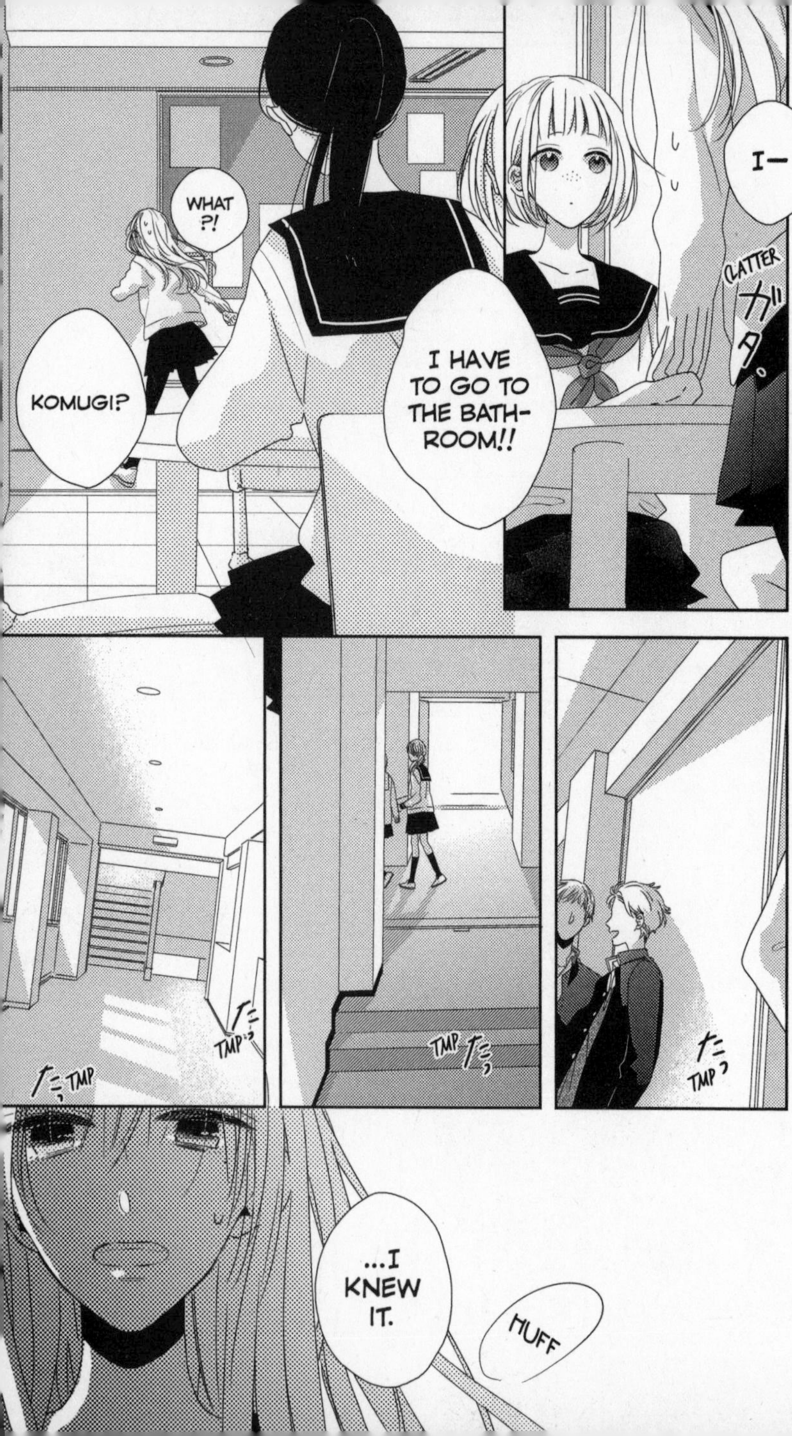
I—
CLATTER
ガタ。
I HAVE TO GO TO THE BATH-ROOM!!
WHAT ?!
KOMUGI?
TMP
TMP
TMP
TMP
...I KNEW IT.
HUFF

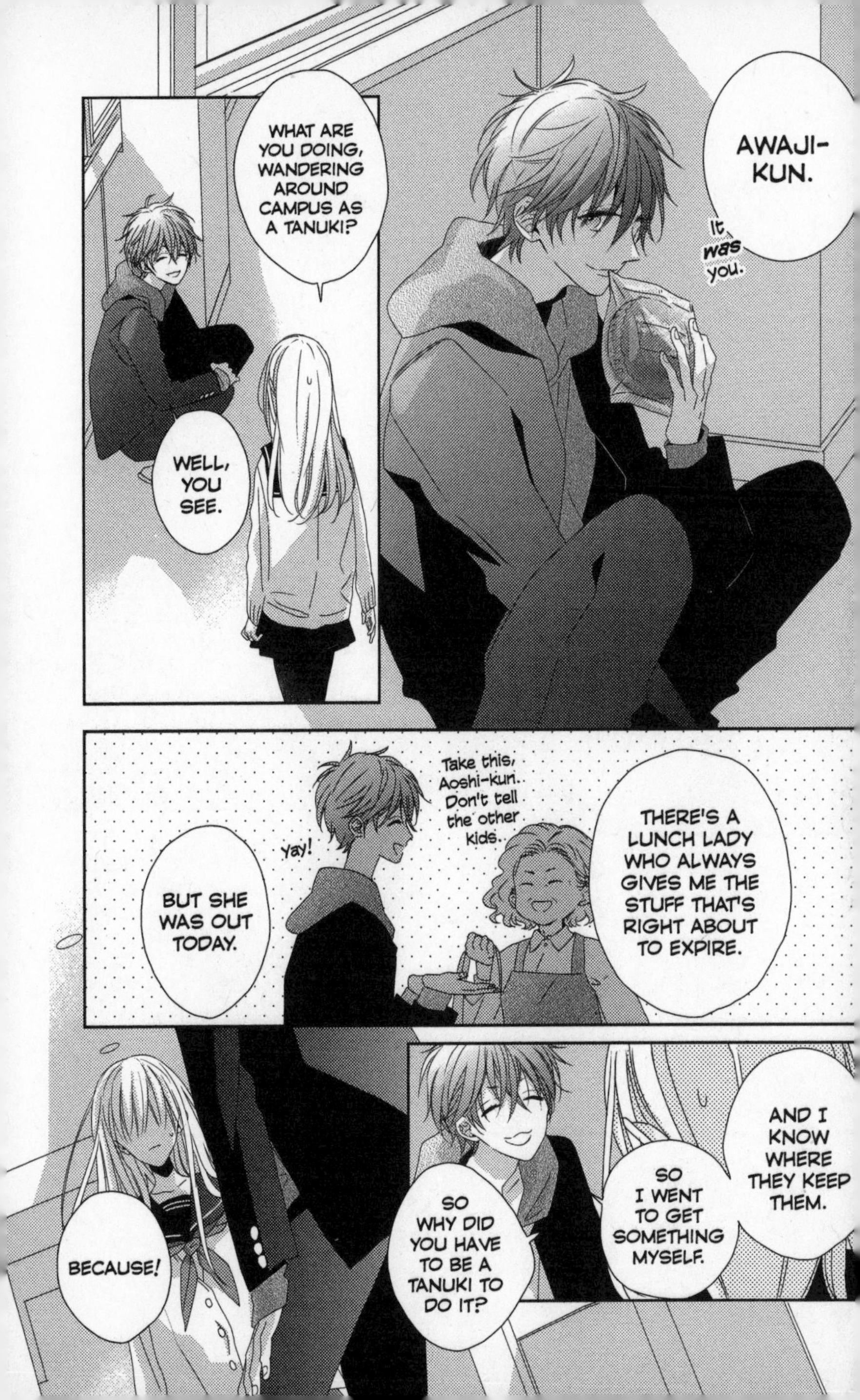
AWAJI-KUN.
It was you.
WHAT ARE YOU DOING, WANDERING AROUND CAMPUS AS A TANUKI?
WELL, YOU SEE.
THERE'S A LUNCH LADY WHO ALWAYS GIVES ME THE STUFF THAT'S RIGHT ABOUT TO EXPIRE.
Take this, Aoshi-kun. Don't tell the other kids.
Yay!
BUT SHE WAS OUT TODAY.
AND I KNOW WHERE THEY KEEP THEM.
SO I WENT TO GET SOMETHING MYSELF.
SO WHY DID YOU HAVE TO BE A TANUKI TO DO IT?
BECAUSE!

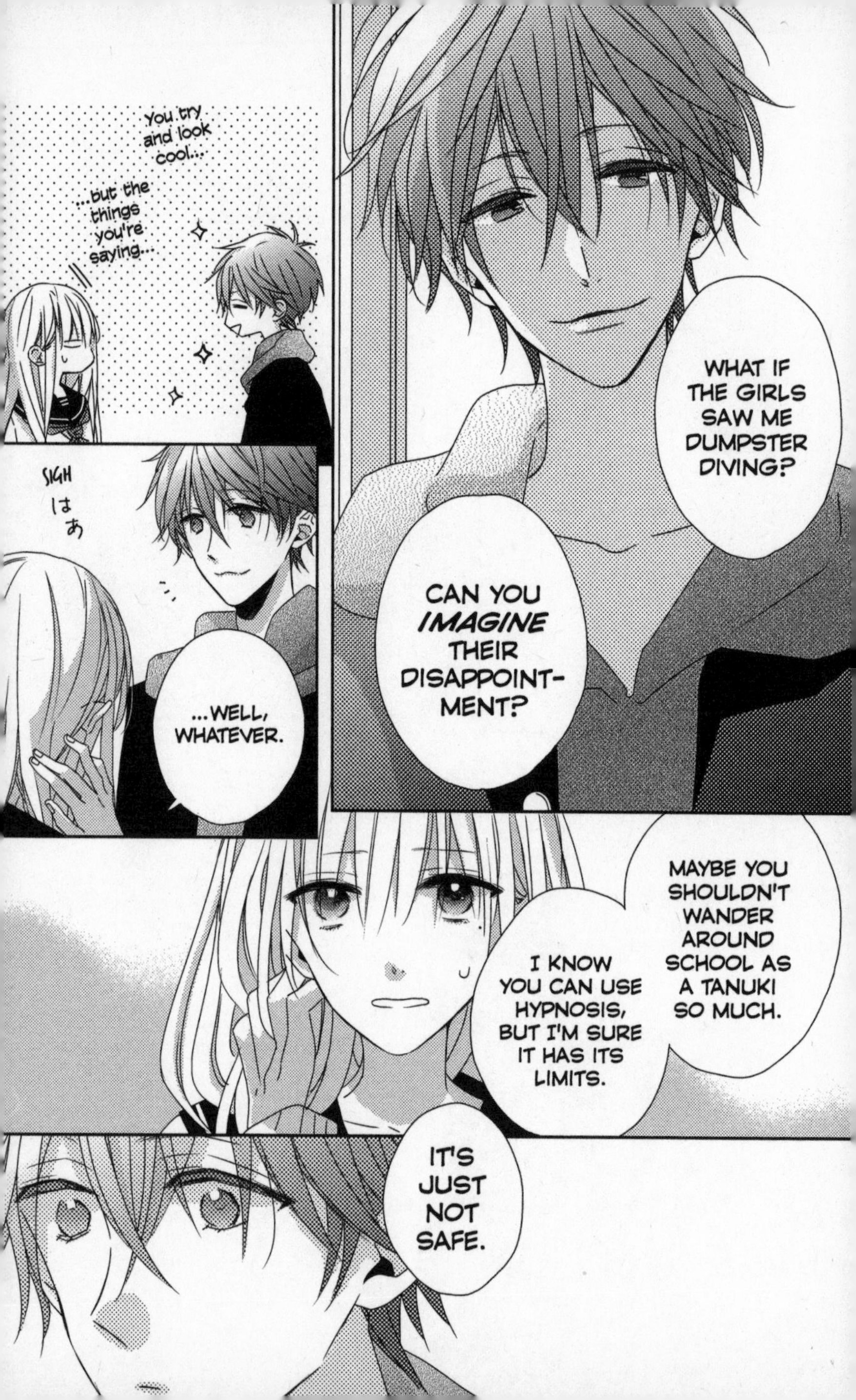

WHAT IF THE GIRLS SAW ME DUMPSTER DIVING?
CAN YOU *IMAGINE* THEIR DISAPPOINT-MENT?
You try and look cool...
...but the things you're saying...
SIGH
はあ
...WELL, WHATEVER.
MAYBE YOU SHOULDN'T WANDER AROUND SCHOOL AS A TANUKI SO MUCH.
I KNOW YOU CAN USE HYPNOSIS, BUT I'M SURE IT HAS ITS LIMITS.
IT'S JUST NOT SAFE.

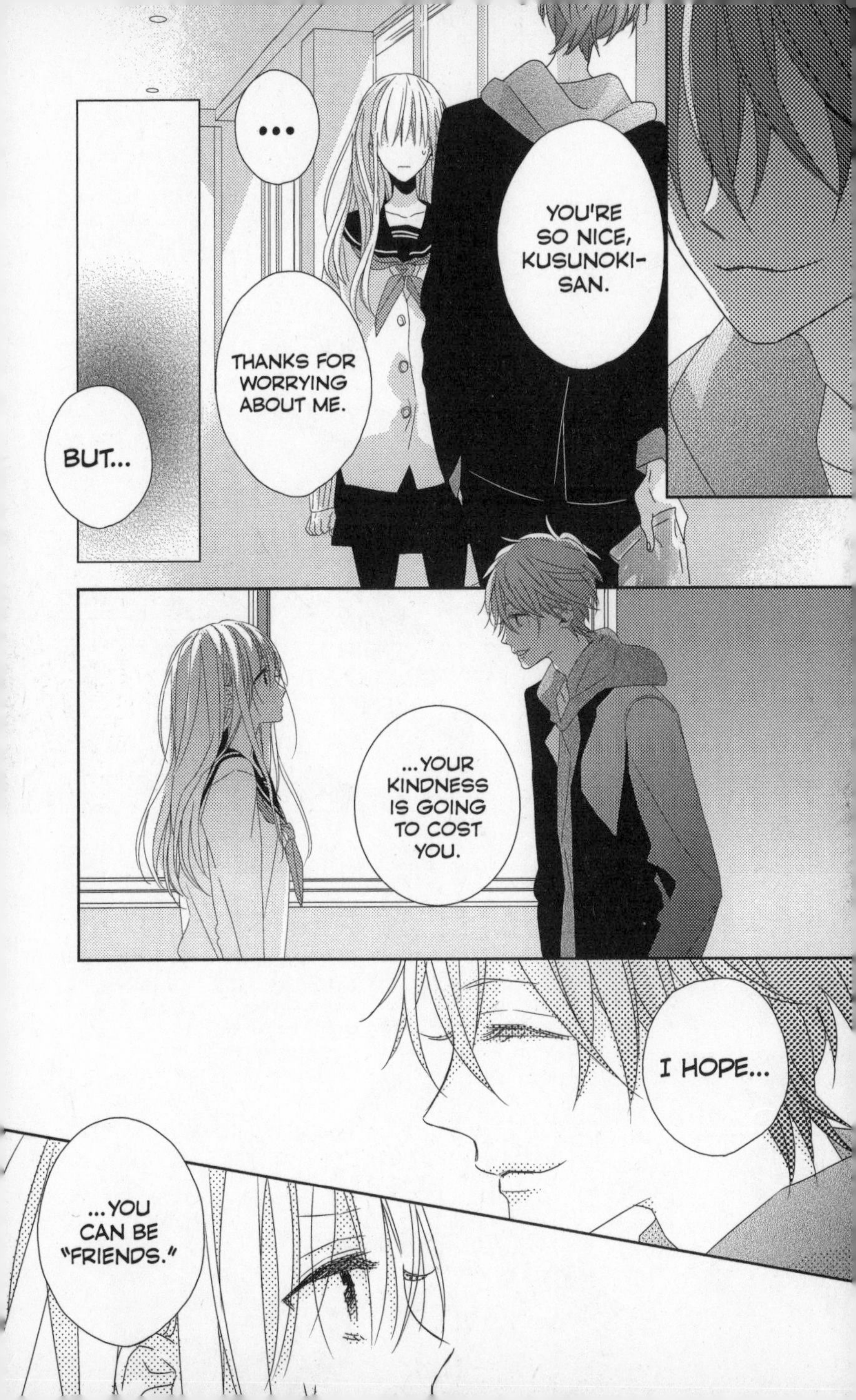
YOU'RE SO NICE, KUSUNOKI-SAN.
...
THANKS FOR WORRYING ABOUT ME.
BUT...
...YOUR KINDNESS IS GOING TO COST YOU.
I HOPE...
...YOU CAN BE "FRIENDS."

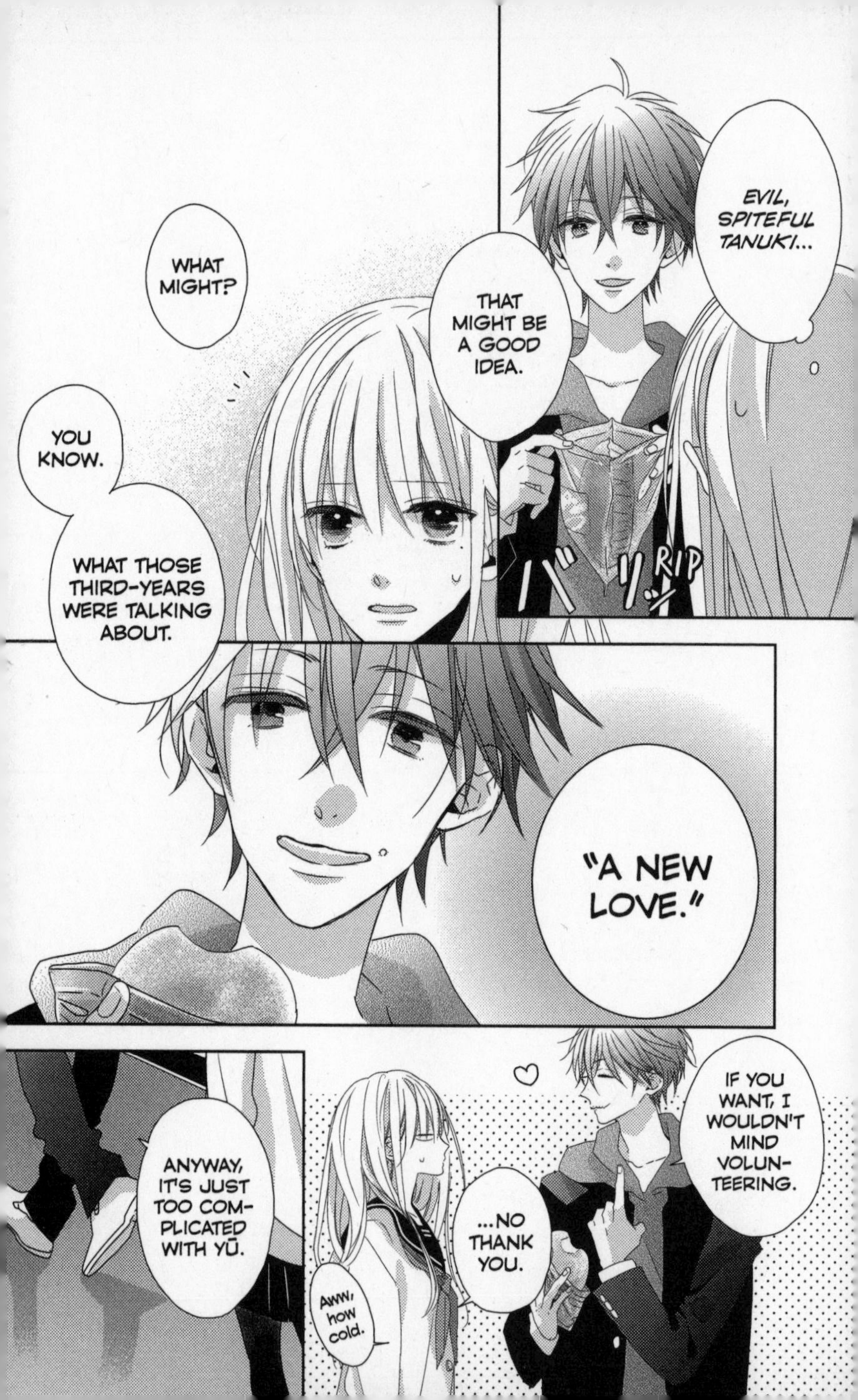
EVIL, SPITEFUL TANUKI...
THAT MIGHT BE A GOOD IDEA.
バリッ RIP
WHAT MIGHT?
YOU KNOW.
WHAT THOSE THIRD-YEARS WERE TALKING ABOUT.
"A NEW LOVE."
IF YOU WANT, I WOULDN'T MIND VOLUNTEERING.
...NO THANK YOU.
Aww, how cold.
ANYWAY, IT'S JUST TOO COMPLICATED WITH YŪ.

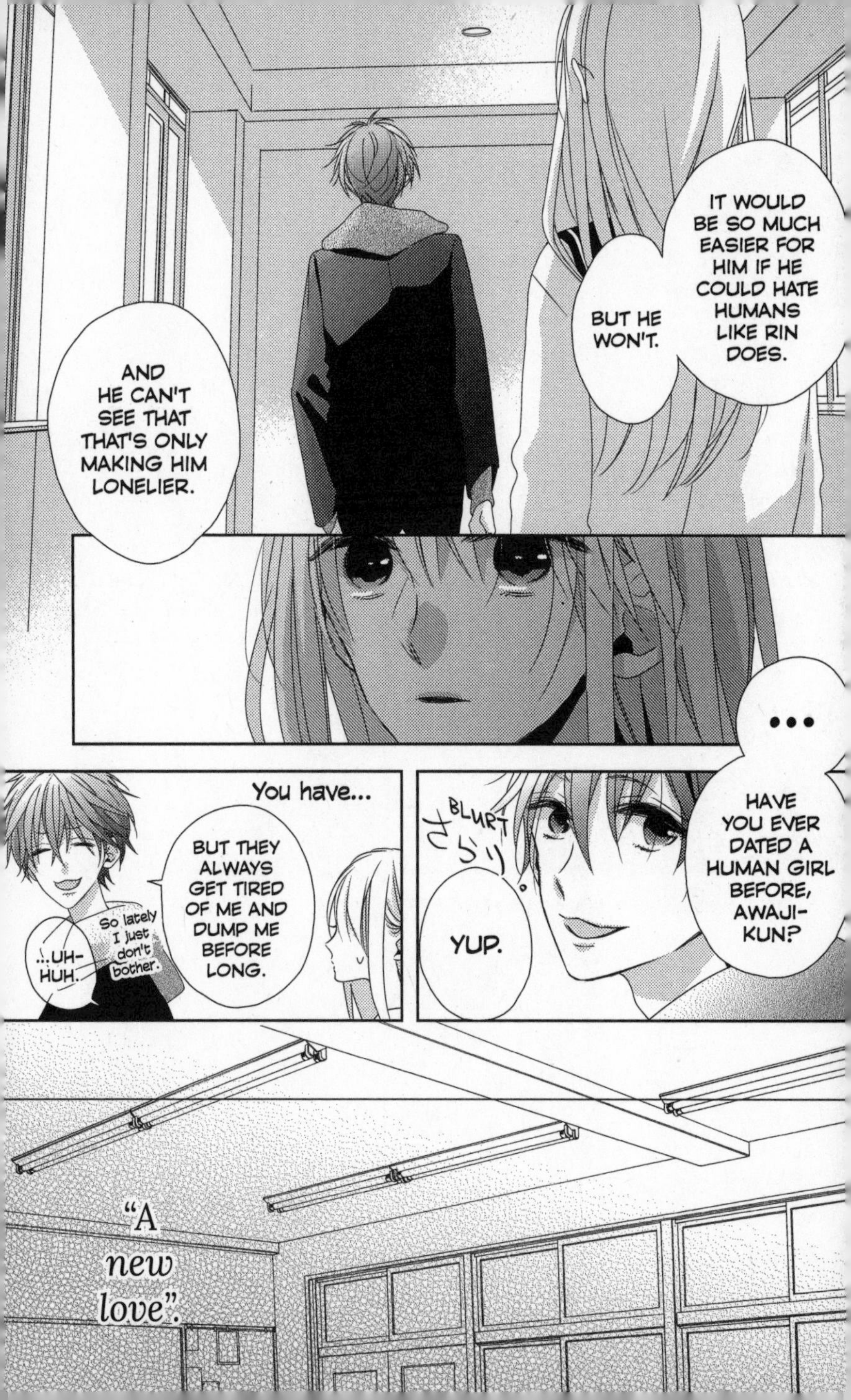
IT WOULD BE SO MUCH EASIER FOR HIM IF HE COULD HATE HUMANS LIKE RIN DOES.
BUT HE WON'T.
AND HE CAN'T SEE THAT THAT'S ONLY MAKING HIM LONELIER.
...
HAVE YOU EVER DATED A HUMAN GIRL BEFORE, AWAJI-KUN?
さらり BLURT
YUP.
You have...
BUT THEY ALWAYS GET TIRED OF ME AND DUMP ME BEFORE LONG.
So lately I just don't bother.
...UH-HUH.
“A new love”.

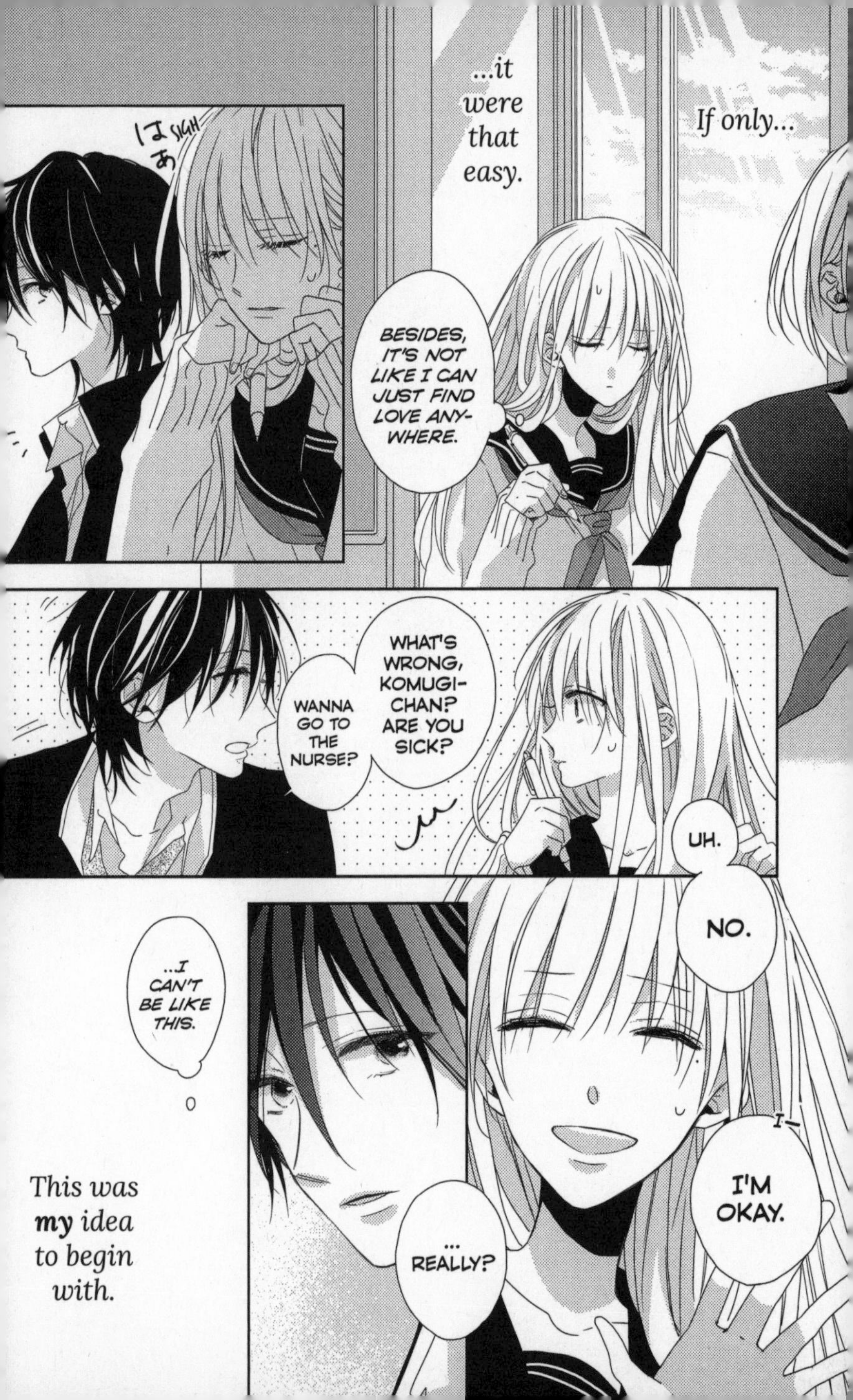
If only...
...it were that easy.
BESIDES, IT'S NOT LIKE I CAN JUST FIND LOVE ANY-WHERE.
はあ SIGH
WHAT'S WRONG, KOMUGI-CHAN? ARE YOU SICK?
WANNA GO TO THE NURSE?
UH.
NO.
I—
I'M OKAY.
...REALLY?
...I CAN'T BE LIKE THIS.
This was **my** idea to begin with.

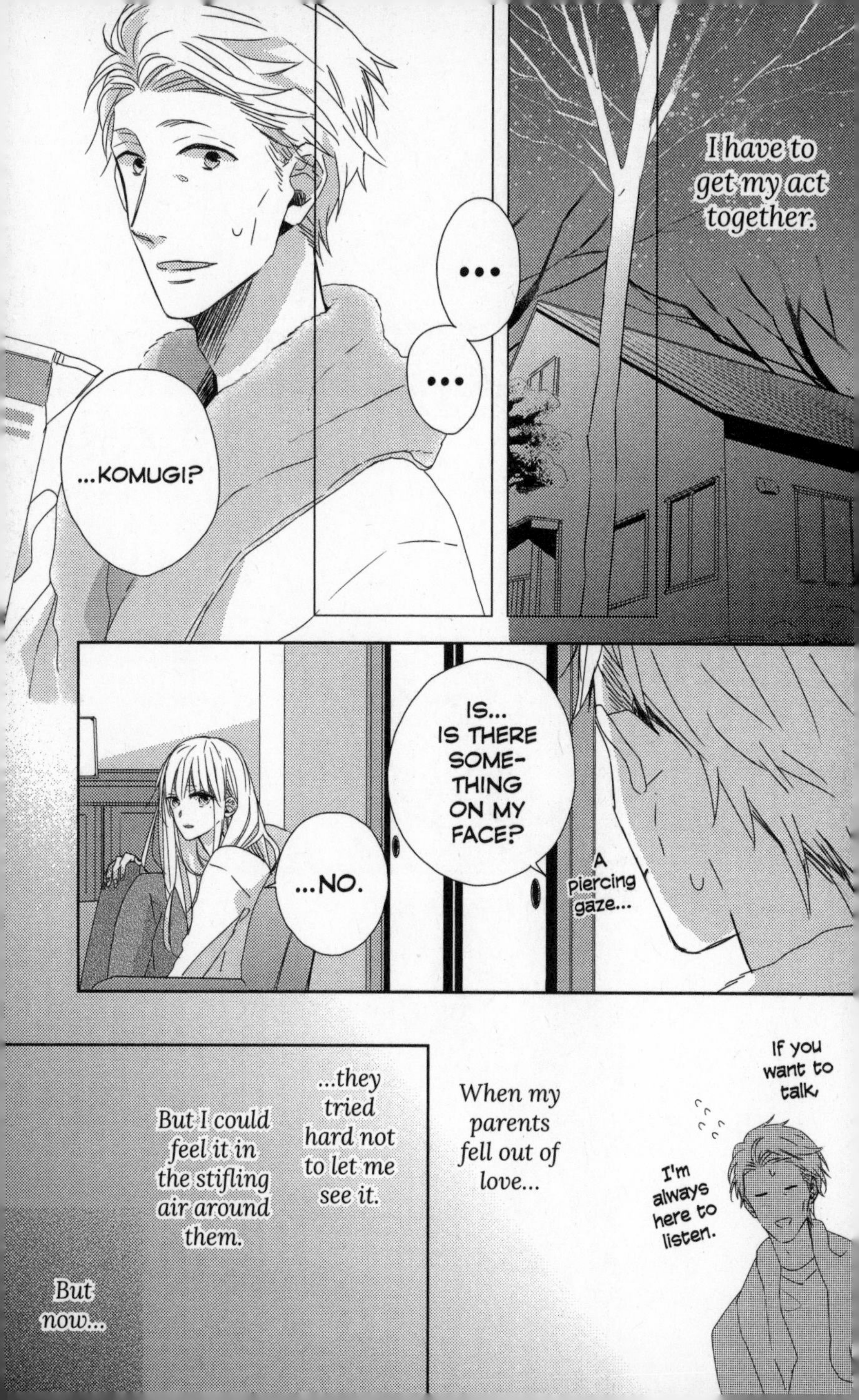
I have to get my act together.
...
...
...KOMUGI?
IS... IS THERE SOME-THING ON MY FACE?
A piercing gaze...
...NO.
If you want to talk,
I'm always here to listen.
When my parents fell out of love...
...they tried hard not to let me see it.
But I could feel it in the stifling air around them.
But now...

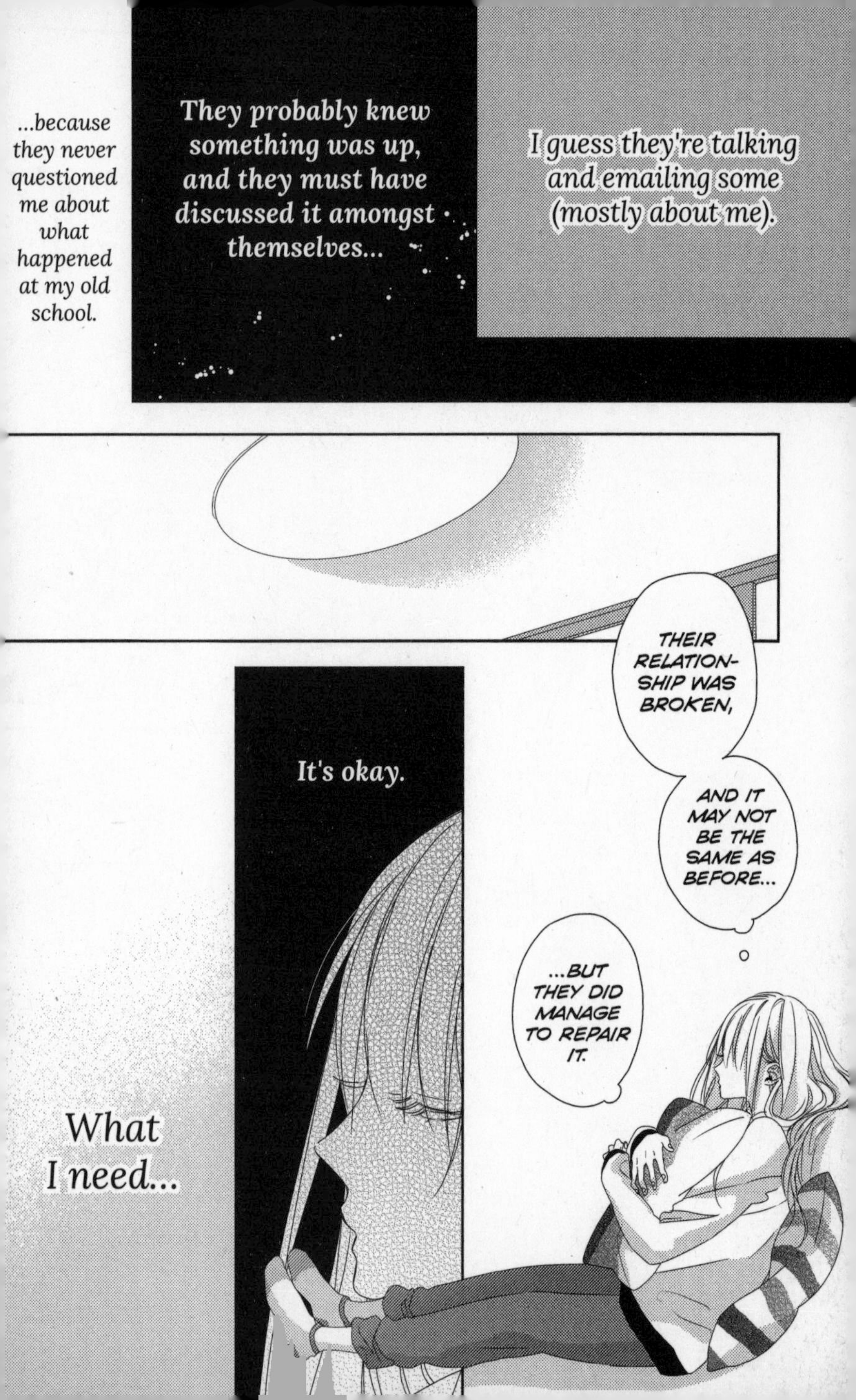
I guess they're talking and emailing some (mostly about me).
They probably knew something was up, and they must have discussed it amongst themselves...
...because they never questioned me about what happened at my old school.
THEIR RELATIONSHIP WAS BROKEN,
AND IT MAY NOT BE THE SAME AS BEFORE...
...BUT THEY DID MANAGE TO REPAIR IT.
It's okay.
What I need...

...is time.

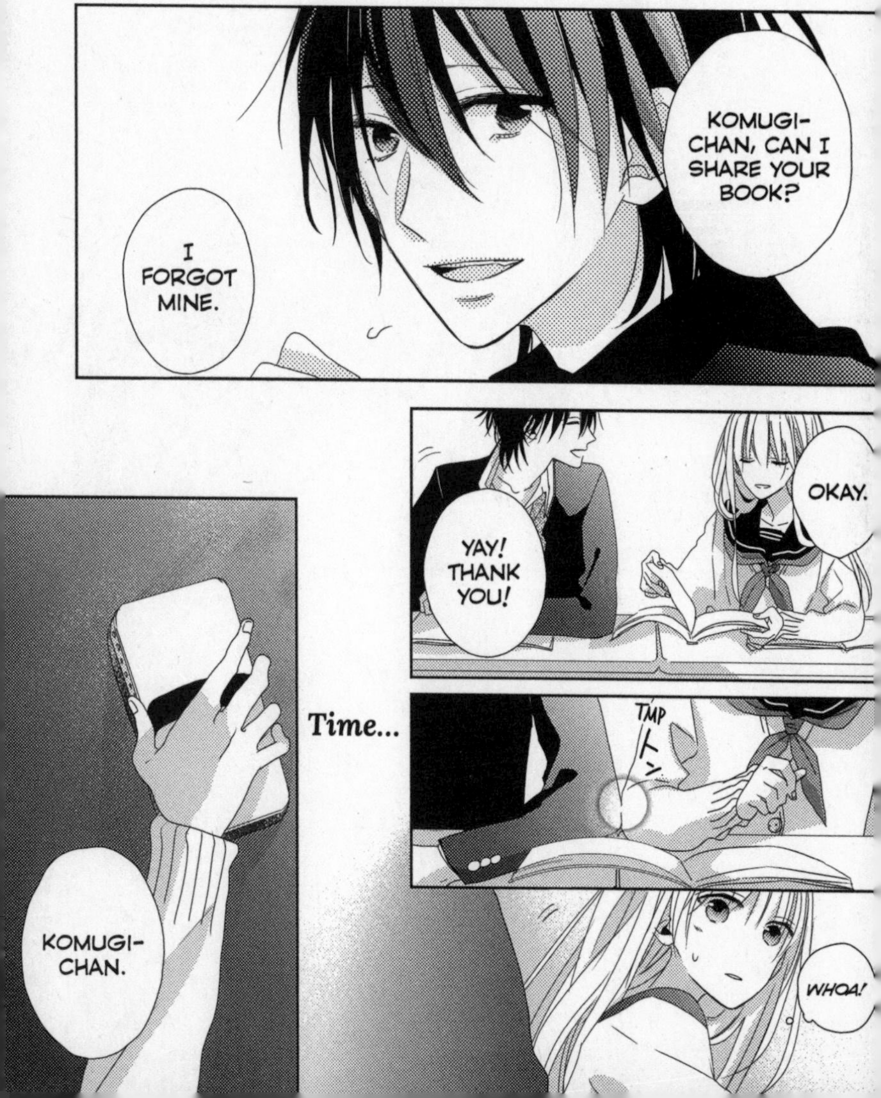
KOMUGI-CHAN, CAN I SHARE YOUR BOOK?
I FORGOT MINE.
OKAY.
YAY! THANK YOU!
TMP
トン
Time...
WHOA!
KOMUGI-CHAN.

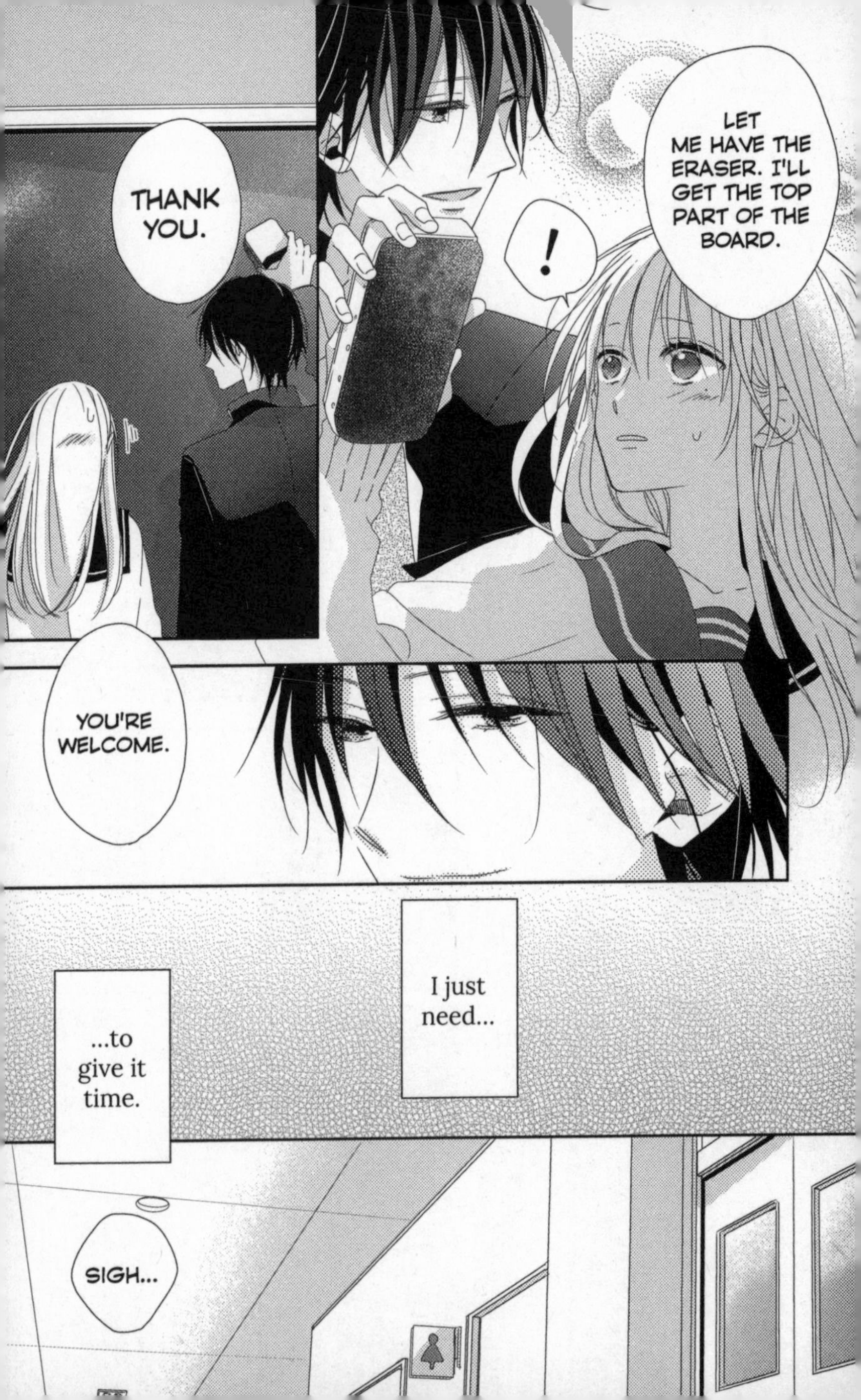
LET ME HAVE THE ERASER. I'LL GET THE TOP PART OF THE BOARD.
!
THANK YOU.
YOU'RE WELCOME.
I just need...
...to give it time.
SIGH...

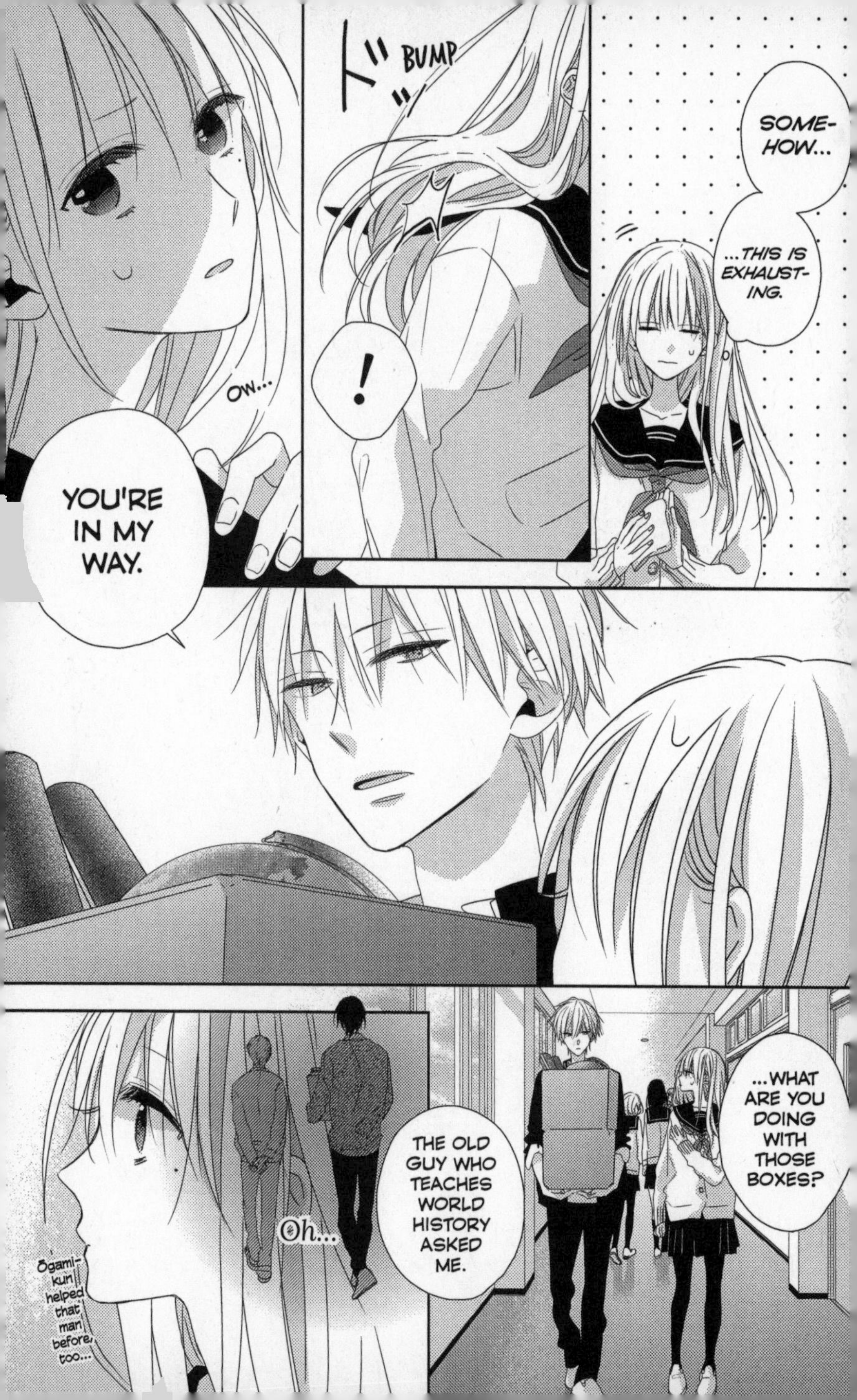
SOME-HOW...
...THIS IS EXHAUST-ING.
BUMP
!
OW...
YOU'RE IN MY WAY.
...WHAT ARE YOU DOING WITH THOSE BOXES?
THE OLD GUY WHO TEACHES WORLD HISTORY ASKED ME.
Oh...
Ōgami-kun helped that man before, too...

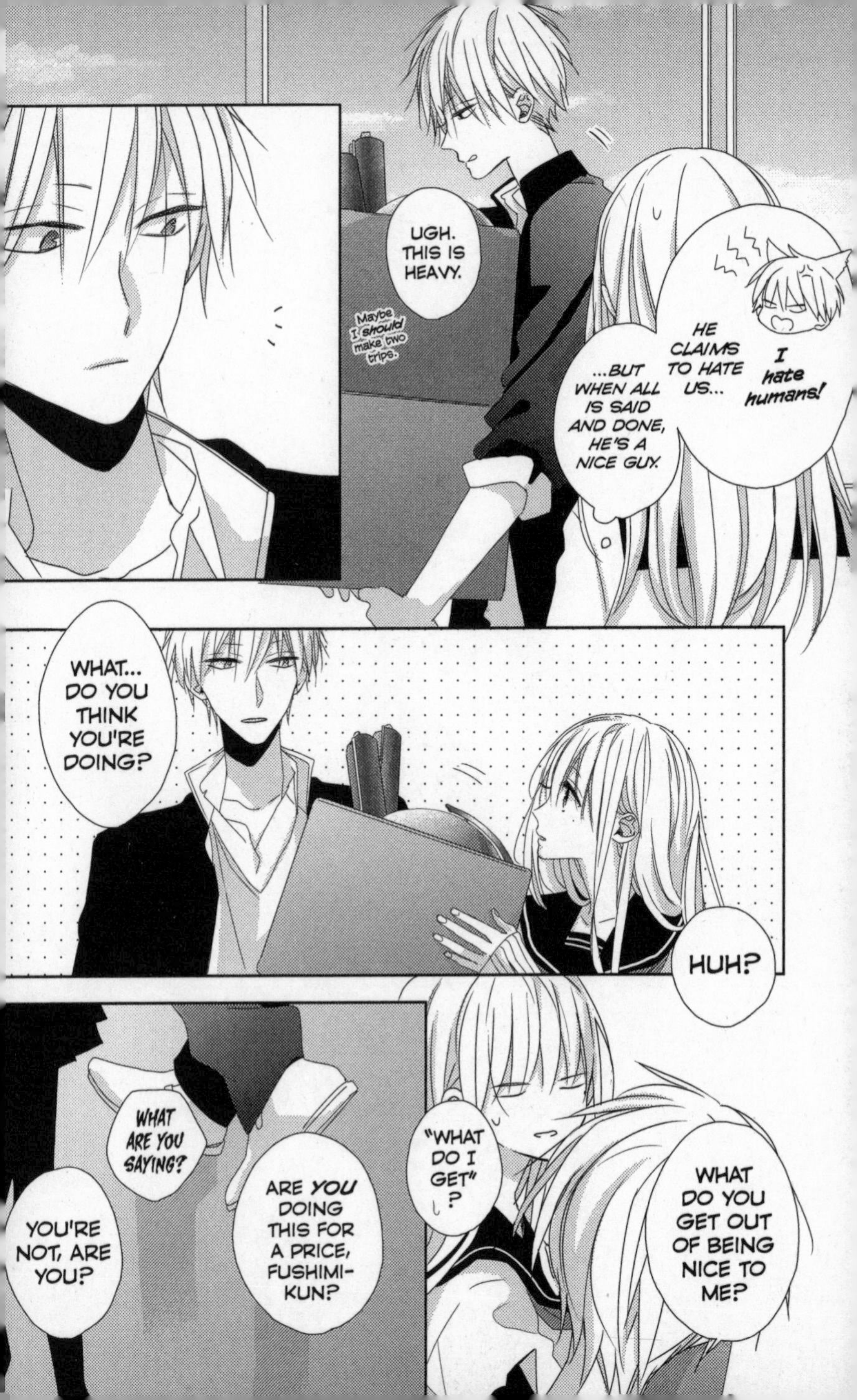
UGH. THIS IS HEAVY.
Maybe I should make two trips.
HE CLAIMS TO HATE US...
I hate humans!
...BUT WHEN ALL IS SAID AND DONE, HE'S A NICE GUY.
WHAT... DO YOU THINK YOU'RE DOING?
HUH?
WHAT DO YOU GET OUT OF BEING NICE TO ME?
"WHAT DO I GET"?
WHAT ARE YOU SAYING?
ARE YOU DOING THIS FOR A PRICE, FUSHIMI-KUN?
YOU'RE NOT, ARE YOU?

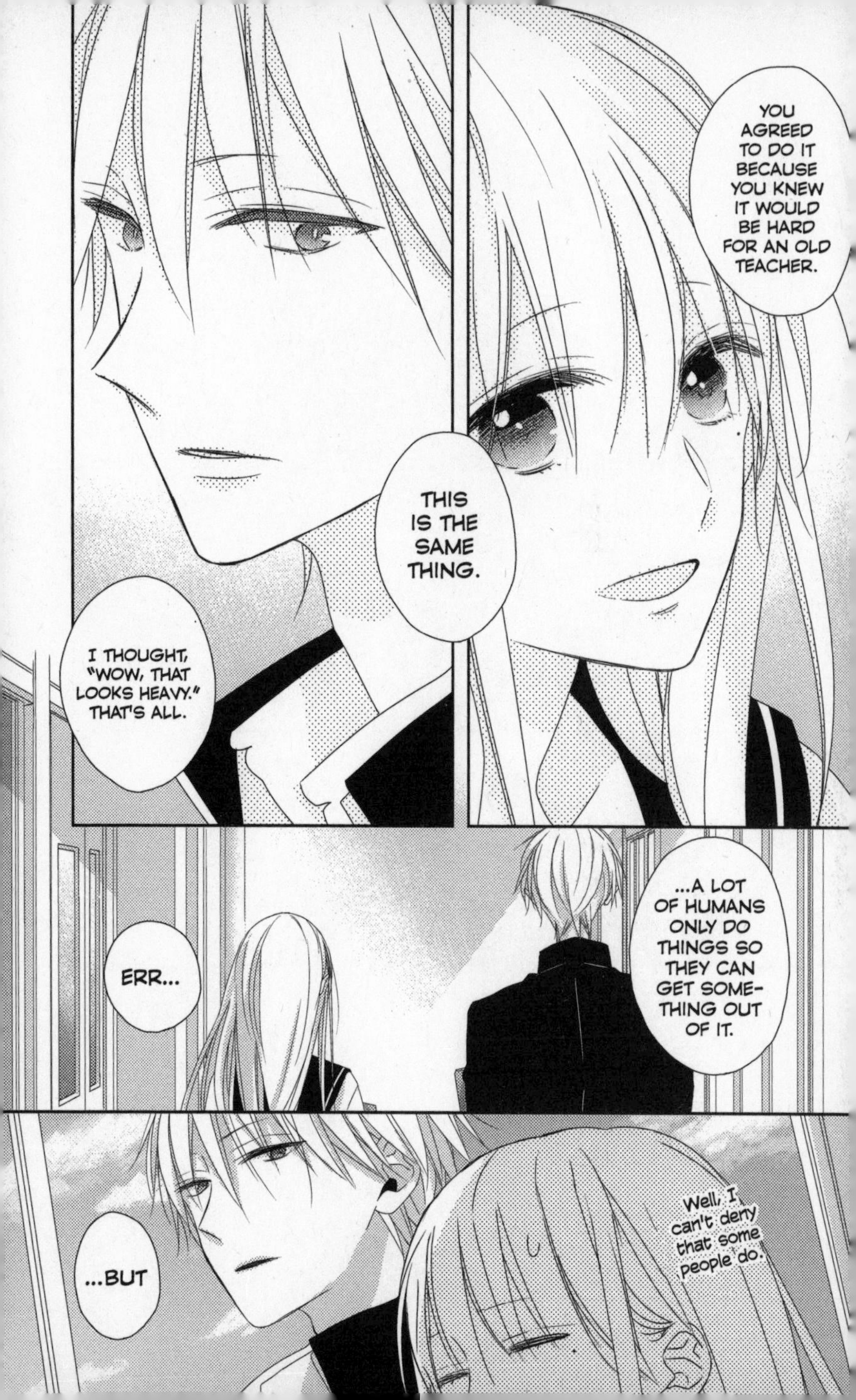
YOU AGREED TO DO IT BECAUSE YOU KNEW IT WOULD BE HARD FOR AN OLD TEACHER.
THIS IS THE SAME THING.
I THOUGHT, "WOW, THAT LOOKS HEAVY." THAT'S ALL.
...A LOT OF HUMANS ONLY DO THINGS SO THEY CAN GET SOME-THING OUT OF IT.
ERR...
Well, I can't deny that some people do.
...BUT

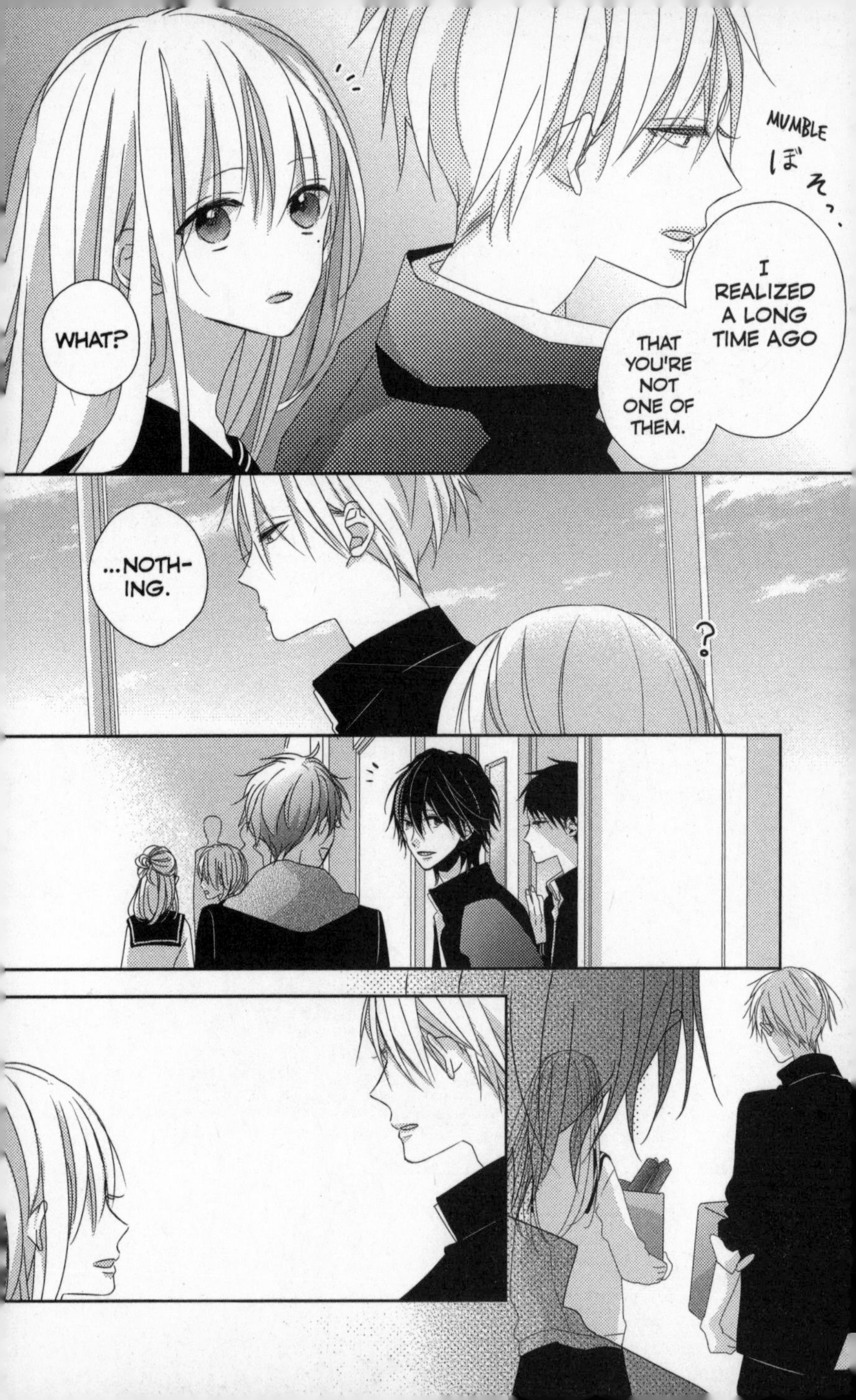
MUMBLE
ぼそっ
I REALIZED A LONG TIME AGO
THAT YOU'RE NOT ONE OF THEM.
WHAT?
...NOTH-ING.
?

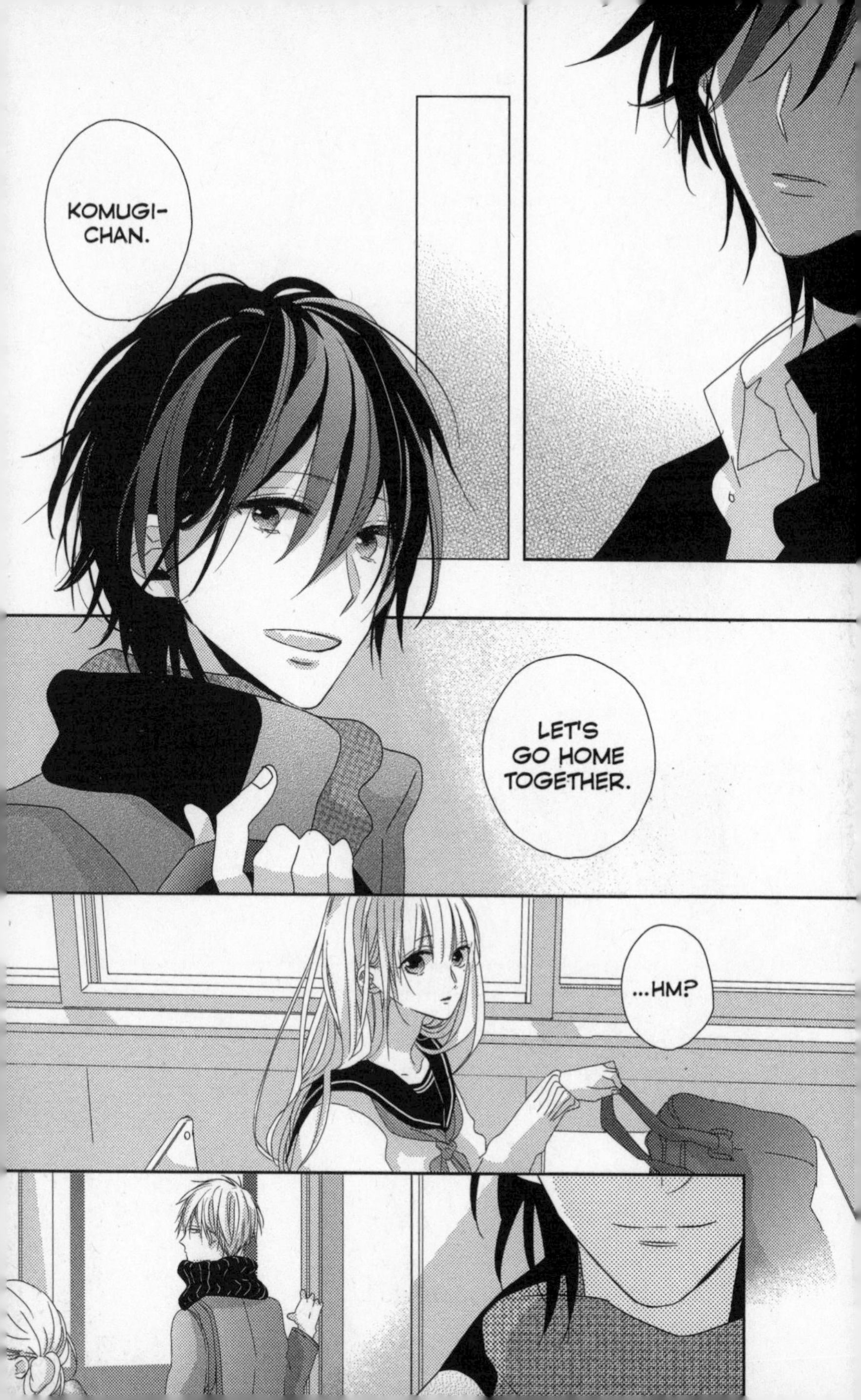
KOMUGI-CHAN.
LET'S GO HOME TOGETHER.
...HM?

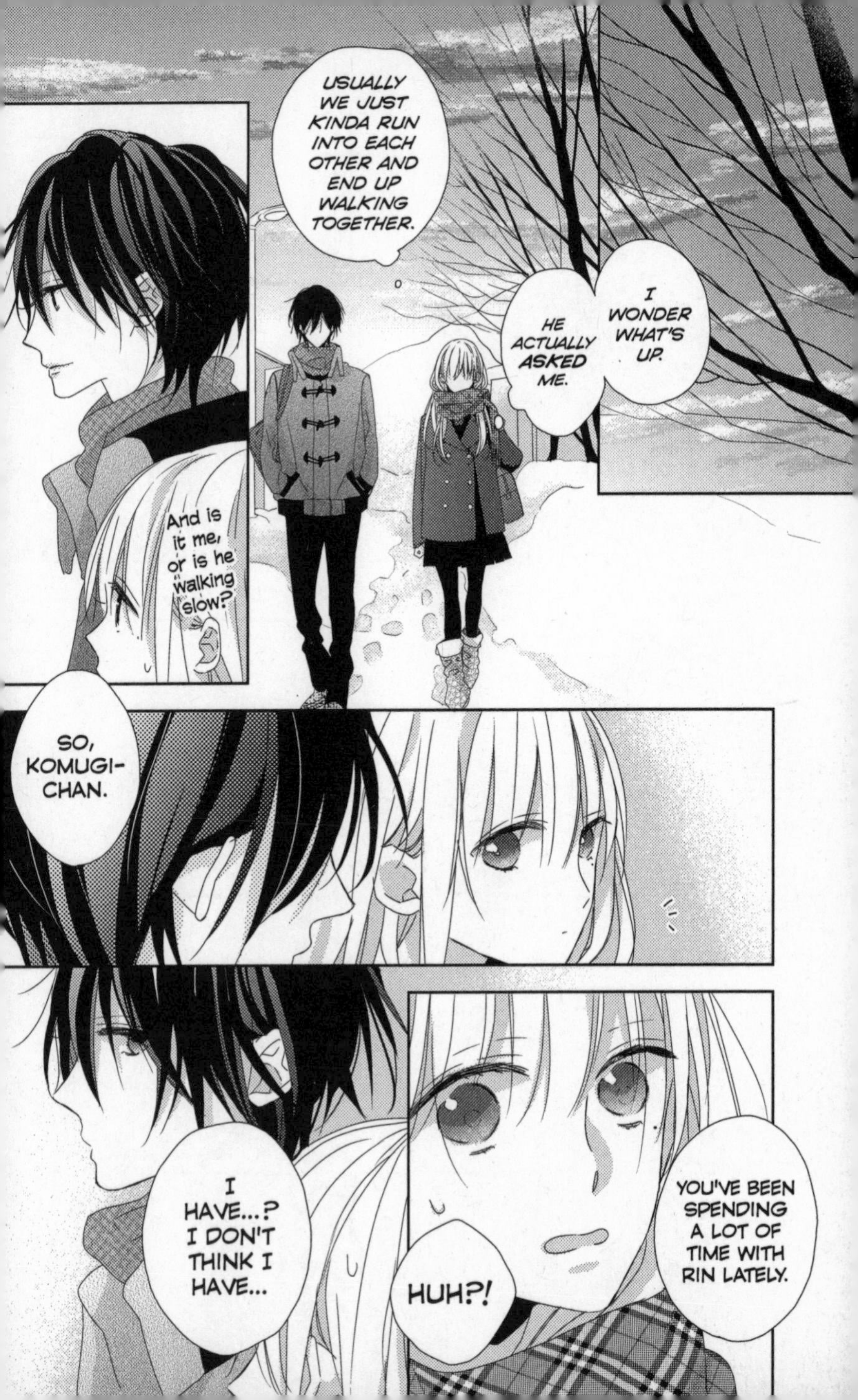
I WONDER WHAT'S UP.
HE ACTUALLY ASKED ME.
USUALLY WE JUST KINDA RUN INTO EACH OTHER AND END UP WALKING TOGETHER.
And is it me, or is he walking slow?
SO, KOMUGI-CHAN.
YOU'VE BEEN SPENDING A LOT OF TIME WITH RIN LATELY.
HUH?!
I HAVE...? I DON'T THINK I HAVE...

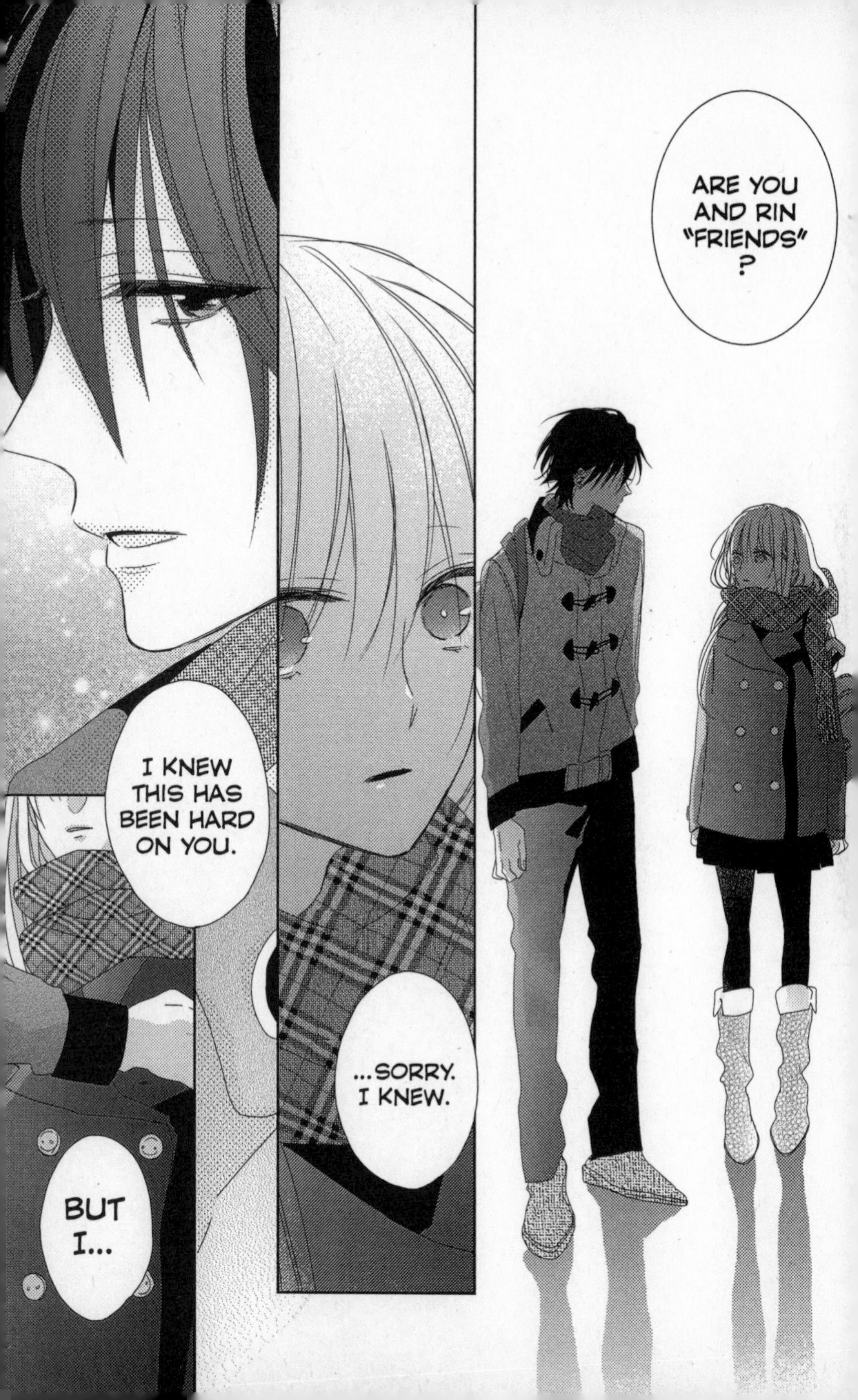
ARE YOU AND RIN "FRIENDS" ?
...SORRY. I KNEW.
I KNEW THIS HAS BEEN HARD ON YOU.
BUT I...

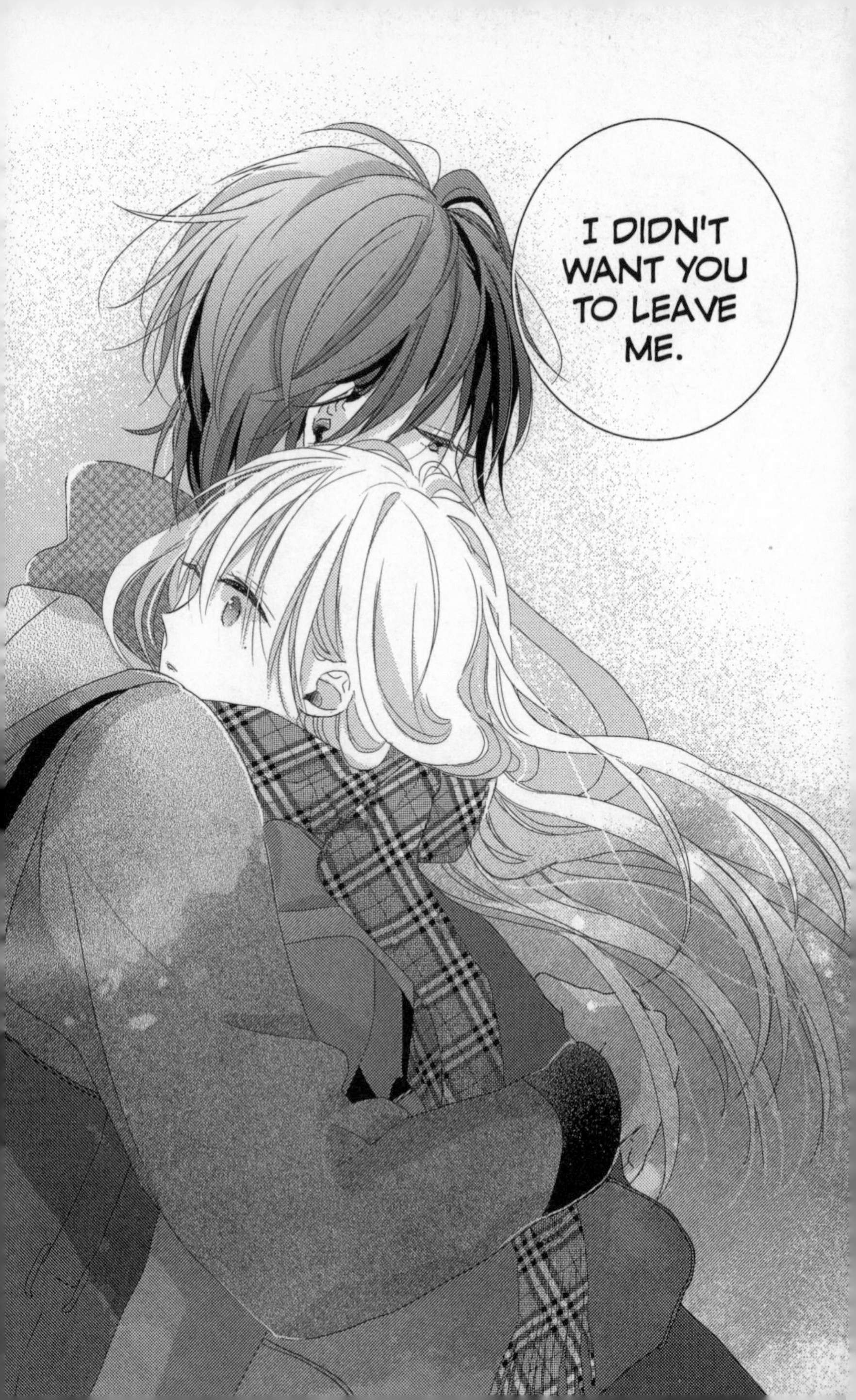
I DIDN'T WANT YOU TO LEAVE ME.

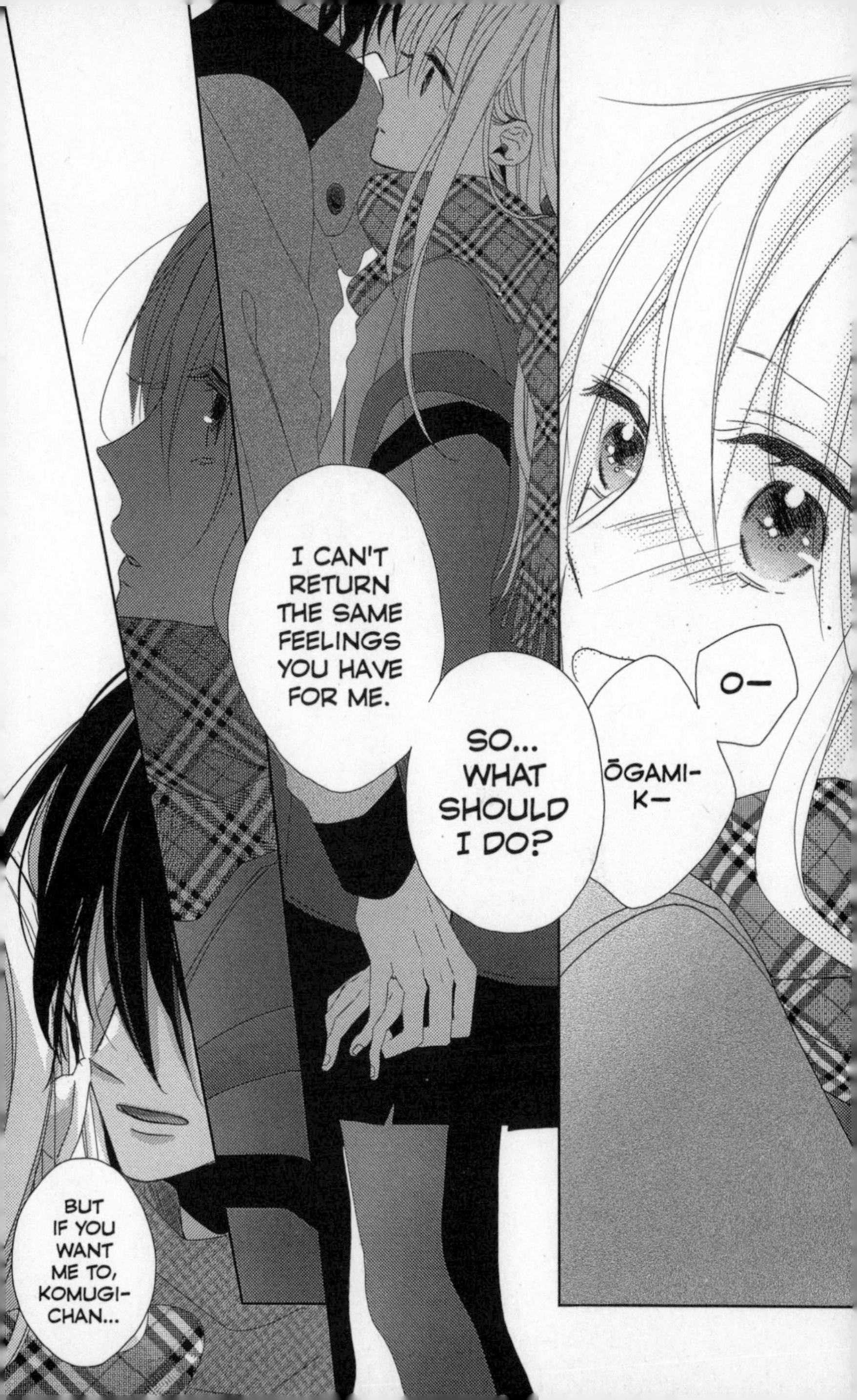
O—
ŌGAMI-K—
I CAN'T RETURN THE SAME FEELINGS YOU HAVE FOR ME.
SO... WHAT SHOULD I DO?
BUT IF YOU WANT ME TO, KOMUGI-CHAN...

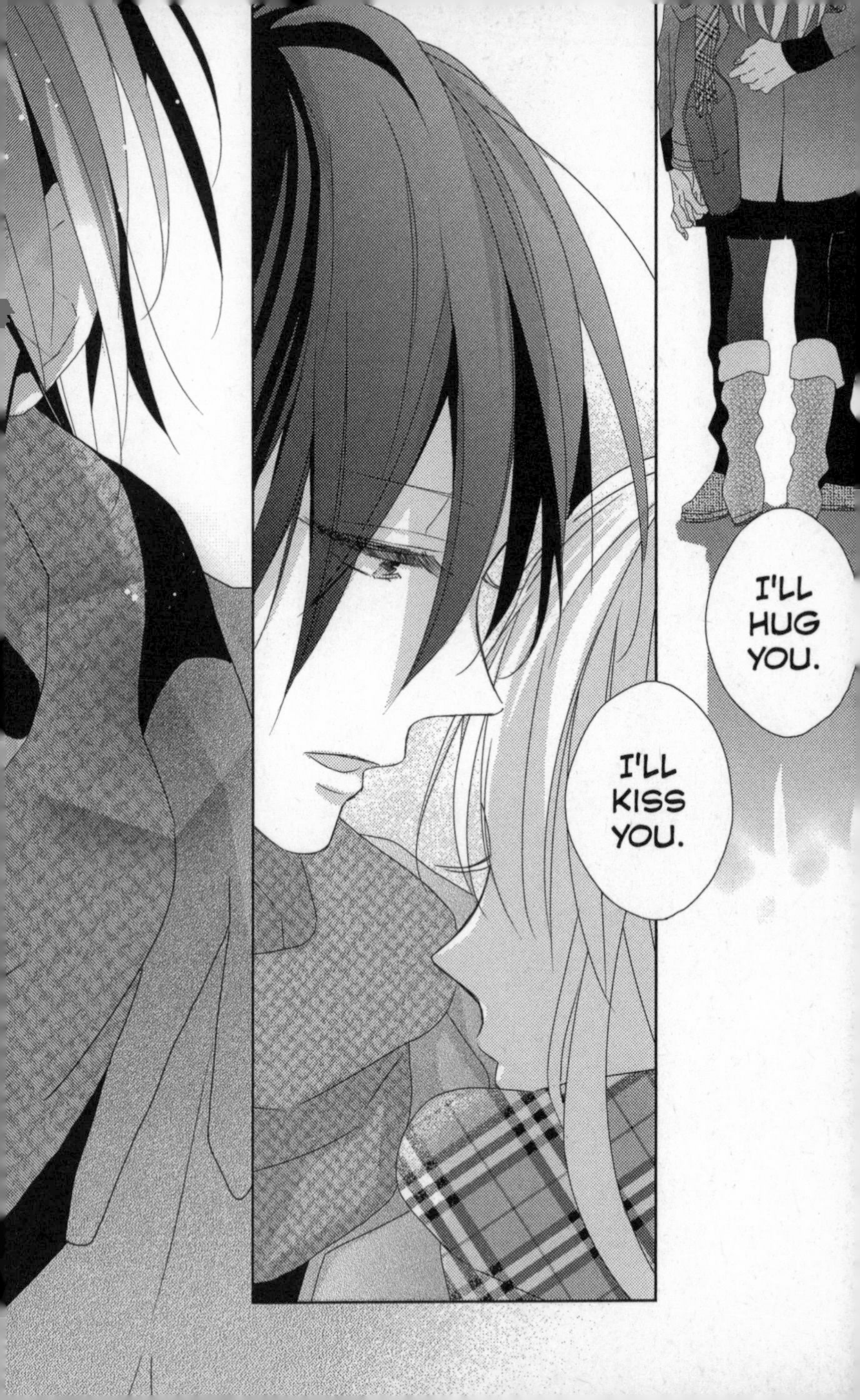
I'LL HUG YOU.
I'LL KISS YOU.

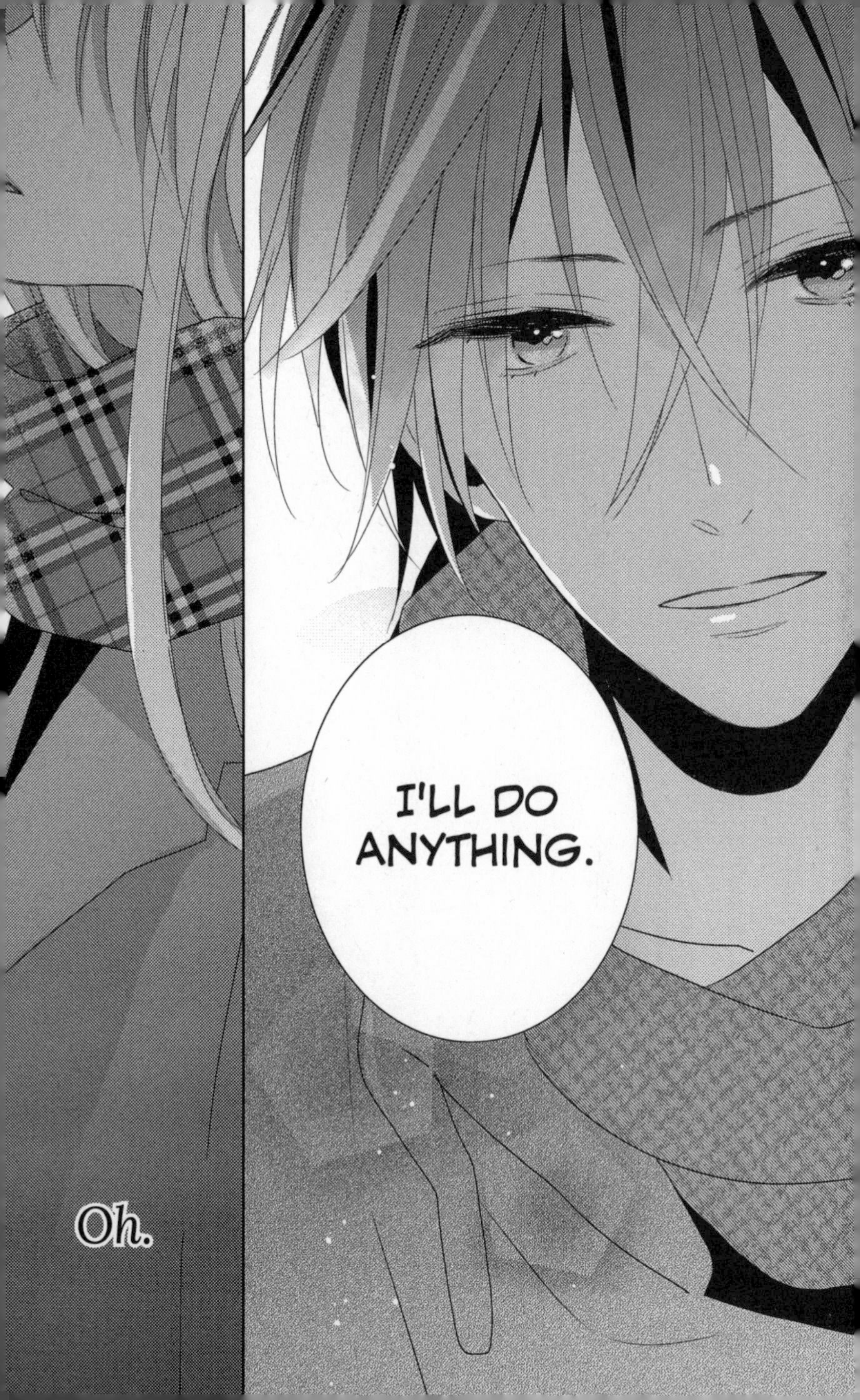
I'LL DO ANYTHING.
Oh.

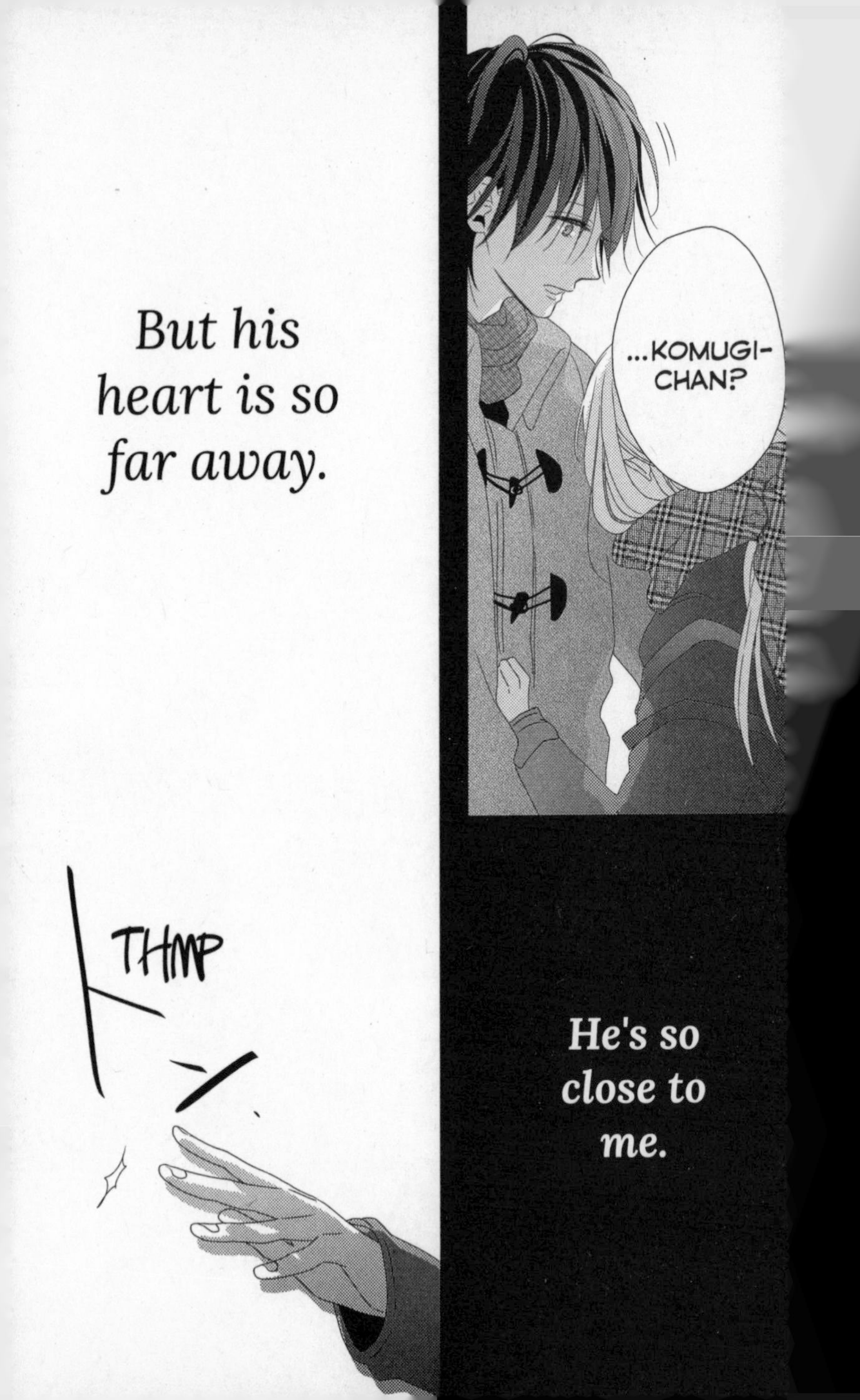
...KOMUGI-CHAN?
He's so close to me.
But his heart is so far away.
THMP

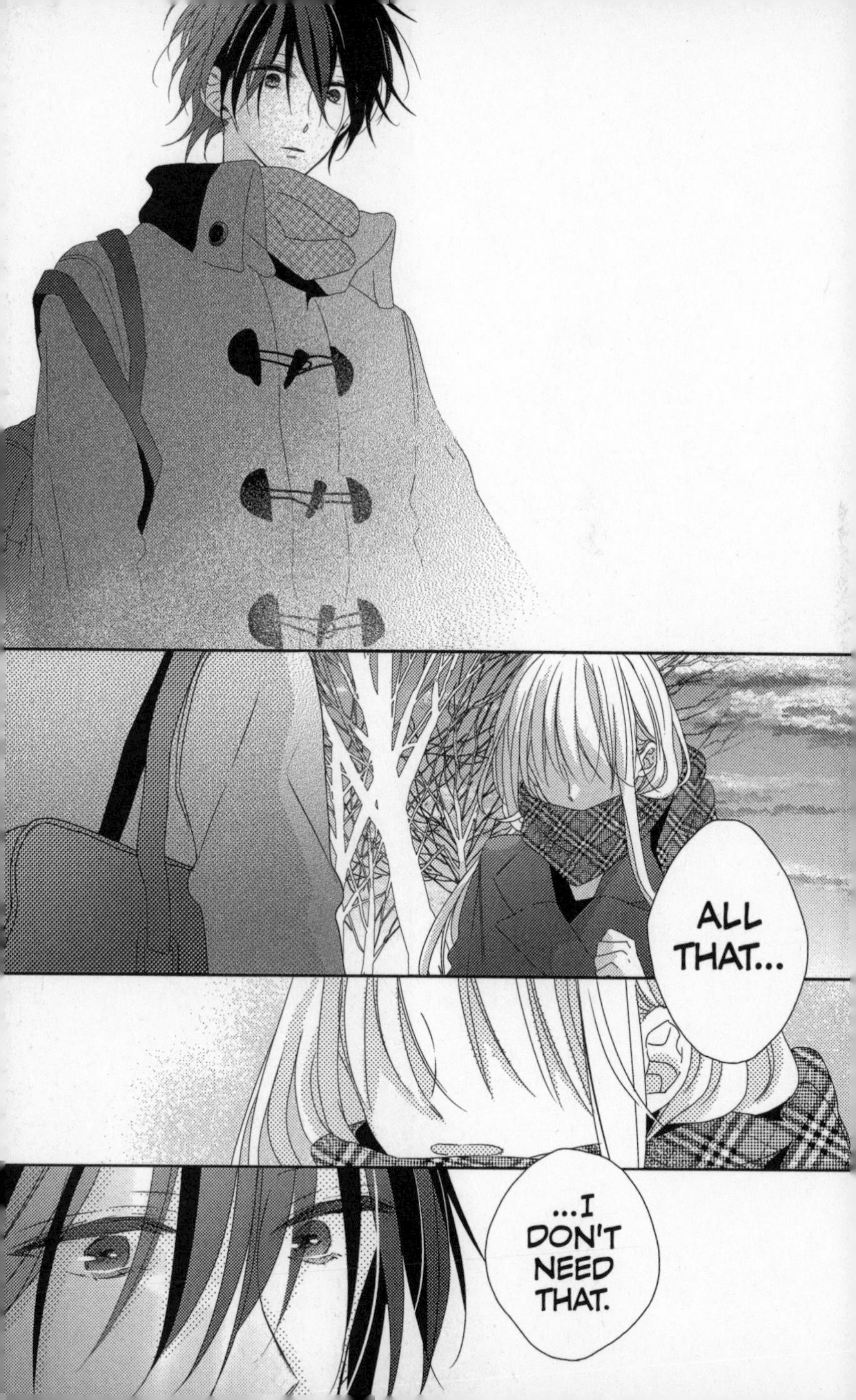
ALL THAT...
...I DON'T NEED THAT.

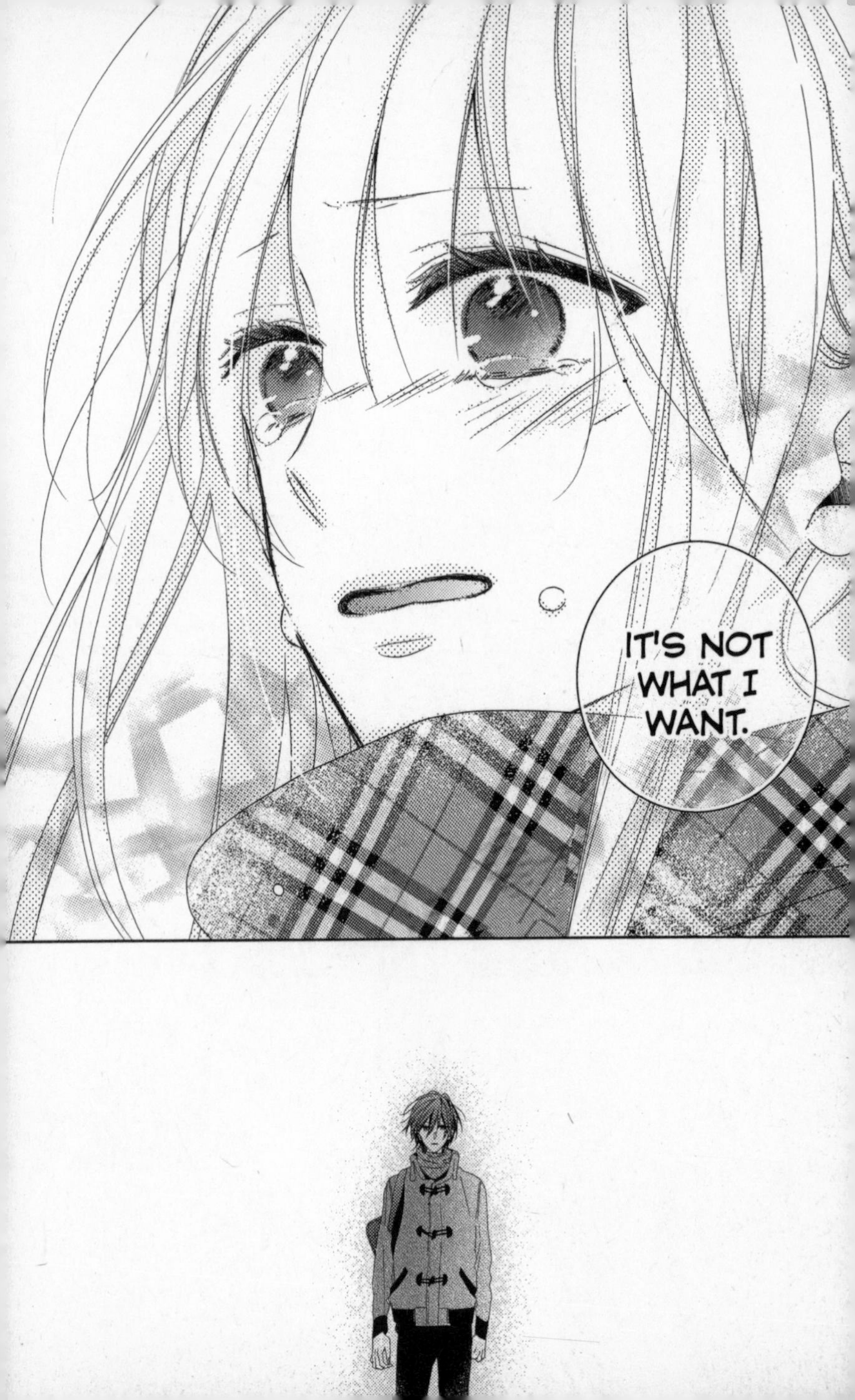
IT'S NOT WHAT I WANT.

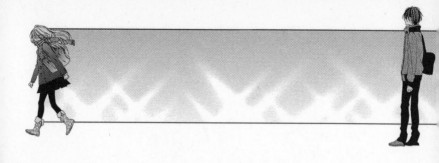

I was so sure
of myself.

But...

...I was so wrong.

That I understood his solitude.

I assumed that I understood him.

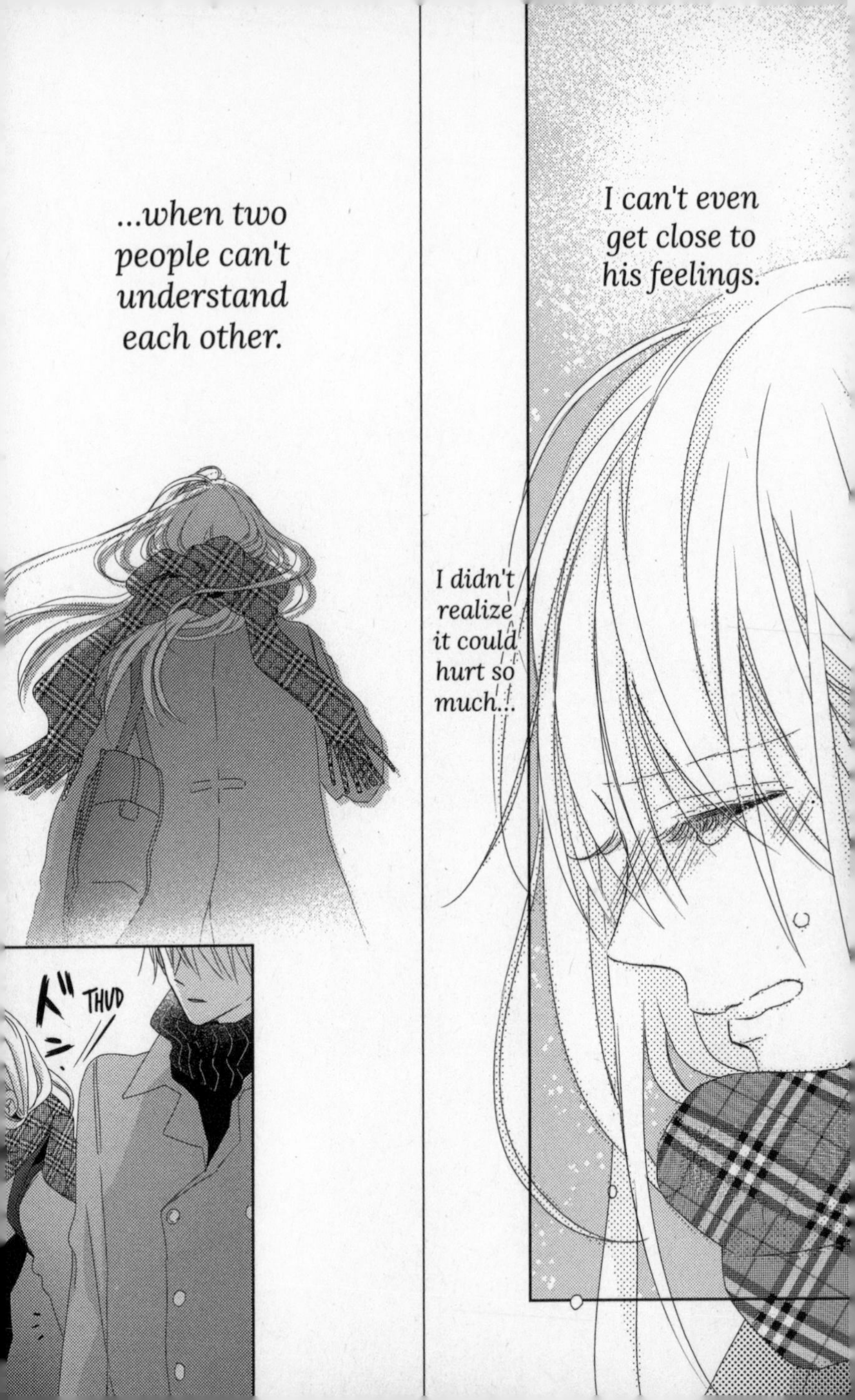
I can't even get close to his feelings.
I didn't realize it could hurt so much...
...when two people can't understand each other.
THUD

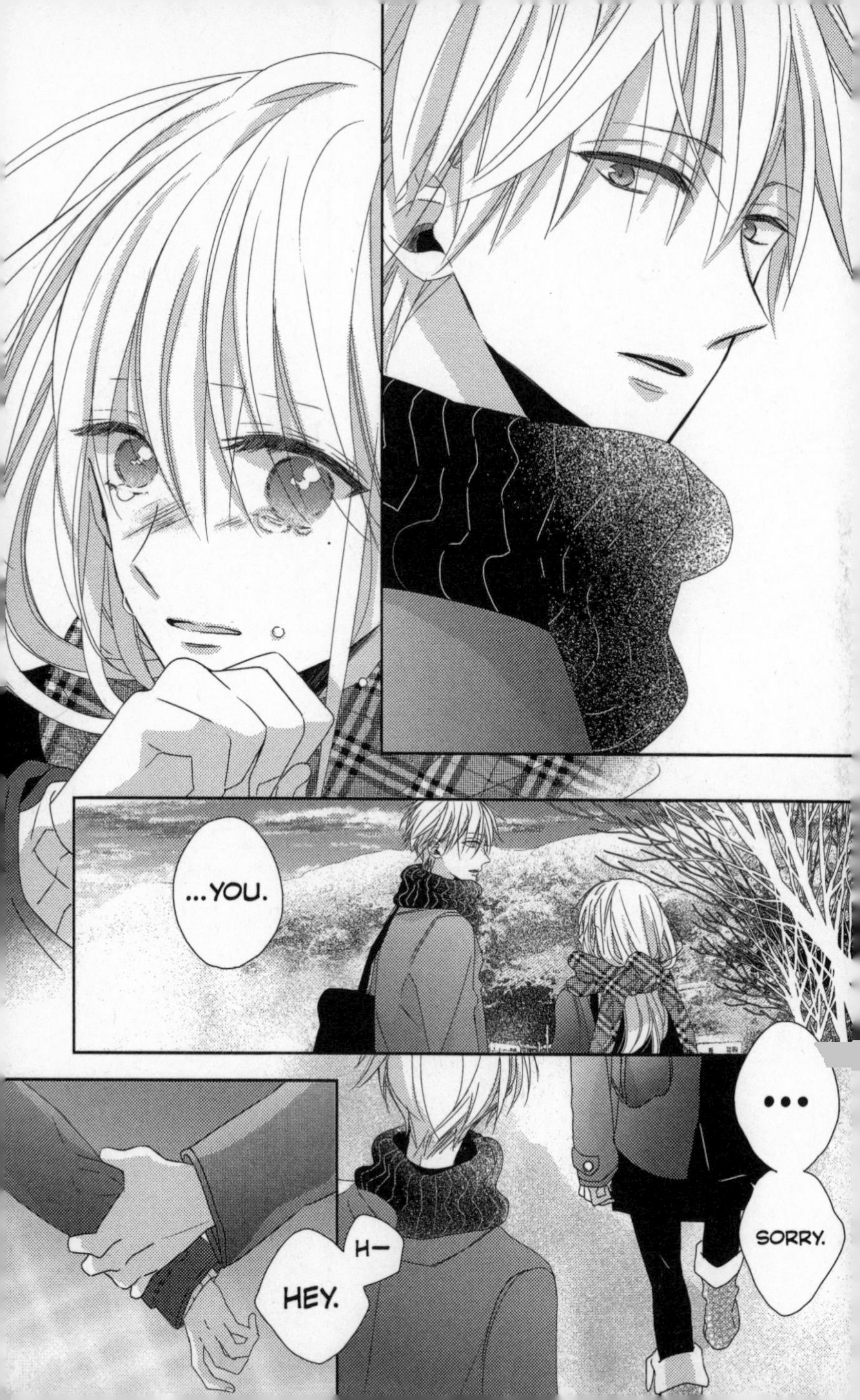
...YOU.
...
SORRY.
H—
HEY.

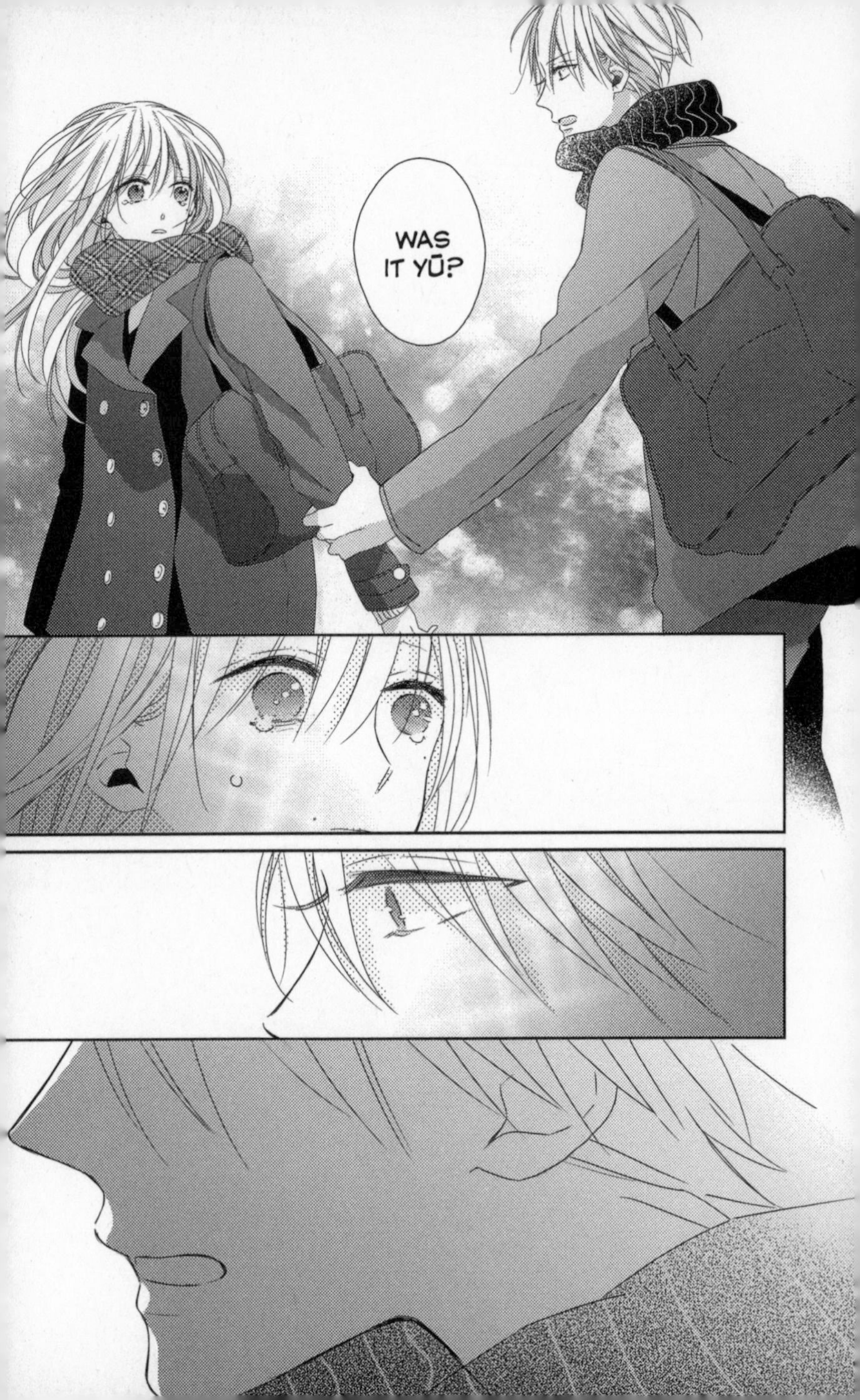
WAS IT YŪ?

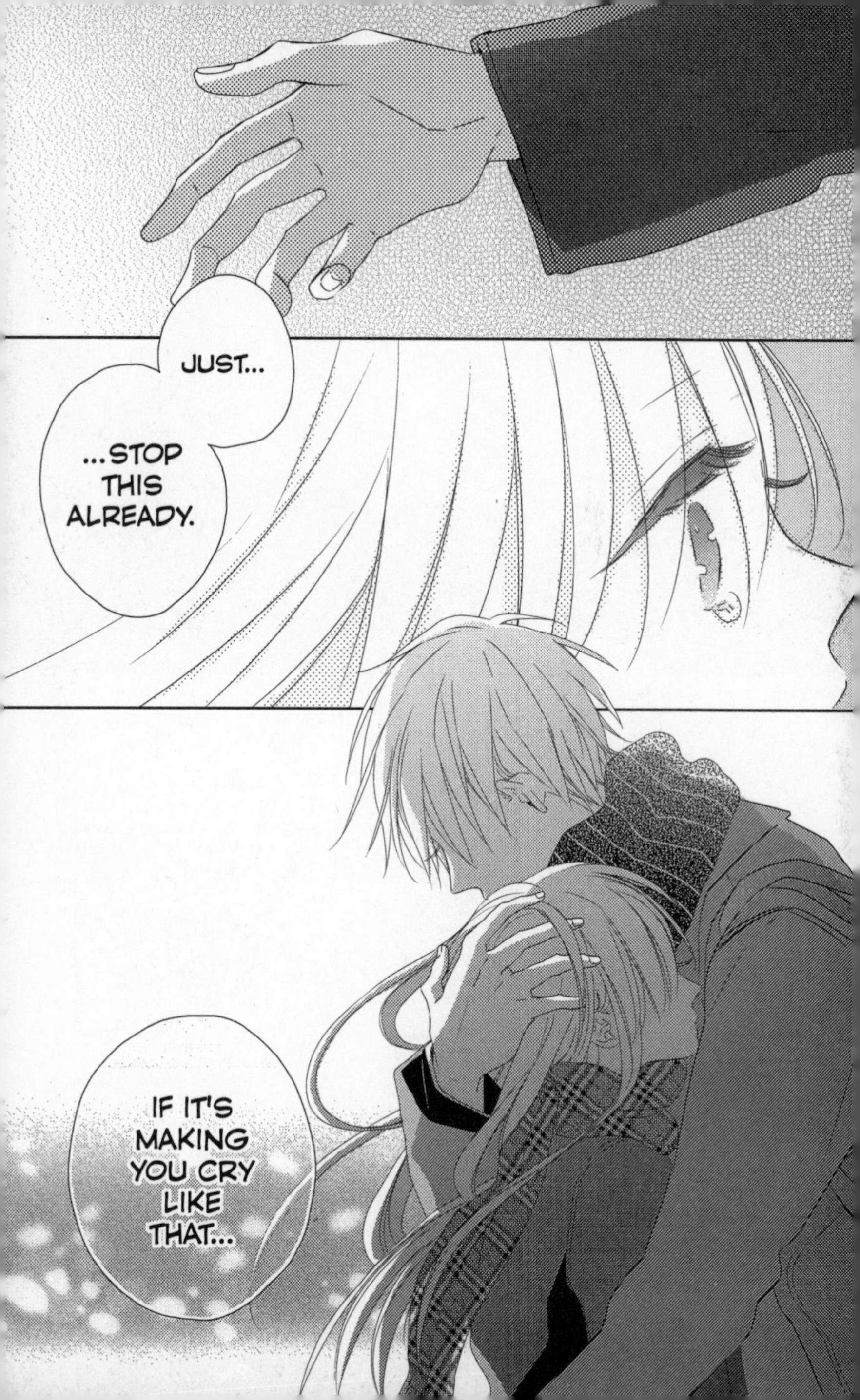
JUST...
...STOP THIS ALREADY.
IF IT'S MAKING YOU CRY LIKE THAT...

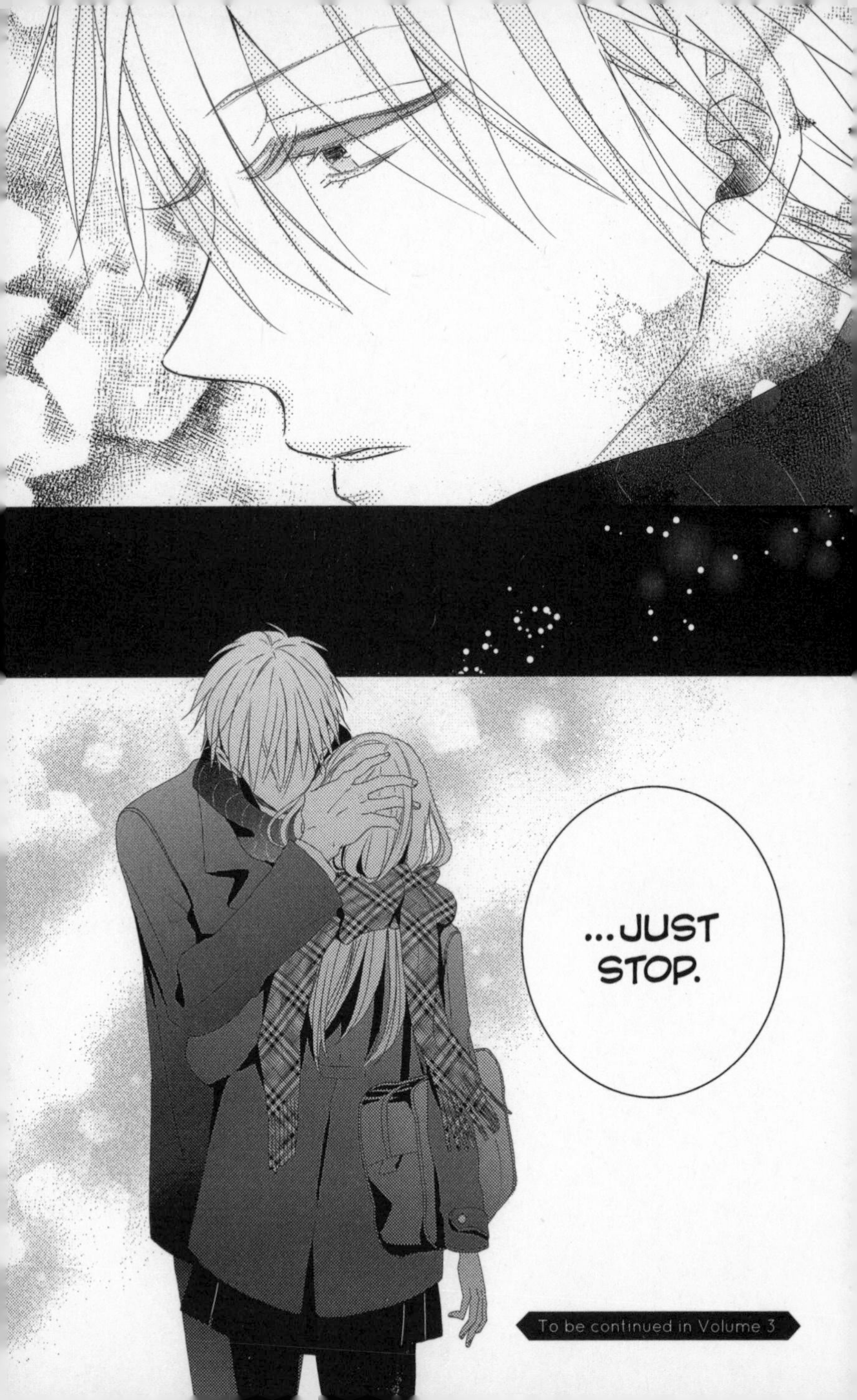
...JUST STOP.
To be continued in Volume 3

That Wolf-Boy is Mine!

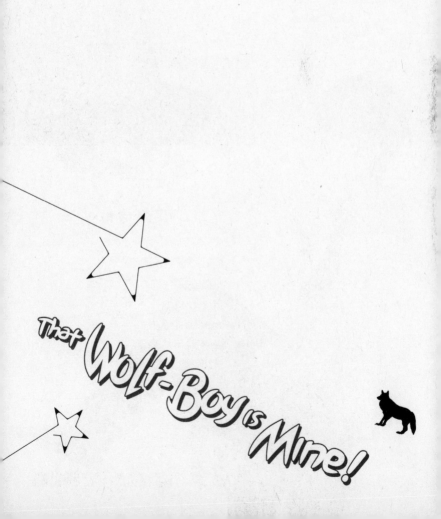

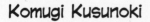

Komugi Kusunoki

Height:	156cm [5'1"]
Birthday:	October 16
Blood type:	O
Favorite food:	Tofu
Least favorite food:	Cucumber
Hobby:	Reading

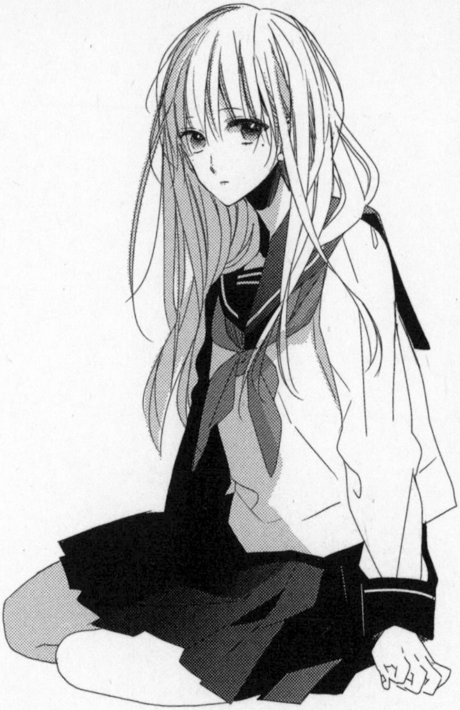

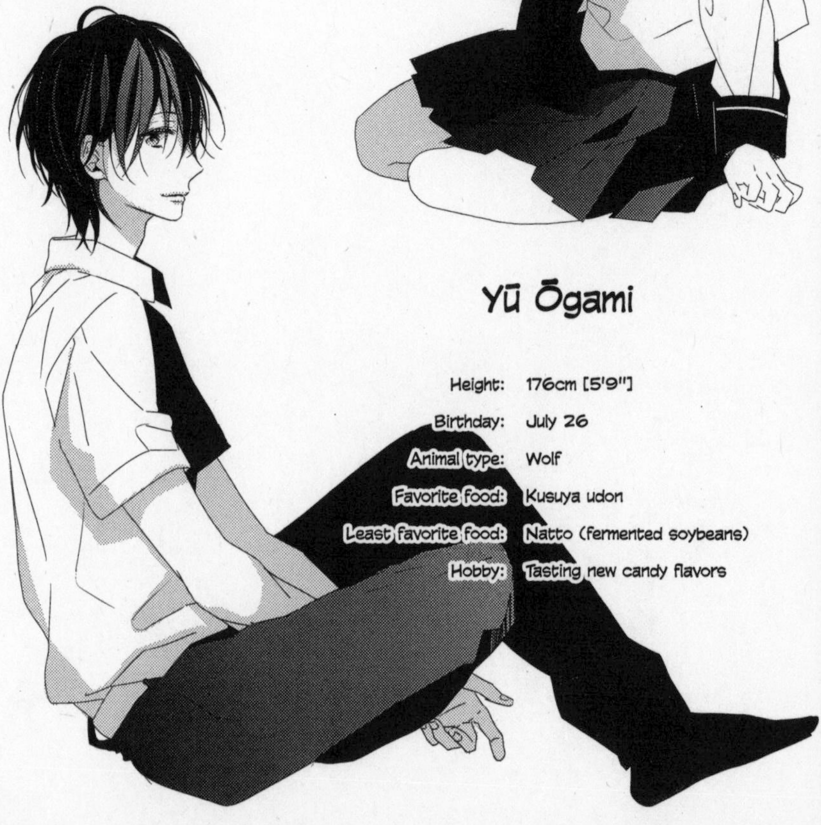

Yū Ōgami

Height:	176cm [5'9"]
Birthday:	July 26
Animal type:	Wolf
Favorite food:	Kusuya udon
Least favorite food:	Natto (fermented soybeans)
Hobby:	Tasting new candy flavors

Rin Fushimi

Height:	174cm [5'8.5"]
Birthday:	September 23
Animal type:	Fox
Favorite food:	Ramen
Least favorite food:	Ankake (thick saucy topping)
Hobby:	Video games

Aoshi Awaji

Height:	173cm [5'8"]
Birthday:	June 15
Animal type:	Tanuki
Favorite food:	Soba noodles
Least favorite food:	Anything sour
Hobby:	Messing with people

Senri Miyama

Height:	171cm [5'7"]
Birthday:	December 23
Animal type:	Two-tailed cat
Favorite food:	Canned tuna
Least favorite food:	Anything spicy
Hobby:	Napping

Kurō Yata

Height:	179cm [5'10"]
Birthday:	Unknown
Animal type:	Three-footed crow
Favorite food:	Saké
Least favorite food:	Nothing in particular
Hobby:	Observing people

Afterword

Thank you very much for picking up this manga!

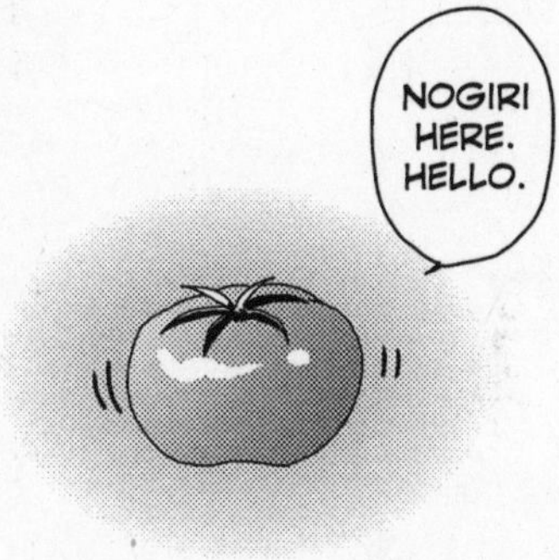
NOGIRI HERE. HELLO.

Thanks to all of you, we have reached two volumes.

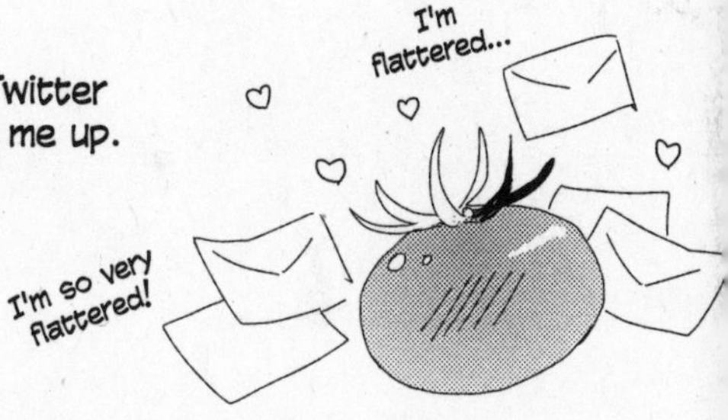
I'm flattered...
I'm so very flattered!

The messages I get on Twitter and in letters really cheer me up.

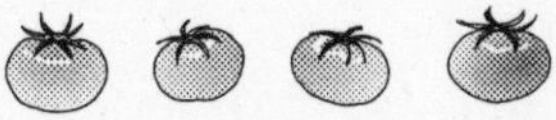

- ✩ To my editor-sama
- ✩ Aki Nishihiro-chan
- ✩ A-H-chan
- ✩ All my friends and family
- ✩ Everyone who read this book

Thank you so much!

I hope you'll read volume three, too!

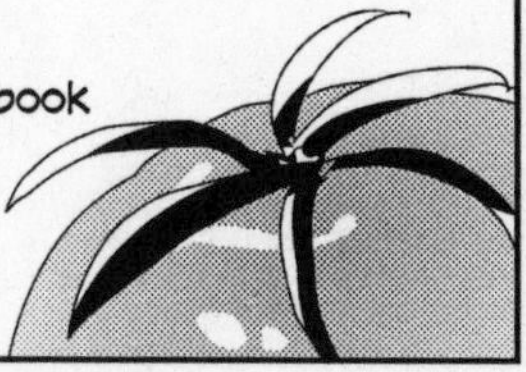

Translation Notes

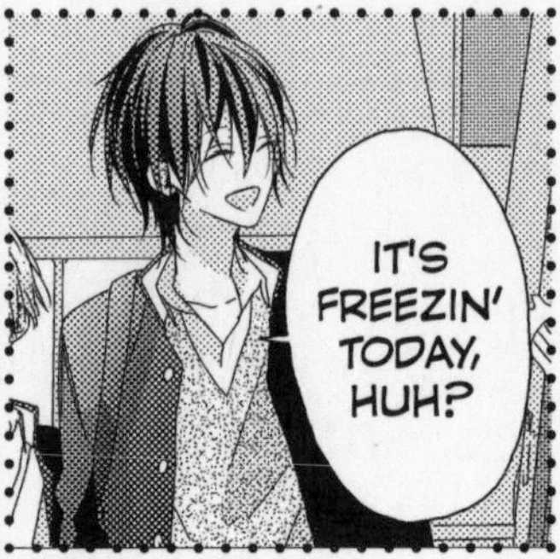
IT'S FREEZIN' TODAY, HUH?

Freezin', page 12
Because this story takes place in Hokkaido, some words that are uncommon in standard Japanese slip into the dialogue. A lot of dialects mixed together in Hokkaido because people from many different regions of Japan once settled there. The term Yū uses here in his regional Hokkaido dialect is *shibareru*, which means "very cold."

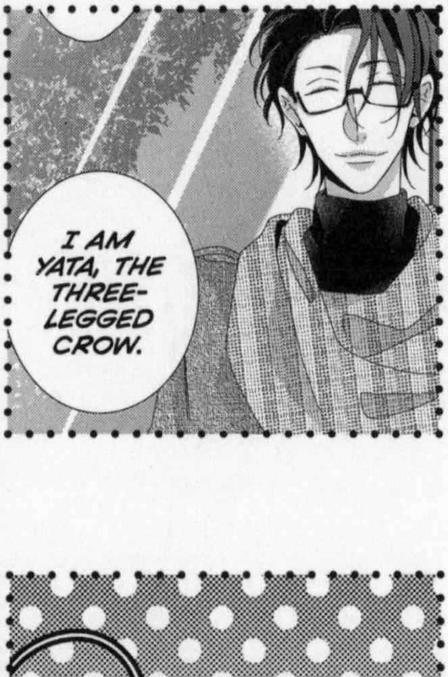
I AM YATA, THE THREE-LEGGED CROW.

Three-legged crow, page 47
The three-legged crow is a part of various Asian mythologies. In Japanese, the *yatagarasu* crow was sent by Amaterasu, the goddess of the sun and universe, to guide one of the nation's first emperors.

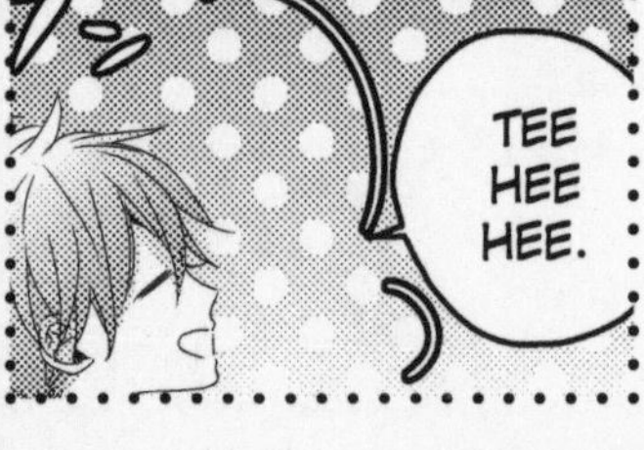
TEE HEE HEE.

Tee hee hee, page 73
To be more precise, Aoshi says "tee hee" followed by a licking sound, as if he were laughing innocently and sticking his tongue out in a cute, childish manner. Incidentally, the leaf on his head is a common accessory for transforming tanuki.

Translation Notes

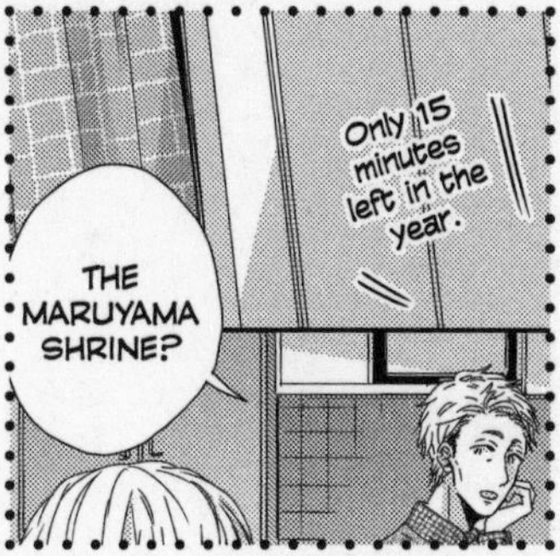
Only 15 minutes left in the year.
THE MARUYAMA SHRINE?

New Year's temple visit, page 87
One of the Japanese New Year traditions is to visit a temple or shrine. Once there, one can make wishes for the new year, make offerings to the temple deities, get amulets and fortunes, etc. People in Hokkaido can go to the Hokkaido Shrine in Sapporo. A popular shrine to visit in Tokyo is Sensō-ji, as mentioned by the New Year's reporters.

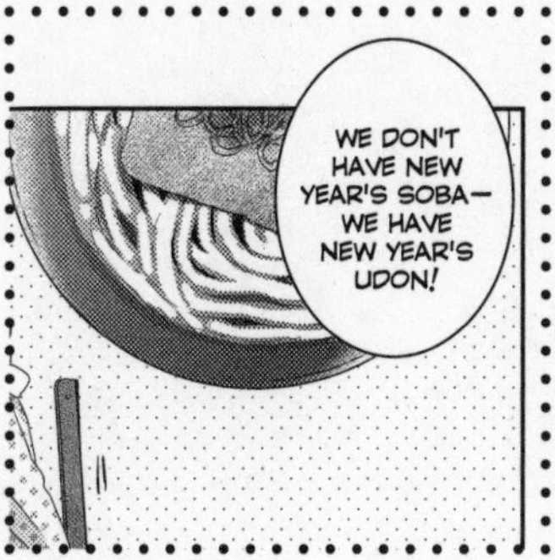
WE DON'T HAVE NEW YEAR'S SOBA—WE HAVE NEW YEAR'S UDON!

New Year's soba, page 88
Another Japanese New Year's tradition is to eat a bowl of soba noodles on New Year's Eve. In Japanese it is called *toshikoshi soba*, or "year-crossing noodles." The noodles are long, representing longevity and long-lasting family fortune, but they're easy to cut, so one can easily cut ties with the hardship and misfortune of the previous year.

OPPOSITES ATTRACT...MAYBE?

Haru Yoshida is feared as an unstable and violent "monster." Mizutani Shizuku is a grade-obsessed student with no friends. Fate brings these two together to form the most unlikely pair. Haru firmly believes he's in love with Mizutani and she firmly believes he's insane.

KC
KODANSHA
COMICS

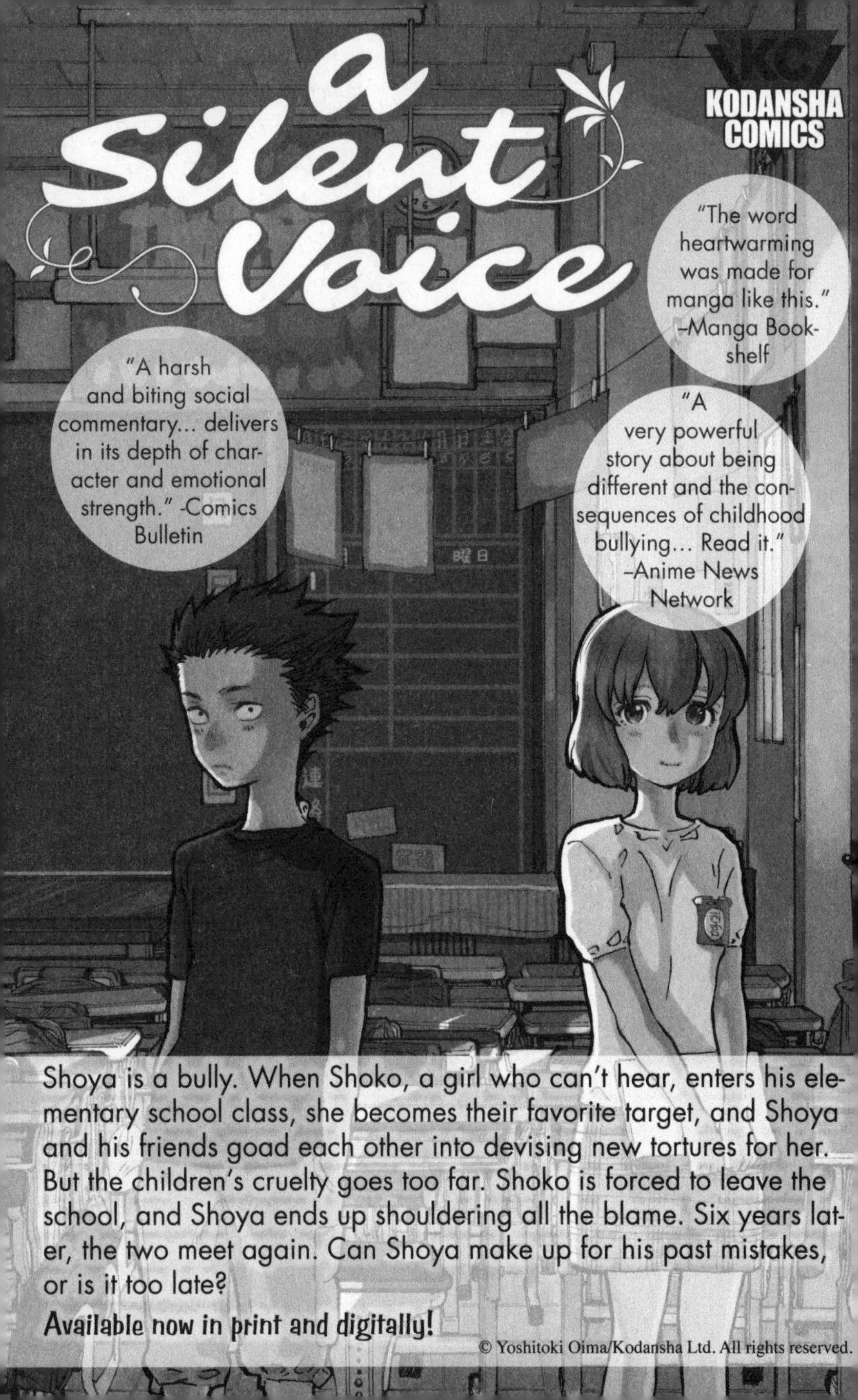
a Silent Voice
KODANSHA COMICS
"The word heartwarming was made for manga like this." –Manga Bookshelf
"A harsh and biting social commentary... delivers in its depth of character and emotional strength." -Comics Bulletin
"A very powerful story about being different and the consequences of childhood bullying... Read it." –Anime News Network
Shoya is a bully. When Shoko, a girl who can't hear, enters his elementary school class, she becomes their favorite target, and Shoya and his friends goad each other into devising new tortures for her. But the children's cruelty goes too far. Shoko is forced to leave the school, and Shoya ends up shouldering all the blame. Six years later, the two meet again. Can Shoya make up for his past mistakes, or is it too late?
Available now in print and digitally!
© Yoshitoki Oima/Kodansha Ltd. All rights reserved.

That Wolf-Boy is Mine! volume 2 is a work of fiction. Names, characters, places, and incidents are the products of the author's imagination or are used fictitiously. Any resemblance to actual events, locales, or persons, living or dead, is entirely coincidental.

A Kodansha Comics Trade Paperback Original

Published in the United States by Kodansha Comics, an imprint of Kodansha USA Publishing, LLC, New York.

Publication rights for this English edition arranged through Kodansha Ltd, Tokyo.

ISBN 978-1-63236-374-9

Printed in the United States of America.

www.kodanshacomics.com

9 8 7 6 5 4 3 2 1
Translation: Alethea and Athena Nibley
Lettering: Sara Linsley
Editing: Haruko Hashimoto
Kodansha Comics edition cover design by Phil Balsman